CREATING A SUCCESSFUL

BUSINESS

Rogene A. Robbins

Robert O. Robbins

ALLWORTH PRESS
NEW YORK

07 06 05 04 03   5 4 3 2 1

Published by Allworth Press
An imprint of Allworth Communications, Inc.
10 East 23rd Street, New York, NY 10010

Cover and interior design by Joan O'Connor

Page composition/typography by Rosanne Pignone, Pro Production

Library of Congress Cataloging-in-Publication Data

Robbins, Rogene A.
    Creating a successful craft business / Rogene A. Robbins and Robert O. Robbins.
        p. cm.
Includes bibliographical references and index.
    ISBN 1-58115-277-9
    1. Handicraft industries—Management. 2. Handicraft—Marketing.
3. Selling—Handicraft. 4. Small business—United States—Management.
I. Robbins, Robert O. II. Title.

HD9999.H363U67 2003
680'.68—dc21   2003008987

Printed in Canada

Contents

Evaluating the Experience • Lessons Learned • Going Home •
Do Your Homework • Need More Help?

My Story • Do Your Homework • Custom Work/Special Orders
Information Form • Tracking Sheet for Article Submissions •
Need More Help?

Lesson 24
DO YOU STILL WANT TO START YOUR OWN BUSINESS?

Appendix A
CAVEAT EMPTOR: RECOGNIZING A LEGITIMATE BUSINESS OPPORTUNITY

Work-at-Home Opportunities • Learn to Recognize a Sales Pitch •
The Internet • Filing a Complaint • Be Aware of Your Community

Appendix B
RESOURCES

Index

List of Worksheets

Introduction

I GREW UP IN A FAMILY OF CREATIVE PEOPLE. A few are professional artists, actors, or singers. Others dabble in creative endeavors for fun and relaxation. For a few, creativity reaches into all areas of daily life.

I still marvel at the exquisitely beautiful clothing designs my grandmother created years ago. The furniture my brother designed and made while a high school student still blows me away. And I have to laugh when I think about some of the craft projects my mom and her best friend undertook.

Yes, I grew up in a family of creative people, but I also grew up in a business-oriented family. I still remember my mother and sister-in-law, both remarkable saleswomen, watching over my shoulder as I interacted with customers in my retail store or at shows. Later, after the customer left, they would pull me aside to give sales advice. My dad always made sure I understood basic business principles and sound financial management. I am also blessed to have a husband with a business degree and many years of business and retail sales experience. Yet with all these people in my life to give me advice and keep me grounded, I have still made many of the mistakes typically made by artists and craftspeople when they try to sell their work. But after selling the work of other artists and listening to artists and craftspeople, both in person and on the Internet, I realized that not everyone has the advantage of built-in (and sometimes live-in) business advisors. I wondered how much more traumatic the transition from a hobby to a business must be for these people. So, I decided to start writing, hoping others could learn from my experience.

This project didn't start out to be a book, however. In the beginning I was going to write a few brief, very focused information sheets that I would make available through my Web site. But soon, the sheer volume of information and the broader vision of my husband took over and those little two-page handouts grew into a book.

✂ HOW TO USE THIS BOOK

This book is a crash course in the basic principles of business, designed especially for artists and craftspeople—"Business 101" for crafters, so to speak. We spent many hours on research for this book, but much of the information here comes from our personal experience. That is why we have included so many personal stories and anecdotes. We have definitely been where you are right now, about to go into new territory, full of hope and ambition, as well as fear and questions. We hope you will be able to learn from our experiences and discover that you can survive even the tough times.

This book is designed to be used as a self-paced business course for artists and craftspeople. In other words, it is something you can use at home as your personal schedule allows. Of course, we also hope it will be used as a textbook in formal craft business classes, but you will still benefit from working on your own at home.

How Is This Book Organized?

You will notice that there is a homework assignment, and often a resource guide, at the end of each lesson. The homework assignments are designed to encourage you to go ahead and do the planning and the work necessary to establish your business. Businesses often fail due to a lack of planning, so these homework assignments are important. Please don't skip over them.

We encourage you to put your answers to the homework assignments in writing. Use whatever form is most comfortable for you. If you prefer to write in a notebook, do that. Or, if you are more of a high-tech type, you may prefer to set up a computer file.

Don't forget the resource section at the back of the book. For your convenience the names of resources pertaining to the information in each chapter are listed at the end of the chapter. You will find the contact information for all of these listed alphabetically in the Resource section at the back of the book.

Use This Book to Help Write Your Business Plan

Every business needs a business plan—even a craft business. It's a basic tool to help you plan and run your business. "So," you may ask, "why, then, is the business plan lesson almost at the end of the book?" Because, in order to complete a business plan, you will need to do a lot of planning and thinking about the kind of business you want to run. Each lesson in this book asks you to consider an aspect of your business that is vital to writing a good plan.

Completing the homework assignments will help you compile and organize the necessary information to write a business plan. Use the Small

Business Administration (SBA) format here or choose your own. There are many fine books and software packages available to help write a business plan. *How* you write your business plan is not as important as *that* you write a business plan. You wouldn't start out on a trip to a new place without a road map. Starting a business is new to most of us, so starting out with a road map is a good idea. A well-thought-out business plan can be that road map.

We hope you will take the time to complete the homework assignments and use at least a few of the resources included in this book. Let them guide you in planning your trip into the world of business. And don't forget your road map!

✂ ABOUT THE AUTHORS

Creating a Successful Craft Business is not just a textbook. It is also the story of Rogene and Bob Robbins and their adventures and misadventures in the craft business.

In 1990, after several miserable years on the craft show circuit, Rogene met Bob, who began teaching her how to apply sound, time-tested business principles to her craft business. In 1991 they opened an experimental store where they successfully sold and distributed clothing and jewelry designed and made by Rogene and her team of "Crafty Ladies." The items sold well in their own store as well as to other retailers for resale. Bob and Rogene eventually closed their retail business in Kansas to move to another state.

With a Bachelor of Science degree in psychology, Rogene has worked as a Qualified Mental Retardation Professional, where she enjoyed using her creativity to work with people with disabilities. Her education and work experience in the rehabilitation field have helped her develop and refine research skills that have been useful in both the running of her business and the writing of this book.

In recent years she has moved away from clothing design to her true love, fabric art. She now divides her professional time between creating original art quilts, writing and teaching about art and business, and answering business questions from artists and crafters.

Bob holds a Bachelor of Science degree in business and a Masters of Education degree in counseling. He, too, has worked in the field of helping people with disabilities, but he also has twenty years of experience in the field of business, mainly in marketing, sales, and customer service.

For the last ten years he has acted as his wife's business manager. Without his knowledge, business experience, and insistence on following sound business principles, her business success would not have been possible.

Lesson 1

DO YOU KNOW WHAT YOU'RE DOING?

As YOU HAVE BEEN PLANNING to start your own business has anyone asked if you really know what you are getting yourself into? I don't remember anyone asking me that question when I decided to start selling my craft work, but they certainly should have. The sad truth is I didn't have a clue. Let me tell you how I started in the craft business.

✂ MY STORY

I found myself single and unemployed in a small town in western Kansas; I was too poor to move back to the city, and there were few employment opportunities where I was. My solution to the problem was to sell my craft work; I fully expected to replace the income from my full-time, professional job.

My first venture into my new career was to set up a booth at the local Founder's Day celebration. I made up a bunch of stuff to sell, nothing especially original, just the kinds of things I saw others selling. Determined to look like I knew what I was doing, I made up hang tags and business cards all hand-lettered on pastel index cards from the discount store. They were a sight! I am not a calligrapher, and the writing was barely legible. I have problems cutting paper (strange for a seamstress to admit, huh?), so the cards were crooked.

When the day of the craft fair arrived I loaded my handmade treasures and borrowed card table into my car and headed for the town square. This was mid-summer in Kansas, which means it was hot! There I went without sunscreen, a hat, lunch, a helper, or even water. Never forget the sunscreen! I looked like a boiled lobster when I got home and had raccoon eyes for weeks from my eyeglasses. When Bob heard this story, he said it was a good thing I forgot the water, because there was no one to watch my booth so I could go to the bathroom.

Oh, but the story gets better—or I should probably say it gets worse. After we all set up our booths they blocked off the streets around the square for the parade. Not a single person came to the booths during the parade, and everyone crowded in front of the booths so we couldn't even see the parade passing by. Then after the parade, the street games started. This I did not expect at all. These games included a water fight between members of the volunteer fire department with fire hoses. Water was flying everywhere, including on me and my booth!

When the people finally started coming to the craft booths they all came at once. All five thousand of them. At least that's what it seemed like. People were packed on the sidewalk like sardines. I don't think anyone could have stopped if they had wanted.

One more important thing I forgot to take with me that day was change. Looking back on that horrible day long, long ago all I can say is, THANK GOD NO ONE BOUGHT ANYTHING!

How can you get off to a better start than I did? A good way to start is to take a look at a few of the realities of starting your own business.

✂ DON'T LET THE AMERICAN DREAM BECOME YOUR WORST NIGHTMARE

We all dream of being our own boss, of not having someone looking over our shoulder while we work. Some of us spend day after day on jobs we hate, dreaming of the day we quit working for someone else and start our own business. But this dream can also turn into a terrible nightmare. Many new businesses will not survive the first year, or worse, the first craft show. Of those that do, more will not make it to five years. Dreams are dashed, life savings are lost, and legal problems abound. That is the downside.

But there are new businesses that *do* survive the first year and make it to five or ten years, even more. So how do you get your business into that elite group of new businesses that actually make it? You plan. You plan. And then you review your plans and plan some more. You also try not to let your emotions cloud your judgment. That means being realistic in both your planning and your goals.

Many new businesses are started out of desperation. You have read my own story about this. There is an old saying: "Necessity is the mother of invention." A few businesses born this way do go on to be tremendously successful, but it is important not to focus on this desperation. What you want to focus on is how to make your idea work. If you fall into the necessity category, planning is even more important. You are one of us who not only want to succeed but cannot afford not to.

Three Keys to Success in the Craft Business

1. *Quality sells.* Don't sacrifice the quality of your work to put a low price on it.
2. *People go to craft fairs looking for original work.* Your work needs to be different from the work of your competitors. Don't just follow what everyone else is doing. Be creative. Use your imagination.
3. *You have to make a profit.* To make certain you make a profit, price so you not only cover your expenses but also have some money after those expenses have been paid. If you do not do this you are not in business, you simply have an expensive hobby. Quality, originality, and profitability are the keys to success in the art and craft world. *Plan* for these three things and you will find yourself on the road to success.

✄— THINGS I WISH SOMEONE HAD TOLD ME ABOUT STARTING A BUSINESS

These are a few of the realities I wish someone had told me before I started my own business. Sometimes I wish they had gotten in my face and screamed them at me. Well, not really. I know I wouldn't have listened if they had; but knowing what I know now, they should have.

No one is ever really her own boss. When you work for someone else you have one boss, or maybe two or three. When you start your own business you will suddenly have hundreds, thousands, or maybe eventually (hopefully) even millions of bosses. These bosses are called "customers." Remember, without them, you do not have a business. Are you really ready for so many bosses?

Starting a business requires a lot of time. There is certainly some flexibility here, but less than most people think. This is where many people get in trouble. To own your own business you must be a self-starter. No one is going to tell you when, how, or where to work. Another aspect of self-employment is that instead of working until your shift is over as in traditional employment, you work till the job is done. In a new business that could amount to well over forty hours a week. Are you willing and able to make that kind of time commitment? Are you willing to sit in an empty store with no customers while building your clientele? Sure, this can be discouraging, but how can customers come in if you are never open?

You won't be making $15 an hour when you quit your full-time job to start your own business. The truth is that, for the first few years of any business, most if not all of the money coming in from the business will have to go right back into the business. Not only that, but if there is not enough money coming in from the business to pay the expenses, you may have to supplement that income with other money. It is not a good idea to expect a new business to support you for the first five years—that is, to provide you with sufficient income to pay all your personal bills. If you have no other means of support, this may be a problem. There are two ways to avoid this. First, you could keep your "day job" and start your business part-time. This allows you to build your business to the point of making a profit *before* you give up the security of your current job. If you use this method, you can use your day job's income as the guideline for when you can make your business your only income. When you get to the point that your business brings in enough income to cover all of its expenses plus your day job's income, benefits, taxes, and Social Security, then you are at the point you can consider letting go of your day job. The second way is to have enough money to live on until the business is ready to fly on its own (two years minimum). This could come from savings, investments, or a spouse with a full-time job.

You need to think about how you are going to replace your benefits from your current job. As I mentioned before, when you quit your full-time job, you will not only lose having a regular paycheck; you will also lose any benefits provided by your employer. This could include health insurance, life insurance, childcare, tuition reimbursement, paid time off (vacation and sick days), retirement programs, and other benefits. Are you prepared to provide these for yourself? Which of your former benefits could you do without? Health insurance is not one of these. Going without health insurance is a terrible risk that no one should take. Please read lesson 7, on insurance, for more information. The time to think about these things is before you quit your full-time job.

✂ DEALING WITH SALESPEOPLE

There is one final thing that most people don't expect when they start their own business—salesmen. *When you announce you are going into business for yourself, people will come out of the woodwork trying to sell you something.* You won't believe the letters and phone calls you will receive. People will try to sell you everything from products for sale in your business to services such as fire or safety "inspections" to fresh fruit. Yes, we did have a fruit salesman show up at our store. We have included a discussion of dealing with salespeople, multilevel marketing, and work-at-home opportunities in Appendix A, "Caveat Emptor: Recognizing a Legitimate Business Opportunity." It will be worth the time to read this information. Even if you think you know about these things, a refresher course never hurts.

I began this book with the story of my first craft fair because I'm pretty sure I was not the first naive, innocent person to venture into the world of business without a clue about what she was doing. I also suspect there will be more to come. But in spite of my disastrous beginning, my adventure in the business world eventually turned into a success story. No, I wasn't able to support myself selling crafts immediately. I did end up going back to work for someone else for awhile, but I did not give up the dream. And I did learn good sound business principles that apply to all businesses, even the business of selling crafts. That does not mean there were not mistakes made, but I also have been learning how to do things right and have learned from my mistakes.

The purpose of this book is to give you a crash course in the basics of business so you can avoid learning the lessons I have learned in the same way I have had to learn them—the hard way. I can't cover it all here, but I will give you enough not only to get you started, but to get you started with confidence.

Incubators Aren't Just for Hatching Chickens

When farmers hear or read the word *incubator,* they think of an egg being kept warm in a special container to assist in its hatching. For an artist, *incubator* is also the term used to describe a certain type of program that seeks to support and encourage the arts by providing studio space, equipment, galleries, classes, sales opportunities, and sometimes even financial support to artists. Some incubators also offer residencies that provide living quarters and studio space, sometimes along with a small financial stipend to allow artists to devote their full time and attention to their work for a period of time. There are a limited number of such residencies and competition is quite stiff. Artists in residence may be required to teach or give talks related to the work of the art center.

While living in Colorado, I became a member of an arts incubator, the Business of Art Center in Manitou Springs. This is where I took my first art business class. I also found the acceptance and support of other struggling artists there. If there is an art center in your community, contact them. They may be a valuable source of help or inspiration.

HOMEWORK ASSIGNMENT

1. Why do you want to start your own business? Take some time to think about this. Be honest, and let your answer come from your heart.
2. Set three goals for your business for the first year. Any time you set a goal you need to be clear about what will define the successful completion of the goal. Be specific. Be realistic. For instance, instead of "to be successful," write a goal that defines success for you, such as sell five hundred widgets.
3. For each of your first-year goals write down the first step you plan to take toward meeting your goal. Why just the first step? Have you heard the saying, "The journey of a thousand miles begins with a single step?" Sometimes a task or goal is so big it seems overwhelming. Just taking that first step is sometimes all it takes to get going down the road toward success. After you take the first step the other steps ahead of you will become clearer.
4. Make a plan to replace the benefits you will lose when you quit your day job. Be sure to include health and life insurance, child care, paid time off, tuition reimbursement, retirement, discounts on products or services, and any other benefits provided by your employer.
5. Make a list of adjustments you will have to make in your lifestyle if you lose certain benefits such as child care or tuition reimbursement.
6. Use the Limited Time Worksheet to help you decide how much time you have to devote to building your business.

Limited Time Worksheet

How Much Time Do You Have for Your Business?

Instructions: Place life task words in the spaces below that represent the hours of each day. Count the times each day you have been able to place the word "business" in a space. (NOTE: Each space represents an hour of the day.) Add daily hours to determine the hours each week you can devote to your business. Is this enough time for success?

Don't forget: Day Job—Eating—Sleeping—Business Entertainment— Shopping—Family—Self—Travel—Education—Other.

	Sunday	Monday	Tuesday	Wednesday	Thursday	Friday	Saturday
12:00 A.M.							
1:00 A.M.							
2:00 A.M.							
3:00 A.M.							
4:00 A.M.							
5:00 A.M.							
6:00 A.M.							
7:00 A.M.							
8:00 A.M.							
9:00 A.M.							
10:00 A.M.							
11:00 A.M.							
12:00 P.M.							
1:00 P.M.							
2:00 P.M.							
3:00 P.M.							
4:00 P.M.							
5:00 P.M.							
6:00 P.M.							
7:00 P.M.							
8:00 P.M.							
9:00 P.M.							
10:00 P.M.							
11:00 P.M.							
Weekly Total							

Need More Help Getting Started?

Literature

Allen, Janet. *Turn Your Passion Into Profits: How to Start a Business of Your Dreams*. New York: Hearst Books, 2001.

American Bar Association Staff. *The American Bar Association Legal Guide for Small Business: Everything a Small-Business Person Must Know, from Startup Employment Laws to Financing and Selling a Business*. New York: Three Rivers Press, 2000.

Arena, Barbara. *The Complete Idiot's Guide to Making Money with Your Hobby*. Indianapolis, Ind.: Alpha Books, 2001.

Brabec, Barbara. *The Crafts Business Answer Book and Resource Guide: Answers to Hundreds of Troublesome Questions about Starting, Marketing and Managing a Homebased Business*. New York: M. Evans and Company, 1998.

———. *Make it Profitable: How to Make Your Art, Craft, Design, Writing or Publishing Business More Efficient, More Satisfying and More Profitable*. New York: M. Evans and Company, 2000.

Broome, J. T., Jr. "A Complete Guide to Getting Your Business off the Ground." *The Crafts Report* (October 2000).

Caputo, Kathryn. *How to Start Making Money with Your Crafts*. Revised ed. White Hall, VA: Betterway Publications, 1999.

Dillehay, James. *The Basic Guide to Selling Arts and Crafts*. Torreon, N. Mex.: Warm Snow Publishers, 1997.

Kammoroff, Bernard B. *Small-Time Operator: How to Start Your Own Small Business, Keep Your Books, Pay Your Taxes and Stay Out of Trouble*. 25th ed. Laytonville, Calif.: Bell Springs Publishing Company, 2000.

Lasley, William. "Getting Started Selling Crafts." *About.com* (cited: July 2002). Available at: *www.artsandcrafts.about.com/library/weekly/aa123099.htm*.

Norman, Jan. *What No One Ever Tells You about Starting You Own Business: Real Life Start-up Advice from 101 Successful Entrepreneurs*. Chicago: Upstart Publishing Company, 1999.

Oberrecht, Kenn. *How to Start a Home-Based Craft Business*. 3rd ed. Old Saybrook, CT: Globe Pequot Press, 2000.

Rosen, Wendy, and Anne Childress. *Crafting as a Business*. 2nd ed. Baltimore: Sterling Publishing Company, 1998.

Staff Entrepreneur Media. *The Entrepreneur Magazine Small Business Advisor: The One-Stop Information Source for Starting, Managing and Growing a Small Business*. New York: John Wiley and Sons, 1999.

West, Susan. "Six Important Things to Know about Setting Up Your Craft Business." Sunshine Glass Works (1 February 2001). Available at *www.sunshineglassworks.com/settingupbiz.shtml*.

WEB SITES
[Contact information is available in Appendix B.]
Arts and Crafts Business @ About.com
Business Forum Online
Business Town
The Idea Cafe
Make-Stuff.com Home Business
Retail Advisors.net
The Small Business Know-How Resource

ORGANIZATIONS
[Contact information is available in Appendix B.]
American Association of Home Based Business
Kansas Small Business Development Center

Service Corps of Retired Executives (SCORE)
United States Chamber of Commerce
University of Central Arkansas College of Business Administration

ARTS INCUBATORS
[Contact information is available in Appendix B.]
Alliance of Artists Communities
Artspace
The Artworks
The Bemis Center for Contemporary Art
The New York Mills Regional Cultural Center
Rockville Arts Place
Torpedo Factory Art Center

Lesson 2

PRESENTING YOURSELF AS A PROFESSIONAL

AN IMPORTANT STEP in taking your art or craft from a hobby to a profession is developing a professional identity. This means thinking, talking, and behaving as a professional. Okay, so how is a professional artist supposed to think talk, and behave? Aren't we different than the rest of the world? You bet. But we still have to live with non-artists, and they are going to, we hope, buy our work. If they don't buy our work, we starve. This means we have to, at least, try to meet them somewhere close to where they live.

✂ DEVELOPING YOUR PROFESSIONAL IDENTITY

The first step in developing your professional identity is to define your medium and become an expert. Artists, and especially craftspeople, often get caught up in thinking they have to be too broad in terms of skills and types of projects, or that they need to follow fads. Having skills in more than one area is not a bad thing, nor is knowing the market, that is, what people are buying. But if you try to change your medium every time the wind blows, so to speak, you will find you do a lot of different things, but none of them especially well.

Find your passion—the one type of art work you *love*. Learn to do it well. Take classes, keep up to date on any changes, especially ones that will make your work easier, but use those skills and information to develop your own style. Make your work your own. Create something that will stand out from the crowd.

Develop your artistic identity. One way to begin is to decide what words you want to use to identify yourself and describe what you do. Do you want to be called an artist, craftsman, craftswoman, crafter, or perhaps craft professional? Or do you prefer to be identified by the type of art or craft you practice? Is your preference to be known as a painter, sculptor, quilter, or maybe a fiber artist or doll maker? My personal choice is fabric artist.

✂ YOUR BUSINESS NAME

The name you choose for your business is very important. This name will identify you and your work to the world. There are many choices available. First you can simply use your name and the type of art or craft you do—your medium. Many artists do this. Examples of this would be John Smith Sculptor, Mary Jones Doll Maker, Rogene A. Robbins Fabric Artist, and so on. Others choose a unique business name. You may want to have a name that is unusual, cute, or trendy. I guess the name of my retail store would fall into this category. We called it The Crafty Lady. I once saw a ceramic artist at a craft show who called his business The Mud Slinger. I really liked that one. Perhaps you would rather have a name that is very professional sounding and businesslike, in which case names like The Walnut Valley Craft Emporium or Artistic Creations might better suit you.

I believe a business name should give at least a hint of what the business is about. This comes from my experience as a consumer looking for goods and services. If a potential customer can't tell what you do by your business name, she may overlook you. If you get too specific, however, you may have problems if you ever want to change the type of work you do without changing your business name.

Of course your business name should be short, sweet, and to the point. Making it easy to read, pronounce, and spell will help your customers find you.

It is a good idea to run your ideas for your business name by other people. Ask what they think of when they hear your business name. Does your idea for a business name have other possible meanings you don't want to be associated with?

After you have chosen your name, the next step is to make sure it is available for use. When you register your business name with your state, the clerks will do a search for you to make sure the name is available in your state. However, in the current world economy this may not be enough, especially if you live on or near a state border or plan on expanding into other states. It is a good idea to search other resources such as the free trademark database on the Web site of the United States Patent and Trademark Office. You might also try a name search on the Internet to see if anyone else is already using the name.

Another reason for searching outside your own state is to be sure you are not guilty of trademark infringement. According to the United States

Patent and Trademark Office a trademark is "a word, phrase, symbol, or design, or a combination of words, symbols, or designs that identifies and distinguishes the source of the goods of one party from those of others" (*www.uspto.gov/web/offices/tac/doc/basic*). A service mark is the same thing, only it applies to a service instead of a product. You can use the TM or SM symbols after your business name even if you do not register it with the Patent and Trademark Office. Remember, though, that you cannot use the federal registration symbol (®) until your trademark is actually registered. Just as with copyright there are advantages to registering your trademark, including giving you the right to fight infringement.

Sometimes you will find a name that works for you and sticks. Other times the name will change and evolve. Try to keep this to a minimum, it possible. Changing your business name can be expensive. Two earlier incarnations of my business name have been The Crafty Lady (my retail store) and Robbins Nest Designs (my design business and clothing label). Now, my work is done under my own name, Rogene A. Robbins, Fabric Artist/Art and Craft Business Consultant.

Of course if you choose to do business on the Internet you will also have to choose a domain name. For more information on this see lesson 19, "Building, Promoting, and Selling from Your Own Web Site."

What's in a Business Name?

You want a business name that will stand out, that people will remember and associate with you and your work. When people look at your business name, do they know what you do or sell? If not, is your business name unique or off the wall enough to draw people in just out of curiosity? Is your business name something you can live with if people decide to call you by your business name? There are still people in my hometown who call my mom Mrs. Benson after the name of the business she and my dad managed for many years. When I had my retail store it was not unusual for me to go to the post office or a local restaurant and hear someone call out, "Hey, Crafty Lady!" I really didn't mind, because everyone in town knew the Crafty Lady and where to find the store.

✄ THE ARTIST'S STATEMENT

Take time to develop an artist's statement. An artist's statement is different than a résumé. A résumé tells people what you've done; an artist's statements tells people who you are. This is your chance to tell the world what you do and why you do it. This is important. As I tried to write a statement to explain my art to others, I began to have a clearer understanding of why I am an artist and what makes my work unique. It also led to a stronger commitment to following my (he)art, to daring to be different, to breaking the rules and being able to live with the consequences and criticism for doing so. An artist's statement may also be used in your printed materials. Your artist's statement, along with your contact information and photos, makes a simple but striking brochure.

The artist's statement is totally individual and very personal. Of course you can get ideas from what others have done but no one else can write your artist's statement for you. Doing this may challenge you and make you stretch. It may even hurt a little, but in the end it will be worth it.

Do I have an artist's statement? After what I just said about how important an artist's statement is do you think I wouldn't have one? Of course I do. You may see my current artist's statement on page 16, following this lesson.

Examples of Artist's Statements Online

Below is a list of artists whose statements you might find helpful:

- Marlene Bulas: *www.sunninghillart.com/statement.htm*
- Aimee Golant: *www.aimeegolant.com/astate.htm*
- Nita Leland: *www.nitaleland.com/bio.htm#statement*
- Mary Leu: *www.batiksbyleu.com/artist_statement.htm*
- Barbara Macdonald: *http://pweb.jps.net/~bmac/bio.html*
- Patty Mitchell: *www.passionworks.org/statement.html*
- Jack R. Slentz: *www.jackslentz.com/statement.html*
- David Walker: *http://www.davidwalker.us/Pages/Artist'sStatement.html*

✄ PROFESSIONAL ORGANIZATIONS

Join at least one business or professional organization. There are many reasons to join an organization. One reason is because it looks good on a résumé. Membership in professional organizations is impressive. Business and professional organizations are also a good source of continuing education. Many organizations offer classes, seminars, or workshops for their members. Membership in an organization is also a good way to stay informed about what is going on in the industry through publications and trade shows. Organizations may also help with networking, which is a big scary word for nothing more than meeting, talking with, and getting to know people.

Joining an organization also gives you the power of having an organization behind you instead of acting alone. It is important to have an organization monitoring new laws that might affect your business and organizing action to protect the interests of its members, or to purchase insurance or other products or services for you at a better rate than you could get by yourself. There is power in numbers.

Many business and professional organizations are able to help replace benefits lost when you quit your day job. Benefits offered by organizations range from insurance to product discounts. Since they will usually address different types of issues, you may wish to join one general small business organization and one professional artist organization.

You may be thinking that all sounds good, but are there drawbacks to joining an organization? Of course there are. The major obstacle to joining organizations may be cost. If money is an issue for you, look around and find an organization that is not quite as costly. But be sure it meets your needs. Otherwise, you will be throwing your money away. To begin with you may wish to join only one and choose either a business or professional organization.

Another drawback is that if you tend to be a joiner you may be tempted to join so many organizations that you either feel overloaded or do not have the time to be active in any of them. Remember, the purpose of joining organizations is to help you with your business. To have a business you must have time to work. When choosing an organization you may want to talk to your peers. What organizations do they belong to? What do they feel are the most important benefits of membership?

An extensive resource list accompanies this lesson, with contact information in Appendix B. This will get you started, but of course it does not include every possible membership organization out there. Choosing the business or professional organization carefully and wisely can help you work more effectively.

✂ CREATE A PROFESSIONAL IMAGE

Carry your business card with you at all times. If we are interested in an artist or a particular work of art, we will often ask for a business card. In our experience, an artist or craftsperson actually having a card to give us is about a fifty/fifty proposition. Business cards are not only expected in the real world of business; they are an excellent way of getting your name out and keeping it in front of your customers and potential customers. Don't be stingy with your business cards. Keep cards out where interested people can take one. If you are concerned about price, shop around. Many full service print shops offer business card specials. This does not have to be a major investment. The Japanese believe that if you do not have a business card, you are not serious about being in business. Could be.

Use high-quality printed materials. If you are going to present yourself as a professional, you will want everything you do to be of the highest quality possible. This includes your written correspondence and the way you give out your contact information. At the very minimum the basics you need are a good quality letterhead and business cards. I know you are thinking, But I'm an artist—can't my printed materials be a means of self-expression? The best rule is that any creative touches should be something you do well and that is related to your work. A pencil sketch, if that is what you do, is great. A hand-lettered card is probably only appropriate if you are a calligrapher. Just be sure it is readable. Calligraphy is beautiful, but sometimes it is difficult to read.

Be on time for appointments. This applies to all appointments, but especially when you are meeting with a buyer or gallery owner. They may not be on time, and often aren't, but that isn't the point. Even if you know you will have to wait, if you have a definite appointment time, keep it. If your appointment is at 2:00 be there at 2:00, or better yet 1:55.

A very important part of having a professional identity is feeling competent in your field of endeavor and therefore having confidence in your abilities. This is no longer a hobby. You are a professional. Work like one. Think like one. Behave like one.

Where's the Artist?

If you are operating a store, gallery, or studio with advertised hours, even if you only post them on the door, have someone there during those hours. Dire emergencies are the only exceptions. If customers come too many times and you are not there they will eventually stop coming. If you give someone a time to return a phone call, be there expecting the call. These two things are basic courtesy but are also part of creating a professional image. If you want to present yourself as a reclusive artist who is hard to find and a little eccentric, that's fine. That is part of your professional identity and, if done correctly, can work. But even this has to be well thought out if you ever want to make many sales. The point here is if you make a commitment, keep it.

✂ ARTIST'S STATEMENT OF ROGENE A. ROBBINS, FABRIC ARTIST

I knew I was an artist when I was fifteen years old and took my first studio art class. It felt like I had come home. I spent the next several years experimenting with various media, finally deciding I was a painter. Several of my acrylic and watercolor works were exhibited in student and community art shows. They are now at rest in my mother's attic, awaiting a proper burial.

I learned to sew from my mother, who learned from her mother, a professional seamstress. Grandma approached her work with skill and boldness, creating beautiful garments with extraordinary attention to detail. My paternal grandmother was a quilter, and a quilting hoop in the living room with a quilt in progress was a familiar sight.

I have sewn my own clothes since I was twelve years old and have designed and sewn clothes for others. But it wasn't until I realized I could use the basic principles of color, perspective, and design learned in art class to create quilts that would be works of art that everything fell into place. Rogene A. Robbins, Quilt Artist, was born. I am proud to work in the medium of my foremothers and attempt to keep alive the artistic tradition of self-expression practiced by generations of women who have come before.

My passion is the art quilt, but I occasionally try to make a traditional quilt. When I first began quilting, I became caught up in the need to follow the rules, but as hard as I tried, I was always breaking them. I also found it extremely difficult to get really caught up in fabric selection. For me, it is much more exciting to create my work around scraps, old clothes, garage sale yard goods, and found objects. Since I use quilting as a means of self-expression, it is much more fulfilling for me to make a quilt my own, rather than reproducing the work of someone else.

—Rogene A. Robbins, Fabric Artist

DO YOUR HOMEWORK

1. Think about how you want to be identified as an artist. What words do you want to use to describe what you do? Once you have decided, try to use this term as much as possible to describe yourself and your work.
2. What is the professional image you want to project as an artist? What can you do to help with this image?
3. If you have not already done so, choose a business name. Keep in mind that people should know what you do from your business name.
4. Take the time to write a general artist's statement. A good way to start is to think about how you would explain to someone else what you do and why you do it. Start writing. Don't worry about grammar, punctuation, spelling, or any other rules. Just write. You can always clean it up later. What is important is that this comes from the heart.
5. If you do not already belong to any business or professional organizations, consider joining at least one of each. Use the directory following this homework assignment if you need help finding an organization. You can also do a Web search using keywords such as small business organizations, artists organizations, craft organizations, quilting organizations, painting organizations, and so on.

NEED MORE HELP?

LITERATURE

Gingerich, Sue. "Choosing a Business Name." *The YEBDC Small Business Information Column on Web site of The Yellowhead East Business Development Corporation.* (July 2002). Available at: *www.yebdc.ab. ca/news/sue53.htm.*

U.S. Patent and Trademark Office. "Basic Facts about Trademarks" (cited: August 2002). Available at: *www.uspto.gov/web/offices/tac/doc/basic.*

INFORMATION ON HOW TO WRITE AN ARTIST'S STATEMENT

Gordon, Molly. "How to Write and Use an Artist Statement" (cited: February 2003). Article reprint available at: *www.contemporaryquiltart.com/ writingTheArtistsStatement.htm.*

Leland, Nita. "Writing an Artist's Statement" (cited: August 2002). Available at: *http://nitaleland.com/articles/statement.htm.*

Schulman, Davida. "Ten Rules for Writing an Artist's Statement" (cited: August 2002). Available at: *www.wetcanvas.com/Articles/Schulman/ artist_statement.html.*

The Artists Foundation. "How to Write An Artist Statement" (cited: August 2002). Available at: *www.artistsfoundation.org/html/afa/freeinfo/ statement.html.*

PROFESSIONAL, TRADE, AND INDUSTRY ORGANIZATIONS

[Contact information is available in Appendix B.]

American Craft Council
Americans for the Arts
Arts and Crafts Association of America
Association of Crafts and Creative Industries
Craft Yarn Council of America
Hobby Industry Association
Home Sewing Association
National Association of Independent Artists

SAFETY

[Contact information is available in Appendix B.]

Arts, Crafts, and Theater Safety

WOMEN IN THE ARTS

[Contact information is available in Appendix B.]

Women's Caucus for Art

SELF-EMPLOYMENT/ SMALL BUSINESS ORGANIZATIONS

[Contact information is available in Appendix B.]

Home-Based Business Owners Association
National Association for the Self-Employed
Working Today

EMERGENCY FINANCIAL ASSISTANCE

[Contact information is available in Appendix B.]

Craft Emergency Relief Fund

HEALTH INSURANCE
[Contact information is available in Appendix B.]
Artists' Health Insurance Resource Center/The Actors' Fund National Headquarters
National Small Business United

CANDLE MAKING
[Contact information is available in Appendix B.]
International Guild of Candle Artisans
National Candle Association

CARICATURES AND CARTOONS
[Contact information is available in Appendix B.]
National Caricaturist Network
National Cartoonists Society

CERAMICS
[Contact information is available in Appendix B.]
American Art Pottery Association
National Council on Education for the Ceramic Arts

CHINA PAINTING
[Contact information is available in Appendix B.]
World Association of China Painters

COLORED PENCILS
[Contact information is available in Appendix B.]
Colored Pencil Society of America

CROCHET
[Contact information is available in Appendix B.]
Crochet Guild of America

DECORATIVE PAINTING
[Contact information is available in Appendix B.]
National Society of Tole and Decorative Painters
The Society of Decorative Painters
The Stencil Artisans League

DECOUPAGE
[Contact information is available in Appendix B.]
National Guild of Decoupeurs

DOLL MAKING
[Contact information is available in Appendix B.]
Academy of American Doll Artists
International Foundation of Doll Makers
National Institute of American Doll Artists
The Professional Doll Makers Art Guild

FOLK ART AND TRADITIONAL ARTS
[Contact information is available in Appendix B.]
Folk Art Society of America
Indian Arts and Crafts Association
National Council for the Traditional Arts

GLASS
[Contact information is available in Appendix B.]
Glass Art Society
Society of Glass Beadmakers

GRAPHIC ARTS
[Contact information is available in Appendix B.]
American Institute of Graphic Arts

INTERIOR DESIGN
[Contact information is available in Appendix B.]
American Society of Interior Designers

KNITTING
[Contact information is available in Appendix B.]
The Knitting Guild of America

METALSMITHING AND BLACKSMITHING
[Contact information is available in Appendix B.]
The Artist-Blacksmiths Association of North America
Society of American Silversmiths
Society of North American Goldsmiths

MINIATURES
[Contact information is available in Appendix B.]
International Guild of Miniature Artists
National Association of Miniature Enthusiasts

MOSAIC
[Contact information is available in Appendix B.]
Society of American Mosaic Artists

NEEDLEARTS
[Contact information is available in Appendix B.]
American Needlepoint Guild
Embroiderer's Guild of America

ORIGAMI
[Contact information is available in Appendix B.]
Origami USA

PAINTING
[Contact information is available in Appendix B.]
National Acrylic Painters Association
National Society of Mural Painters

PASTELS
[Contact information is available in Appendix B.]
Pastel Society of America

PHOTOGRAPHY
[Contact information is available in Appendix B.]
The African American Photographers Guild
American Society of Picture Professionals
North American Nature Photography Association
Photographic Society of America

POLYMER CLAY
[Contact information is available in Appendix B.]
National Polymer Clay Guild

QUILTING
[Contact information is available in Appendix B.]
American Quilter's Society
National Quilting Association Inc.
Studio Art Quilt Associates
The Appliqué Society

SCULPTURE
[Contact information is available in Appendix B.]
International Sculpture Center

SEWING

[Contact information is available in Appendix B.]
American Sewing Guild
Home Sewing Association
The Professional Association of Custom Clothiers
The Smocking Arts Guild of America

SOAP MAKING

[Contact information is available in Appendix B.]
The Handcrafted Soap Makers Guild

STAINED GLASS

[Contact information is available in Appendix B.]
Association of Stained Glass Lamp Artists
Stained Glass Association of America

WATERCOLOR

Contact information is available in Appendix B.]
American Watercolor Society
National Watercolor Society

WEAVING

[Contact information is available in Appendix B.]
The Handweavers Guild of America Inc.

WOOD CARVING

[Contact information is available in Appendix B.]
Affiliated Wood Carvers Ltd.
National Wood Carvers Association

WOOD WORKING

[Contact information is available in Appendix B.]
American Association of Woodturners

Lesson 3

LAWS, RULES, AND REGULATIONS

WHEN IT COMES TO INFORMATION about the laws, rules, and regulations governing your business it is important not to rely solely on Aunt Sadie, urban legends, or the current self-proclaimed expert in the Internet chat room. These people can be helpful. They may be able to help you get started in your search for information, but whenever you get information that does not come directly from the source, check it out.

✂ GET TO KNOW YOUR UNCLE SAM

Information is expensive. But did you know there are sources of information and services available for people starting a new business that you have already paid for? Yes, that's right, you have paid for information and services you do not use. You probably are not even aware they exist. The source is the Federal government, and your tax dollars are being used to pay for them, so why not use these resources?

The following government agencies are listed as a starting point. As you get started you will find others. These agencies all have Web sites, and you may want to start there to get an idea of the programs and services offered. Government agencies are listed following this lesson, and contact information, including Internet addresses, may be found in Appendix B.

The Small Business Administration or *SBA* is a wonderful source of information. You may go to your local SBA office if there is one near you, or visit the Web site. I recommend visiting the Web site first even if you do plan on going to the office, just to get an idea of what the SBA has to offer. The Small Business Startup Kit, available online, is a good place to get started. This will walk you through the basics of starting a business, any business.

Other services offered by the SBA include training seminars and courses and information on business plans and business counseling. This is also one of the best places for help to get started writing a business plan.

The *Internal Revenue Service* or *IRS* has tax information especially for small businesses. Ask for Your Business Tax Kit. Check out the IRS Web site and go to the Small Business Corner. When it comes to tax information it is always best to go to the source—that is, the IRS.

The *United States Copyright Office* is the source of information on copyright laws and how they effect you as an artist or craftsperson. Again, go straight to the source on this one, either the Copyright Office or a copyright attorney. I am not an expert in this area, but there seem to be things being said and written about copyright in the art and craft community which may not be part of the literature from the copyright office or other resources. These may be popular myths. Do not rely on rumors; go to the source.

Copyrights, patents, or trademarks are not the same. *The United States Patent and Trademark Office* is the source of information if you think you have a product that needs patent or trademark protection.

The National Endowment for the Arts is a great source of inspiration as well as a funding source for arts-related organizations and projects. It is also a source of information on making the arts accessible to people with disabilities.

The Consumer Information Center in Pueblo, Colorado, is a good source of free and low-cost government-sponsored publications on a wide range of topics. You may have seen their advertisements on television.

If you have or plan to have employees, you should contact the *United States Department of Labor,* the *United States Immigration and Naturalization Service,* and the *Occupational Safety and Health Administration,* also know as *OSHA.*

The services and information available from the federal government can help you get started. Remember, your tax dollars pay for them. But most of the laws, rules, and regulations governing business depend on the state, city, and county where you live. How do you find this information? And why do they think they can tell you how to run your business anyway?

✂ ATTITUDE IS EVERYTHING

You can look at the laws, rules, and regulations governing your business in one of two ways. First you can see them as a burden, as interference from or coercion by "big brother," and as something you are being forced to do against your will. Or you can instead look at them as guidelines to help you start your business and be successful at it.

You certainly can choose the first approach, but that is a hard road, and no matter how hard you try to fight, you will most likely end up complying anyway. Believe it or not, most laws, rules, and regulations are intended for your benefit. For example, local building codes protect you, your work, and your customers. An annual safety or fire inspection can give you valuable information. Another example of how laws, rules, and regulations can help you involves taxes. Yes, taxes. A properly filed income tax return can become your annual report concerning the financial status of your business (profit or loss, etc.)

✂ HOW DO YOU FIND LOCAL AND STATE LAWS, RULES, AND REGULATIONS?

In most cases, the source for local information will be the agency or branch of government responsible for enforcing the laws and regulations governing businesses in your area. Those laws and regulations vary greatly from state to state, city to city, and county to county, so finding what applies directly to you in your specific location is very important.

A good place to start is city hall. The clerks there will be able to tell you about city regulations concerning location, signs, any applicable city taxes, and so on. Some cities will have very specific city ordinances governing small businesses. Some locations may also require a special city business license. You will also want to find out about local zoning laws.

Check with your county and state for any information they may have for small business owners. In some states information on starting a business may be in printed form and available free of charge at various locations. Check this out first. It could save you a lot of running around. Be sure to ask if there are any required business licenses. This is usually up to each local jurisdiction.

You must register your business name if you are using a fictitious business name, which is something other than your own legal name. In my state, Nebraska, this is done through the County Recorders Office. In other states where we have lived and done business, this was automatically done when we applied for our tax resale number. A search will be conducted to make sure your name is not already in use. This is for your protection.

In most states you will need a resale tax license often called a tax number. Even if you are not selling your work directly and collecting sales tax, you still need this for the purchase of your supplies. These are usually issued by your state, although you will want to find out if your city collects its own sales tax. Some jurisdictions will have a "use tax" on your supplies, and some charge a "value added tax." That is why it is so important to check with city, state, and county officials for information on regulations governing businesses.

There may also be a few federal laws that will apply to your business. For instance, if you are planning to have a retail store, studio, or gallery, you will want to look into the Americans with Disabilities Act to find out how to make your building physically accessible to people with disabilities. This is not just the law, it is good business. Why would you want to turn away any potential customers?

If you are planning on having employees, you will need to find out about applicable employment and tax laws. Your business advisor or attorney should be able to help you here.

Many artists use hazardous chemicals in their work, such as paint, thinners, and cleaners. If your work involves chemicals, you should become familiar with procedures for their safe use and disposal. These laws are designed for your protection. Check local jurisdictions concerning this. The Environmental Protection Agency (EPA) is also a good source of information on this. Occupational Safety and Health Administration (OSHA) safety standards are also good outlines for any business, whether or not you have employees.

DBA?

Have you ever wondered what DBA means? It is really not all that mysterious or complicated. DBA simply stands for "doing business as" and applies to you if you are using a fictitious business name—that is, something other that your own legal name. These three little letters connect you to your registered business name. This will most often be used by your bank and will usually appear with your name. For example, Mary Smith DBA Crafters Corner.

YOUR TEAM OF ADVISORS

Right now you may be thinking, Okay, so there are laws governing my business. There are a lot of laws, rules, and regulations, and you are telling me they vary from state to state, county to county, and city to city. How do I find out what applies to me? Good question. That gives me a chance to talk about the importance of good advisors. Think of your advisors as your team of experts. You will want a variety of people on your team.

The first person you will want on your team is your *business advisor.* This might be a person who works for the Small Business Administration, your local Economic Development Agency, or a local college or university. These people may not understand the aspects of your work that are unique to arts or crafts, but they can be a great help with the economic side of starting any business. Better yet, find a non-artist who can catch your vision. Bob and I used the Small Business Development Center at our local university several times for information and advice. The information we received there was very helpful. We also consulted a volunteer with the Service Corps of Retired Executives (SCORE).

Your *business attorney* is also an important person to have on your team. This needs to be an attorney who works with small businesses. Do not start even a very small business without one. A good business attorney will be able to answer legal questions about your business and point you to the proper agency if needed. We started out with an attorney early in the establishment of our retail business, and later we were so glad we did. He was very helpful.

Don't forget you *accountant/tax preparer.* You could do this for yourself, but remember that this is business. It is a whole different ball game than your personal taxes and accounting. Remember to monitor the work of your accountant or tax preparer. Know what he is doing with your money and, as with any situation, never sign anything without reading it first. If you do not understand what you read, ask. It is her job to explain.

Successful business people can also be an excellent source of information. This may be where you get information specifically related to the art or craft business. However, a word of caution is in order here. Misinformation can easily be spread from person to person. Always verify information that does not come from the source.

✄ OTHER SOURCES OF INFORMATION

You may also have other sources of local information including the following:

- *Your local Chamber of Commerce* should be able to offer you information on starting a business in your community. There may even be classes available.
- Look for *local publications* on starting a business in your area. Perhaps your local newspaper puts out a small business edition listing local laws and resources. In Nebraska, we have the Small Business Guide, put out by the district office of the SBA. This forty-page booklet is available for free at local libraries and other locations across the state.
- Discover the *business section of your local library.* This is a valuable free resource. Go in and spend some time just looking around. After you have done that, ask the business librarian for help in learning about available business resources.

You may miss something. In most cases you will be notified and given a chance to correct the problem. There may be penalties involved, such as fines or back taxes, but just work with the appropriate agency to correct the problem. Now that does not mean you do not have to try to find out about the laws, rules, and regulations and be in compliance. Just do your best, find good advisors, and listen to them.

Finding Federal Agencies on the Internet

This is not as difficult as you may think. Government agencies have Web addresses ending in ".gov." First, try entering the agencies name or initials followed by ".gov." For example, *www.ssa.gov* is the Web address for the Social Security Administration. Or you can use a search engine and enter the name of the agency. You may also use the U.S. Business Advisor at *www.business.gov* to find governmental information on the Web.

DO YOUR HOMEWORK

Your homework assignment for this lesson is to go out and gather as much information as you can on the legalities of starting a business in your city, county, and state. This is not nearly as difficult as it sounds. Reread the lesson carefully for hints if necessary.

You may gather this information by phone, mail, Internet, or, of course, in person. Remember, the agency in charge of making or enforcing the rules has the final word, so it is best to get your information there if at all possible.

We have tried to make this information gathering process easier by providing worksheets for you to use to both collect and record the essentials. Although this may seem like a tedious, time-consuming, and sometimes useless activity, it is much easier and less expensive to do things right when you start out than to have to correct problems later.

LAWS, RULES, AND REGULATIONS WORKSHEET—STATE

	DATE	CONTACT NAME	PHONE #	NOTES
SALES TAX				
INCOME TAXES				
REAL ESTATE & PROPERTY TAXES				
DISABILITIES & ACCESSIBILITY LAWS & REGULATIONS				
EMPLOYMENT LAWS & WORKMEN'S COMPENSATION				
HAZARDOUS CHEMICALS & ENVIRONMENTAL LAWS & REGULATIONS				
OTHER Note: Make your notes in this section specific to the needs of your business. Remember, the laws for your business will most likely be different from your friend's business, so check this out for yourself.				

LAWS, RULES, AND REGULATIONS WORKSHEET—FEDERAL

	DATE	CONTACT NAME	PHONE #	NOTES
INCOME TAXES (IRS)				
COPYRIGHT (Library of Congress)				
HAZARDOUS CHEMICALS (OSHA)				
DISABILITIES & ACCESSIBILITY LAWS & REGULATIONS				
EMPLOYMENT LAWS				
ENVIRONMENTAL LAWS & REGULATIONS (EPA)				
OTHER Note: Make your notes in this section specific to the needs of your business. Remember, the laws for your business will most likely be different from your friend's business, so check this out for yourself.				

LAWS, RULES, AND REGULATIONS WORKSHEET—COUNTY

	DATE	CONTACT NAME	PHONE #	NOTES
INCOME TAX				
SALES TAXES				
REAL & PERSONAL PROPERTY TAXES Remember, in most states, counties collect property taxes for the state they are in, but they may have their own taxes as well.				
HAZARDOUS CHEMICALS & ENVIRONMENTAL LAWS & REGULATIONS				
OTHER Note: Make your notes in this section specific to the needs of your business. Remember, the laws for your business will most likely be different from your friend's business, so check this out for yourself.				

LAWS, RULES, AND REGULATIONS WORKSHEET—CITY

	DATE	CONTACT NAME	PHONE #	NOTES
BUSINESS LICENSE				
SALES TAXES				
FIRE, HAZARDOUS CHEMICALS & ENVIRONMENTAL LAWS & REGULATIONS (Fire Department)				
ZONING & PROPERTY USE LAWS				
OTHER Note: Make your notes in this section specific to the needs of your business. Remember, the laws for your business will most likely be different from your friend's business, so check this out for yourself.				

Need More Help?

Federal Information
[Contact information is available in Appendix B.]
Federal Consumer Information Center
Internal Revenue Service
The National Endowment for the Arts
Small Business Administration
Social Security Administration
United States Copyright Office

United States Patent and Trademark Office
United States Postal Service

Web Sites
[Contact information is available in Appendix B.]
Abbreviations and Acronyms of the U.S. Government
U.S. Business Advisor

Lesson 4

WORKING FROM HOME

WORKING FROM HOME has become a rapidly growing trend in recent years. People who are tired of long commutes and the lack of quality time with their families are leaving the fast-paced corporate world and seeking the peace, tranquility, and simplicity of working at home. However, working from your home may not be that idyllic or simple. Matters become especially complicated if you share you living space—now also your work space—with children.

✂ TIPS FOR SUCCESSFULLY WORKING AT HOME

There are simple ways to organize your home workspace as well as your time to help make working at home a pleasant and profitable experience. This does take some planning, however. The following are a few ideas to get you started.

Set regular work hours, just as if you worked outside the home. If your children are of school age and you are working at home to have more time with them, then perhaps the best time for your work is while they are at school.

Have space dedicated to your work, a place you actually go to when you are at work. A spare bedroom, converted garage, waterproofed basement, loft, or attic may be used for studio space. Keep in mind your medium when making this decision. For example, working with permanent dyes would be better suited for a garage or basement with concrete floors than a bedroom with plush carpeting. Likewise, be sure that electric outlets, water, and other utilities are available as needed. If your work calls for large amounts of water, how far do you really want to carry it? If you use any type of chemicals in your work (including paint), remember that you will need adequate ventilation. This means windows that open and exhaust fans. This is an especially serious point; do not take it lightly. Chemical fumes cause serious illness and even death as well as increasing the risk of fire and explosion.

Invest in a good answering machine or voice mail service. Make it a practice not to take phone calls during work hours, unless you have a separate business line in your home workspace. Make sure that, when giving your home number out to friends, PTA members, church members, and others, you also give the best time to call. Print these times on your business cards. Most people will try to respect that. If you are concerned about missing emergency calls from your children or spouse, carry a pager and give the number only to people who might need to make emergency contact with you.

If your family includes children, especially toddlers, you have probably already childproofed your home. *Do not forget that you must also childproof your work space.* When working with chemicals or sharp objects, you will need to consider ways of keeping these away from your children. This means at least storing dangerous chemicals, paints, carving tools, knives, needles, and other supplies in a locked cabinet. It might also be a good idea to have family rules concerning mom or dad's work space. Keep your studio or office door locked when you are not working. Children are naturally curious. If you are an artist, the tools of your trade can also be fun to play with and very inviting to little or not so little ones.

The same guidelines apply if you have indoor pets. As people owned by a cat, we know that most people with pets would never intentionally do anything to harm their beloved animals; but what about the hidden dangers? Pet proofing is important if you work from home with furry children around.

✄ KEEPING CITY HALL HAPPY

That was the personal side of working at home. Now just a little bit about the relationship between your home-based business and the city, county, or state where you live. Your local jurisdiction may have special rules or regulations for home-based businesses.

Much of the concern over home-based businesses in residential areas is related to *traffic*. Will your home-based business increase traffic in a residential neighborhood? Do you plan to put up a sign and encourage drop-in customers? This may not be allowed. Check local zoning regulations.

Some locales *require a city business license*. Even if you are not selling from your home, check if this applies to businesses in your area.

If you are already a working artist and use hazardous chemicals, you should already be familiar with *local regulations concerning the use and disposal of such chemicals*. If not, why not? The life of your business and possibly yourself could depend upon this knowledge. City or county safety departments can usually give you general outlines of these regulations without a lot a questions. The fire department may also be able to advise you on the safe storage and disposal of chemicals and other supplies if you simply ask.

This is why it is so important to go to city hall and the county courthouse early in your planning stages. There may be laws and ordinances governing business that you are not even thinking about. Many local governments will not have a problem with you having your studio in your home, as long as you are not posing a threat to public health or safety.

With the proper planning, working from home can be a rewarding, convenient, and even profitable experience. Use this lesson to help begin making your own plans so working at home will work for you.

DO YOUR HOMEWORK

1. Contact your city and county governments for their regulations on running a business out of a private residence.
2. Decide which room or rooms of your home will be devoted to your business.
3. Use the Working from Home Checklist to help determine if any changes need to be made in your workspace or your life and the lives of your family to accommodate your business.
4. Make the changes needed in consultation with family members and the appropriate building professionals.

Working from Home Checklist

FINDING TIME TO WORK

When will you have uninterrupted time to work?
- ❏ While spouse is at work.   Time of day._____
- ❏ While kids are at school.   Time of day._____
- ❏ While baby is napping.   Time of day._____
- ❏ While spouse is napping.   Time of day._____
- ❏ Other_____   Time of day._____

What arrangements might be necessary to have uninterrupted work time?
- ❏ Child care
- ❏ Voice mail or pager
- ❏ Modified work schedule (if keeping day job)
- ❏ Other_____

FINDING SPACE TO WORK

Where is the best place in your house or apartment for your work area?
- ❏ Spare bedroom
- ❏ Loft
- ❏ Converted garage
- ❏ Attic
- ❏ Waterproofed basement
- ❏ Other_____

Does this space meet your needs?
- ❏ Floor covering (tile, carpet, etc.)_____
- ❏ Availability of water
- ❏ Electrical outlets
- ❏ Ventilation
- ❏ Other_____

PROTECTING CHILDREN AND PETS

Is your workspace child- or pet-proof?

❏ Sharps, chemicals, paints, and other supplies in locked cabinet
❏ Childproof locks on studio doors
❏ Security systems on your computer
❏ Other_____

YOUR HOME BUSINESS AND THE GOVERNMENT

Have you checked out the following as they apply to your home business?

❏ Business licenses
❏ Zoning
❏ Parking
❏ Signs
❏ Disposal of hazardous chemicals
❏ Other_____

Need More Help?
Literature
Backer, Noelle. "No Place Like Home: A Practical and Comprehensive Guide to Starting Your Home-Based Business." *The Crafts Report* (December 2001). Available at: *www.craftsreport.com/december01/noplace.html.*

Brabec, Barbara. *The Crafts Business Answer Book and Resource Guide: Answers to Hundreds of Troublesome Questions about Starting, Marketing and Managing a Homebased Business.* New York: M. Evans and Company, 1998.

Edwards, Paul, and Sarah Edwards. *Working from Home: Everything You Need to Know about Living and Working Under the Same Roof.* Los Angeles: J.P. Tarcher, 1999.

Evans, Poppy. *Your Perfect Home Based Studio.* 3rd ed. Cincinnati, Ohio: F&W Publications, 2001.

Gould, Meredith. *Working from Home: Making It Work for You.* Pownal, Vt.: Storey Books, 2000.

Miyashiro, Marlo. "How to Look Professional When Your Office Is a Dining Room Table." Craftbits.com (cited: March 2003). Available at: *www.craftbits.com/html/articles/sellingcrafts/officedesk.htm.*

Oberrecht, Kenn. *How to Start a Home Based Craft Business.* Edited by Paula Brisco. Old Saybrook, CT: Globe Pequot Press, 2000.

Szerman, Millie. *A View from the Tub: An Inspiring and Practical Guide to Working from Home.* Redondo Beach, Calif.: Stairwell Press, 2000.

Young, Pam, Peggy Jones Smith, and Sydney Craft-Rosen. *Sidetracked Home Executives: From Pig Pen to Paradise.* New York: Warner Books, 2001.

Organizations
[Contact information is available in Appendix B.]
American Home Business Association
Home Based Business News
Home-Based Business Owners Association

Publications
Entrepreneur Magazine
Home Business Magazine

Web Sites
Home Working Mom.com
Mom's Homework

Lesson 5

GETTING THE MOST OUT OF THE WEB AND YOUR COMPUTER

How can a computer help an artist or crafter? If you have not yet jumped onto the information super highway you will not believe what a computer can do for you. Your computer may be used to find patterns, instructions for new techniques, or hard-to-find craft supplies. Did you know you can even take classes online? A computer with the right software will also greatly simplify the mountain of paperwork any business owner must deal with. A computer can even help you sell your work by helping you find craft shows in your area or by giving you a new forum for advertising or actually selling your work online. You can even publish your own books, newsletters, and craft patterns, right from your own PC.

✂ FINDING YOUR WAY AROUND THE INTERNET

The computer revolution has quite literally put unbelievable amounts of information at our fingertips. The Internet is a valuable source of information. The interactive nature of the Internet has made it possible to meet and talk to people around the world through e-mail, message boards, or live chat. This is something that until a few years ago most of us never dreamed we would do. This opens new opportunities for networking that can be helpful to artists and craftspeople.

So what exactly is out there? You will not believe what you can find on the Internet! So let's take a look at some of the information on the Internet that might benefit you as an artist and a businessperson.

Many manufacturers of art or craft supplies and materials now have Web sites. You may have questions about a certain material you are working with.

41

Often you will find your answers there. You can also find contact information such as e-mail, postal addresses, or phone numbers. For example, maybe you are a quilter. If you have a question about quilt batting you can go to the Web site of Mountain Mist, a leading manufacturer of batting, and look for the answer there. The address is *www.stearnstextiles.com/ mountainmist*. Often Web sites will have a section called FAQ, which stands for frequently asked questions. That is a good place to start if you have a specific question. The answer may already be there.

Web sites sponsored by manufacturers of art or craft supplies are also often a source of inspiration and just plain fun. As a way of selling their products manufacturers often put out patterns using their products. You will find new craft ideas, project sheets, and even photos of finished projects online.

Professional and special interest organizations will often have an online presence through a Web site. For example, the Web site for the National Craft Association is located at *www.craftassoc.com*. This is a good Web site, packed with lots of information on selling crafts, so it is worth a visit even if you aren't looking for a membership organization. Visiting a Web site is also a good way to find initial information about an organization you may wish to join. There are also organizations that exist only on the Internet. For instance, National Online Quilters is a virtual guild, with many of the same activities of a more traditional quilt guild, only everything is done by computer. They may be found online at *www.noqers.org*

Newsletters and E-zines are available online in abundance. It is now possible to sign up and have information delivered right to your e-mail. Can you imagine that? Sometimes this will be in the form of a newsletter with actual articles, or sometimes the newsletter will be a series of links to articles on one or more Web sites. It is convenient to have the information sent directly to you, but as someone who loves to sign up for newsletters, I can tell you that if you are not careful you will end up with an overwhelming amount of e-mail. From time to time it may be a good idea to "unsubscribe" to any newsletters you do not actually read.

✂ NETWORKING ONLINE

Many people are using the Internet as a networking tool. That is, as a place to meet other people and share experiences and knowledge. A word of caution is in order here. Please remember that personal opinion on the Internet is just that. It is up to the individual user to check out the validity and accuracy of information given on the Internet, especially when the information does not come directly from the source.

But, you say, the person who gave me the information is a lawyer, the head of a major company, a doctor, an art "expert." Do you really know that? One of the great advantages—and at the same time one of the disadvantages—of the Internet is anonymity. You do not have to give your real name online. Just be aware that not all people online claiming to be professionals or experts in any given field really are. Do not worry too much about this, just use your head.

Now that we have the warnings out of the way, we will look at the ways the Internet can be used for networking. One way to meet people and share information online is through *online bulletin boards,* sometimes also known as message boards or forums. You post a message, question, or request and wait for someone to post an answer. If you need an immediate answer this may not be the way to go as it may take days, weeks, or months for someone to decide to answer. It is usually up to you to check back to see if someone has responded to your posting.

If you need an immediate response you will want to try *live chat,* which is just that. You are actually talking to other people in real time by typing your end of the conversation on your computer keyboard. Your words, as well as the words of the other people in the chat room, appear on your computer screen.

E-mail lists are made up of groups of people with similar interests who share information, opinions, and advice via e-mail. Everyone sends e-mails to a list administrator or coordinator who then forwards them on to the other members of the list. You may choose to receive individual e-mails as they come in or you may choose the digest version—a collection of e-mails that are sent once a day, twice a week, or whatever the administrator decides is best. These are often high volume, so don't join unless you are prepared to deal with a large amount of e-mail. Many people love e-mail lists, but others may find the sheer profusion of mail difficult to deal with.

Keep in mind that when you join an established list you may be joining in the middle of a discussion. I once joined an e-mail list in the middle of a heated discussion on copyright. The first message I received was very angry and directed at one individual who was being accused of infringing on the writer's copyright. Since I was new to the list and this was the first message I had received, I wondered who this person was and what I had done to offend her. Finally, as I received more messages, I realized what was going on and that the e-mail was not personal. However, the angry accusations continued, and after two weeks I decided that I could take no more and dropped out of that particular list. If I had joined at another time I might have reacted quite differently.

✂ USING SEARCH ENGINES

I have been doing Internet searches for so long it has become automatic. However, even with all of this experience, I was at a loss when it came to trying to explain Web searches to you. Since this was the case, I asked Floyd Conaway, the computer manager at my local library, for his help. The information available on the Internet is so vast that finding what you want may be difficult. If you know the address of a specific site, you can go there directly. But what if you don't have a clue? Maybe you are looking for a list of craft fairs. What do you do? The easiest way to find information on the Internet in a fairly short time is to use a search engine. You are probably familiar with the most popular ones, such as Ask Jeeves, Look Smart, Lycos, Yahoo, Overture, and Google. There are also search engines that search all the other search engines, such as Dog Pile or Mamma. After awhile you will develop your favorites as you learn which search engines are best for certain types of information.

When you do an online search, the keywords that you use for your search are important. They will help you narrow down your search. For example, Floyd and I did a search on Google using the keyword *crafts*. We came up with 2,170,002 Web sites related to crafts, also known as "hits." I don't know about you, but I just don't have time to wade through over two million Web sites. So we decided to narrow it down a little and try *selling crafts*. That narrowed it down to 264,002. That many hits might not all be useful, however, because the computer would search for each word separately as well as together. Finally Floyd suggested using the keywords *"selling crafts"* again but this time in quotes. The number of hits with that search was 2,832. Now we're starting to get things a little more manageable and closer to the information I want. Another way to get more specific is to add a city name to your keywords—such as *"selling crafts Toledo."* You will also find as you start going through the results of your search that some entries will stand out as not what you are looking for and you can just skip over those.

Floyd also showed me several Web sites with search engine tutorials, including his own. This information may be found under "Need More Help?" at the end of this lesson.

The best way to learn to do an Internet search is to do one. As you go along, you will refine your skills and get quite good at finding information quickly.

✂ A COMPUTER HAS MORE TO OFFER THAN JUST THE INTERNET

There is much more that a computer has to offer to crafters and people in business than Internet access. A personal computer is a valuable *recordkeeping tool.* Your tax records, purchase orders, invoices, payroll, inventory, and profit and loss statements are just a few of the important business records capable of being stored on a computer. Think of it as paperwork without the paper. This saves time as well as space. Your directory of business contacts may also be kept in a computer file. Yes, you can say good-bye to your old faithful Rolodex. One word of caution about keeping important information and business documents on your computer is in order here. Be sure to make a backup disk of this information and update it regularly. Keep this disk in a safe place such as a safety deposit box. This way if something bad should happen to your hard drive you still have your business documents.

Do you remember when *typesetting* had to be done at the print shop? I do, but maybe you're not that old. Back in the olden days when we wanted to have business cards, advertising brochures, or other printed materials made up, we took a rough idea of what we wanted to the print shop. They made up a sample, which we would go in, look at, and either approve or change. Now it is possible to do your own typesetting at home and with the right equipment even to produce and copy your own finished documents. Or, do your own typesetting and take your document to the print shop camera-ready. All of this takes just a fraction of the time and cost of doing it the old-fashioned way.

Finally, your computer may be used as a *design tool.* Draw out new designs to scale and even try various color combinations, all from your computer. You might be able to use your existing software or special software might be available to meet your specific needs.

If you have not yet discovered the benefits of computer use, at least think about doing a little exploring. You do not have to jump right into the deep end on this. You can sit on the edge and dip your toe in the water to start. You do not even have to run out and buy a computer to get started. In fact, I suggest you take a class first. Be sure it is a very basic introductory class appropriate for a computer newbie. Talk to the teacher first if you're in doubt. Computer classes are available through many sources. Check your local community college, but also do not forget your community center, senior center, and public library. Speaking of the library, many libraries now have computer access available for patrons. All you have to do is present your library card. It is a high-tech world. Computers may be a little intimidating at first. I know. I was dragged into the information age kicking and screaming. But once you start learning the basics, a computer can become your best friend.

If you can hardly wait to jump in and sell your work online, you might be disappointed that I didn't cover that here. You will be glad to know that I devoted an entire lesson to creating a Web site and selling online. So be patient and have fun with lesson 19, "Building, Promoting, and Selling from Your Own Web Site."

Take a Class on Your Computer?

What will they think of next? Interested in learning a new technique but cannot find anyone in your area who is teaching it? Check the Internet. Sometimes individuals or companies will print instructions for using new materials or techniques right on their Web sites. There are also interactive online classes. Some of these are free, some are not. Sometimes a free class is offered as a "sample" of classes available for a fee.

DO YOUR HOMEWORK

1. If you do not have a computer at home, check around your community for free or low-cost computer access.
2. If you are not familiar with the Internet, do some exploring. You will be surprised by what you find. If you need help, take a basic Internet class or ask a twelve-year-old.
3. Go to your local office supply store or computer store and look at software. See what you can find to help with the record keeping for your business. Be sure any programs you decide to purchase are designed for small business.
4. If your computer is also for personal use, set up separate files for your business. Be sure to carefully label all files as either personal or business.
5. If you have not already done so, experiment with setting up a computer file for names, addresses, and phone numbers of business contacts.

NEED MORE HELP?

LITERATURE

Ashford, Janet. *The Arts and Crafts Computer: Using Your Computer As an Artist's Tool*. Berkeley, Calif.: Peachpit Press, 2001.

———, and John Odam. *Start with a Scan: A Guide to Transforming Scanned Photos and Objects into High Quality Art*. 2nd ed. Berkeley, Calif.: Peachpit Press, 2000.

Bolyston, Scott. *Creative Solutions for Unusual Projects*. Cincinnati, Ohio: How Design Books, 2001.

Crabe, Genevieve. *Crafter's Internet Handbook: Research, Connect and Sell Your Crafts Online*. Cincinnati, Ohio: Muska and Lipman Publishing, 2002.

Dillehay, James. *The Basic Guide to Selling Crafts on the Internet*. Torreon, N. Mex.: Warm Snow Publishers, 2000.

Gordon, Herschell, and Gordon Lewis. *Effective E-Mail Marketing: The Complete Guide to Creating Successful Campaigns*. New York: AMACOM, 2002.

Laury, Jean Ray. *The Photo Transfer Handbook: Snap It, Print It, Stitch It*. Edited by Vera Tobin and Liz Aneloski. Lafayette, Calif.: C & T Publishing, 1999.

Monroy, Bert. *Photorealistic Techniques with Photo Shop and Illustrator*. Indianapolis, Ind.: New Riders Publishing, 2000.

ONLINE INSTRUCTION

[Contact information is available in Appendix B.]

Artistic Purr-suits
Animation Artist
Crafter's Community
Crafty College
Craft Link
Cressida's Transformations
Hearts 2 Hands
Penny Soto-Steps to Watercolor
Quilt University

E-MAIL NEWSLETTERS

[Contact information is available in Appendix B.]

Craft Finder
Craft Marketer
My Free

Knitting Goddess
Quilters Review
Selling Your Art Online
Sew What's New
The Virtual Quilt

FORUMS

[Contact information is available in Appendix B.]

Arts and Crafts Business @ About.com
Art and Craft Show Yellow Pages™
Craft Planet
Craftsmarts™
Entrepreneur Magazine
Knitting Goddess
Michaels
Textile Source
The Woodburner

E-mail Lists

[Contact information is available in Appendix B.]

National Craft Association
Onelist
Professional Crafters Mailing List

Search Engine Information

[Contact information is available in Appendix B.]

Web Resource Center
Search Engine Guide
Search Engines.com

Lesson 6

REASONS YOU MIGHT NEED A BUSINESS ATTORNEY

You may be wondering why you need an attorney just to start a craft business. The simple answer is, you need an attorney to help keep you out of trouble. The time to build a relationship with a good business attorney is *before* there are problems.

✂ WHY DO YOU NEED AN ATTORNEY?

An attorney can *help you meet the legal requirements of your city, county, or state.* You might need specific legal advice in certain situations, such as when you want to request a zoning variance. In general, you need to let your attorney know what you have done in terms of business legalities just to make sure you haven't missed anything.

Your attorney will also be able to *help you determine the legal structure of your business* (sole proprietorship, partnership, corporation, cooperative, etc.) and file any necessary paperwork. If you decide on anything more complicated than a sole proprietorship, you will definitely need the expertise and experience of your attorney.

Another reason for having a business attorney is to *write, approve, and negotiate contracts.* Don't hesitate to pay attorney's fees to have a contract read. Attorney's fees of a few hundred dollars could save thousands of dollars and much grief later. Never assume that a contract is legal in your state, or that it is in your best interest. It doesn't matter if it is written in legalese. It doesn't even matter if the other party says his attorney drew up the contract. The job of the attorney for the other party is to make sure that the contract is in the best interest of *her* client. It is up to your attorney to determine if the contract is also in *your* best interest. Remember, however, that your attorney will be looking mostly at the legalities of the contract. It is still up to you to decide if it is something you can live with.

A contract sets the ground rules for any business relationship and is for the protection of both parties. Sure there are one-sided contracts, but do you really want to be in a relationship where there are no benefits to you?

As you become established in your business the need may arise to get an attorney involved in *collection of past due accounts* or *checks returned for insufficient funds.* Although your general business attorney may not do this for you, she should be able to refer you to someone who can. Do not assume that this will never happen to you. Anyone who accepts checks is vulnerable. We only had this situation arise once, but when it did we were grateful to our business attorney for knowing where to refer us.

Finally, while no one wants to think about this, you might need an attorney to *defend you in a legal action.* This is why it is important to keep your attorney aware of any problems that could escalate into a lawsuit. Your attorney may be able to resolve problems before they become lawsuits. By all means, if you receive official notification on an issue such as copyright infringement or product liability, take it directly to your attorney. She will advise you on how to handle the situation. Remember, your attorney is the expert in the law. She is also not emotionally involved in the situation, so pay attention to her.

✄ HOW DO YOU FIND A BUSINESS ATTORNEY?

You find a business attorney in the same way you find any professional. One way *many people find professionals is through referrals* from friends, relatives, and business associates. This is a fine and acceptable way of doing so. Keep in mind, however, that individuals will have different needs, standards, and ways of evaluating whether or not any given professional is a good one. A good attorney for your neighbor may not be good for you.

Your *local bar association may have a referral service.* This is another way of finding an attorney, but it is important that you know you may simply be given the next name on the referral list.

Recommendations from your business advisors may also be helpful in your search for an attorney. If one of your advisors is someone who is currently in business, ask for the name of his attorney.

If you are a member of a *prepaid legal services plan* you may be able to get a referral there. Your membership may entitle you to certain services with no further charge. This is how we found our business attorney and it worked for us; however, this may not be the best option for you.

Last but not least, you can always look in the Yellow Pages. Most of us have done this at some time or other, whether looking for an attorney, a dentist, or even a plumber. If you have done this you know that sometimes you find the perfect professional and sometimes you find a perfect nightmare.

Anytime you have a first visit with any professional you are entitled to ask questions to help you decide if this is the right person for you. If you find an attorney who offers a free consultation this is ideal. Remember that you need an attorney who is experienced in small business issues. You do not have to stay with an attorney you are not comfortable with or whose expertise does not meet your needs. If, however, you insist that your attorney know the ins and outs of crafts you will probably be disappointed. Your business attorney is your legal advisor; that is her job. You are an artist or craftsperson, your job is thinking creatively and putting that creativity in tangible form. Letting your attorney do her job gives you the freedom to do yours. A good attorney is one of your greatest allies. Don't start a business without one.

Contracts

As you make the transition from crafting as a hobby to becoming a professional you may have to change the way you look at things. Whenever you sign a written agreement you need to start recognizing it as a contract. These are a few of the types of business agreements you may need to sign as a business owner:

- Your Building Lease
- Consignment Agreements
- Craft Mall Agreements
- Custom Orders or Commissions

Have you ever thought of these as contracts? Is this an area where you may need to change your way of thinking about business?

DO YOUR HOMEWORK

If you do not already have one, now is the time to start looking for a business attorney.

1. If you already have an attorney for personal matters, ask if he could also represent you in business matters. If not, ask if he could refer you to someone.
2. Ask friends or family members who own their own business for the name of their business attorney. If you have a business advisor, do not forget to ask for her help with this.
3. Look in your local Yellow Pages under attorneys. If you live in a large city you may find listings by specialty. Remember that you are looking for someone who deals with small businesses, not Fortune 500 companies. When I looked in my local phone book under Attorneys: Business, Corporation, and Partnership, I found two with small ads that stood out. One said, "small business attorney," and the other offered "small business planning/consulting." I would probably start by contacting both of these.
4. Call your local bar association for a referral.

NEED MORE HELP?

LITERATURE

American Bar Association Staff. *The American Bar Association Legal Guide for Small Business: Everything a Small-Business Person Must Know, from Startup Employment Laws to Financing and Selling a Business.* New York: Three Rivers Press, 2000.

Campanelli, Melissa. "Dot.common Sense." *Entrepreneur Magazine* (May 2002).

Crawford, Tad. *Business and Legal Forms for Authors and Self-Publishers.* New York: Allworth Press, 2000. (Includes CD-ROM.)

————. *Business and Legal Forms for Crafts.* New York: Allworth Press, 1998. (Includes CD-ROM.)

————. *Business and Legal Forms for Fine Artists.* New York: Allworth Press, 1999. (Includes CD-ROM.)

————. *Business and Legal Forms for Photographers.* New York: Allworth Press, 2002. (Includes CD-ROM.)

————. *Legal Guide for the Visual Artist.* 4th ed. New York: Allworth Press, 1999.

Crawford, Tad, et. al. *The Artist-Gallery Partnership: A Practical Guide to Consigning Art.* New York: Allworth Press, 1998.

"Developing a Solid Relationship with Your Attorney." *Entrepreneur Magazine* (6 May 2002).

Doherty, M. Stephen. *Business Letters for Artists.* New York: Watson-Guptill Publications, 1993.

Du Boff, Leonard D. *The Law (In Plain English) for Crafts.* New York: Allworth Press, 1999.

Emereson, Robert W., and John Harwicke. *Business Law.* (Barron's Business Review Series.) Hauppauge, NY: Barron's Educational, 1997.

Lisante, Joan E. "Legal Aid." *Entrepreneur Magazine* (28 April 2000).

Maple, Stephen M. *The Complete Idiot's Guide to Law for Small Business.* Indianapolis, Ind.: Alpha, 2000.

Silver, Judith. "The ABC's of Web Site Law." *Entrepreneur Magazine* (13 May 2002). Available at: *www.entrepreneur.com/Your_Business/YB_SegArticle/0,4621,299623,00.html.*

WEB SITES

[Contact information is available in Appendix B.]

Findlaw

Lesson 7

DO YOU HAVE INSURANCE?

ARE YOU COVERED? By insurance that is. If your answer to this question is no, you are taking one of the biggest risks you can take.

✂ GET TO KNOW YOUR AGENT

This is an area where you *must* talk to a professional. The best place to start is your current insurance agent—the person who handles your automobile and homeowners policies. He already knows you and your current coverage and should be able to give information on your existing policy as well as any additional coverage you may need for your business. That does not mean you have to stay with the same company. By all means shop around. Compare coverage and prices, but an informal conversation with your current agent is a good place to start.

We have generally been blessed with wonderful insurance agents. Our agent when we started our retail business was a real jewel. We called and made an appointment, telling the receptionist we were starting a business and needed to discuss business coverage. The first meeting was very casual. We spent some time talking about crafts and our vision of the business. We then talked about our specific insurance needs. Our agent said she would send one of her staff agents out to look at our building and then call to schedule another meeting. When we arrived for the second meeting she handed us a printed proposal outlining what she saw as our minimum insurance needs and other options for additional coverage. Her proposal also addressed minor problems with our building that were uncovered during her agent's inspection. After asking any additional questions we had, we went home to study her recommendations and make our decision.

When we finally signed the paperwork, we felt we were making a well-informed decision.

I realize we had an exceptional agent. In fact, when we relocated our business to another state we tried to talk her into going with us. Actually, we got down on our knees, begged, pleaded, and shed a few tears. But even if your agent isn't a candidate for the "Agent of the Year Award," he is still your best source for insurance information. Remember, you have choices. Shop around for the best rates for the best coverage.

✂ WHAT TYPE OF INSURANCE DO YOU NEED?

The following are just a few types of insurance that might be helpful to you. These are not all required or necessary in every circumstance. Insurance is a personal decision concerning the amount of risk you want to assume and what you think you should share with others.

Do not, I repeat, do not go without *health insurance.* Not having health insurance is nothing short of gambling, and if you lose, you lose big. If you are married and your spouse is still employed outside the home, you may have or be able to obtain coverage there. Individual health plans are available but expensive. It is still a good idea to get a quote from an agent for comparison. Many organizations offer group plans for their members. You may already be a member of such an organization. Contact the Artists' Health Insurance Resource Center sponsored by the Actors' Fund for help in finding such a group. Do not be concerned about the name of the sponsoring organization. This is for all artists. One unexpected illness or accident could easily wipe you out financially without insurance. It is a big risk and not one worth taking. Find a way to get the best deal you can, but get it!

Property insurance covers damaged or destroyed equipment, buildings, and so on. Be sure you know the specific types of losses that are covered and not covered. Get it in writing. The last things you need are surprises when disaster strikes. The time to find out you do not have flood insurance is not when you are knee deep in mud. Do not assume anything. If it is not written in the policy, and you feel you need a particular coverage, make sure it gets there. If it is there, and you don't need it, ask how much you would save to have it removed. Be sure also to consider fire, theft, electrical storms, wind damage, falling objects, malicious intent, collision, and other uncontrollable and damaging events.

You will also want to check into *liability insurance.* There are *three basic types of liability insurance. General liability* covers business premises owned or leased by you to protect you in the event of an accident resulting in injury to anyone while visiting your place of business. If you lease space at craft fairs, some contracts place liability responsibility on you if a person is injured while in your leased space or in front of it. Get your insurance agent to write a rider clause that this possibility is covered when buying your general liability insurance. If you have a retail gallery or open your studio to customers, you will also want to look at liability insurance to protect you if someone is injured on your premises. This should also cover business sidewalks, parking lots, and surrounding property. Product liability insurance covers injuries incurred by others from products made by you.

If you work at home, you may need to update your *homeowners or renters policy*. Your basic policy may or may not cover office equipment, work in progress, or other business property.

Is your *automobile insurance adequate?* You may need special coverage if you use your personal vehicle for business purposes. This usually depends on the percentage of time the vehicle is used for business purposes. Get specific with your agent on this one.

As with health insurance, you may suddenly find yourself without *life insurance* when you quit your full-time day job. Life insurance gives your spouse, family, and business partners assurance that they can continue financially without you in the event of your untimely death. The best rule of thumb is to figure your portion of both your personal and business budget times five for your minimum amount of life insurance coverage.

Disability insurance is personal income assurance in the event of the loss of your ability to do a job that brings you income. Make sure you know if the policy covers either short- or long-term disability and the types of disabilities covered. Also be certain it defines the type of work you are doing as legitimate work or employment and what is required to prove income.

Business interruption insurance is more important if you are in business with other people and are a prime factor in their ability to continue the business. If the others in the business may eventually be able to recuperate after a period of time and continue in the business without you, then this is a good policy. If not, consider more life insurance to help your partners get reestablished.

Good, adequate insurance that will meet the needs of both your business and your family is important. These are, however, personal decisions only you can make after discussions with your family, business partners, and, of course, your insurance agent. The worksheet included with this lesson may be used to gather and record information to assist you in making these decisions.

DO YOUR HOMEWORK

Have you ever asked someone for information, then, thirty minutes later, couldn't remember the details? This has happened to me, more than once. That is why I have included worksheets in this book, to give you a place to write down information received from other people.

Talking to your insurance agent is one occasion when information is going to be flying in all directions and you might have a hard time catching it. Be sure to write down the important details and get as much in writing from your agent as you can.

To use the insurance worksheets, determine if each type of insurance is required for your business now, if you can wait, or if you are willing to assume the risk yourself—the latter is known as self-insurance. Write down the names of companies, price quotes, and any notes you think are important. Obtain quotes from at least two different companies. Make copies of the worksheet as needed to record this information.

Insurance Worksheet

TYPE OF INSURANCE

❑ Health Insurance
❑ Property Insurance
❑ Liability Insurance
❑ Homeowners Insurance

❑ Automobile Insurance
❑ Life Insurance
❑ Disability Insurance
❑ Business Interruption Insurance

❑ Other _____

Company Name: _____

Agent: _____

Phone Number: _____

E-mail: _____

Quoted Rates: _____

_____

_____

_____

_____

Coverage: _____

_____

_____

_____

_____

_____

_____

_____

_____

_____

_____

_____

_____

Notes: _____

_____

_____

_____

_____

NEED MORE HELP?

LITERATURE

Coughlin, Kirsten, and Marcy Newbold (compilers). "Health Care Insurance for Craftspeople." *The Crafts Report* (September 1998).

Finnerty, Bernadette. "A National Health Care Crisis: How to Cover the Working Uninsured." *The Crafts Report* (July 2002).

Godin, Seth. *If You're Clueless about Insurance and Want to Know More.* Chicago: Dearborn Trade, 1997.

Grant, Daniel. "To Your Health-Insurance Plans for Artists." *Sunshine Artist Magazine* (July 1999).

Norman, Jan. "How To: Insure Your Homebased Business." *Business Startups Magazine* (May 1998).

Rohland, Pamela. "Quick Guide to Insurance." *Entrepreneur Magazine* (September 2000).

Tiffany, Laura. "Insure Your Business." *Entrepreneur Magazine* (22 March 2001).

MORE INFORMATION ON
HEALTH INSURANCE
[Contact information is available in Appendix B.]
Artists' Health Insurance Resource Center
Insurance Information Institute
Insurance Resources for Craftspeople

MEMBERSHIP ORGANIZATIONS OFFERING
HEALTH INSURANCE AS A BENEFIT
[Contact information is available in Appendix B.]
The Alliance for Affordable Services
American Association of Retired Persons

Chicago Artist's Coalition
National Association for the Self-Employed
National Small Business United
New York Artists Equity Association
Small Business Service Bureau
Working Today

Lesson 8

MONEY, MONEY, MONEY, MONEY

WHATEVER YOUR MOTIVATION for going into business, finding your startup money is one of the most difficult and frustrating parts of starting a business. The most frustration comes from having a dream with no means of making that dream reality.

If you have the money to get your business started, but are expecting the business to support itself or your family immediately, chances are your days as a business owner are numbered. We have all heard of the dramatic exceptions, but this is not the way things usually happen.

✂ SO, WHERE DOES THE MONEY COME FROM?

The most obvious source of startup money for your business is your *personal savings*. This can go a long way toward getting you started, but do you have enough to keep you afloat for two years while you build your business? Be careful about draining your savings account dry. Remember to keep enough money on hand for personal emergencies that may arise, such as the car breaking down, the dog getting sick, or a loan payment coming due.

Your business may also be financed by liquidating or borrowing against any *personal investments* you have such as IRAs, stock, or life insurance. Remember, if you take money out of a retirement account such as an IRA or 401k that was not taxed before it went into the account, you will have to pay taxes on that money when you withdraw it. You may also have to pay other penalties for early withdrawal, not to mention the fact that your retirement money will not be there when you want or need to retire. The same goes for life insurance policies. Some policies have a cash value you can borrow against, but you could leave your loved ones with a major financial burden if you should die before you repay the money borrowed. It is also not a good idea to take money from savings intended to pay for your children's education. No matter how well intentioned you are about replenishing the money, you have no guarantee the money will be there to do so. Please do not gamble with your children's education.

Family and friends may be able to help with your startup money, but a strong word of caution is in order here. We all know there can be complications from borrowing from or lending to friends and family. Families have been torn apart and friendships lost over money. Do not borrow money from anyone, not even your grandmother, without some sort of written agreement spelling out the duration of the loan, when and how repayment is due, and any interest issues. This is something I personally think is just better not to do, but only you can determine if your personal relationships will stand up to borrowing money. A somewhat safer but also problematic alternative would be to have your friend or family member cosign a conventional bank loan for you.

There is always the option of taking on a *business partner;* but this, too, is somewhat dangerous. Be careful when choosing a partner, even a silent one. Legally, you and your partner become co-owners of everything. If the partner takes on a debt that she cannot pay, even a personal loan, you become liable. Your business partner must also be someone you can work with, someone who shares your vision. While a partner may be able to point out problems or needs you do not see, if you are always miles apart in your thinking on important issues it may be difficult to get anything accomplished.

There are people and corporations looking for businesses to invest in. These are known as venture capitalists. They are not the best source of funding for artists and craftspeople, however, because they see your business purely as an investment. Their one goal is to make money and lots of it. Are you ready for this type of pressure?

Special loan or grant programs may be available to help you start your business. These may depend on your gender or ethnic background. There may be special programs available to help start a business if you are a single parent, a displaced homemaker, or if you fall into the category of being economically disadvantaged. Contact your state social services agency, the local YWCA, or your local community action program for information on these programs. The Small Business Administration or your local Small Business Development Center may also have information on these for you. There may also be money available through economic development funds for locating your business in certain areas of your city.

✂ APPROACHING YOUR BANKER

Bankers and other investors will gladly invest their money in your business if you can prove you have a strong possibility of making them money, but that is the only way they will do so. The Small Business Administration has several loan guarantee programs that are worth looking into if you really feel you must borrow money. Information on these is available on the SBA Web site.

Don't even think about approaching a banker about a business loan unless you are prepared and organized. Go in with a formal, written business plan that includes how much money you need, why you need it, and how you will pay it back. For more information on how to approach a lender, the best place to start is the Small Business Administration (see *www.sba.gov*); your banker and the business department of a local college can also be very helpful.

Expect a difficult road if you go to your banker for financing. The fact is that artists and crafters simply are not considered a good risk. This may be because we too often do not understand business, and this is something you will have to overcome. This is where a business plan is essential.

There are business books and articles that recommend using credit cards to finance your business. Please do not even consider this. It is not something we will ever recommend. In fact, except in those very rare instances when you anticipate immediate income possibilities (within thirty-day absolute payoff situations) we believe it could be foolish. It is just too easy to forget that when you use a credit card to pay for anything you are borrowing money, and at what is usually a very high interest rate. I doubt anyone ever puts a purchase on a credit card without the intention of paying the bill, but anyone who has ever used a charge card knows how easy it is for credit card debt to get away from you.

✂ THERE IS ALWAYS ANOTHER WAY TO GO

The best way to finance a small art or craft business, I believe, is to keep it small and work at it part-time until you simply cannot fill your orders any other way than by quitting your day job. If you have a working spouse or domestic partner, sit down together and decide if you can live on one income while you start your business. This must be a mutual decision. Don't let your dream of your own business cost you your family.

Reinvestment is the key. Put any money you earn from your art right back into it.

Any form of financing is very time-consuming, expensive, and in most cases very frustrating. Remember, art is an expression of freedom. The more your business is financed by other people, the more investors will want to control that freedom of self-expression.

How did we finance our business? The money to start our business came from personal savings, investments, and a small inheritance. When I read those words, I think to myself, "This sounds like we were wealthy"—we were not. We did have to decide what our priorities were when it came to using what money we had. We chose to invest in our business rather than making major purchases such as a house or a new car.

The way you choose to finance your business must fit your personality; your lifestyle; and your moral, spiritual, and ethical beliefs—especially your beliefs about money. Remember, whenever you borrow money the day will come to pay it back. Will you be ready?

DO YOUR HOMEWORK

1. Get your business plan in order. This is talked about more in lesson 22, but keep in mind that building your business plan is what this whole book is about.
2. Estimate how much money you are going to need to get started.
3. Don't have a clue? Begin by estimating the following expenses:

_____ Building rent
_____ Equipment
_____ Advertising
_____ Business phone
_____ Utilities
_____ Business licenses
_____ Product and supplies
_____ Office supplies (receipt books, letterhead, etc.)
_____ Professional services (attorney, accountant, etc.)
_____ Other (specify)

4. Where is the money you need to get started?

❑ Don't have a clue
❑ Personal savings
❑ Income of spouse or partner
❑ Investments
❑ Keeping your day job
❑ A family member (parents, in-laws, rich uncle)
❑ Private investors
❑ The bank
❑ The government
❑ A business partner

5. Learn about any special programs offering funding or services for which you may qualify.
6. Before borrowing money make a plan for how you are going to repay the loan. Be as realistic and specific as possible.
7. Be sure that any potential business partners or investors share your vision. This is important! How much are you willing to sacrifice to please your investors?
8. Are you really financially ready to quit your day job?

NEED MORE HELP?

LITERATURE

Dillehay, James. *Directory of Grants for Crafts and How to Write a Winning Proposal.* Torreon, N. Mex.: Warm Snow Publishers, 2000.

Evenson, David R. *Where to Go When the Bank Says No: Alternatives for Financing Your Business.* Princeton, N.J.: Bloomberg Press, 1998.

Godin, Seth. *The Bootstrappers Bible: How to Start and Build a Business with a Great Idea and (Almost) No Money.* Chicago: Upstart Publishing Co., 1998.

Green, Charles. *The SBA Loan Book.* Holbrook, Mass.: Adams Media Corp., 1999.

Long, Mark H. *Financing the New Venture.* Holbrook, Mass.: Adams Media Corp, 2000.

Magos, Alice H., ed. *Small Business Financing: How and Where to Get It.* Chicago: Commerce Clearing House, 1998.

Radeschi, Loretta. "Tips for Financial Stability and Growth." Crafts Finance Column. *The Crafts Report* (June 2002).

Robbins, Stever. "Asking Friends or Family for Financing." *Entrepreneur Magazine* (October 2001).

Spaeder, Karen E. "Pre Startup Checklist." *Entrepreneur's Startup Magazine* (December 2001).

WORKSHEETS
[Contact information is available in Appendix B.]
Entrepreneur Startup Costs Work Sheet

Lesson 9

HANDLING CASH AND OTHER FINANCIAL MATTERS

ONE OF THE FIRST PEOPLE you will want to sit down and have a chat with is your banker. Do not try to discuss business money matters with a teller. Ask to speak to the branch manager or an officer. She will take you to her desk or office where you can sit down and visit for awhile. It is a good idea to take a list of questions along with you to make certain you cover everything.

OPENING A BUSINESS ACCOUNT

You will want to open a separate checking account for your business. Your banker can explain your options to you. You may be thinking, *Why do I need a business checking account?*

One reason you need a business account is *to keep your business finances separate from your personal finances.* Never mix business money with personal money; it is unprofessional and causes confusion when dealing with financial professionals and the IRS.

Another reason you need a business account is for *tax purposes.* Bank statements and canceled checks will help provide you with a legal form of record keeping.

Having a separate business checking account is also *part of your professional image.* A business check is one form of proof of your business status that is acceptable to wholesale suppliers, if you buy your supplies this way.

It is imperative to have a running record of all income and expenses as they occur if you are attempting to keep your bookkeeping procedures as simple as possible. Your checkbook can act as your accounting ledger— either in your actual checkbook or in electronic form. Use this to keep track of all of your costs and sales. But this is effective only if you are persistent in entering all of your transactions into your check record book. This means that all income, no matter how small a dollar amount the sale might be, must be deposited into the checking account and entered into the record book as a separate deposit to make it possible to be traced in the future if necessary. Likewise, all purchases made for the business must be made through the checking account, regardless of how small. If purchases are made in any other way, then the checkbook loses its value as a replacement for a bookkeeper's ledger, and all check records must then be transferred from the checkbook to a posted accounting ledger. If there is income you receive for your business that you do not put into your business checking account, then once again you have destroyed your check record book as your ledger.

If you have not decided what types of payment you are going to accept, talk this over with your banker. She may have valuable information for you.

✂ HANDLING CASH

The best way to assure you will be paid, of course, is to have a *cash-only business*. This option is not without its dangers, however. For instance, anyone who runs a business should go to the bank and ask for instruction in spotting counterfeit bills. Ask your banker to explain what you should look for. Be sure your employees also know this information. This might not totally protect you from receiving counterfeit bills, but knowing what to look for will help.

When the new bills first came out—you know, the ones that look like monopoly money—Bob happened to be at the bank. One of the vice presidents, who was also a personal friend, was holding a handful of the new bills and asked Bob, "Have you seen one of these yet?" Bob said no, and our banker friend proceeded to explain the new bills to him. It was a quick and easy lesson. Don't be afraid to ask your banker to do this; it is part of his job.

Another danger associated with a cash-only business is that having large amounts of cash on hand could make you a target for robbery. Routinely making bank deposits when your cash on hand exceeds a predetermined amount will help reduce the risk. This might require making more than one trip to the bank during the day. Another commonsense tip is to never count your cash in front of customers or where someone could walk in on you. Either count your cash after store hours, with the door locked, or go into an office or a separate area of your store or gallery and lock the door.

Be aware that if you run a cash-only business you will turn away potential customers. Not everyone who comes into your retail store or to your booth at a craft show will be carrying cash. If you sell higher-priced items this customer loss will be especially true, as most people are not used to paying cash for larger purchases.

Don't Flash Your Cash at Craft Shows

When working an art or craft show, and dealing with large amounts of cash, don't flash it around. Remove excess cash to a safe place, and don't leave your cash box unattended. Many crafters now use cash registers, and these are ideal, but remember that you need an electrical outlet. I do not recommend aprons for cash at a show. The tops of the pockets are open, and money may be easily seen as well as work its way out of the pocket. My personal preference is a fanny pack because I am able to keep it on my person and it has a zipper closure. It is not easy to keep your eye on a cash box and wait on customers at the same time.

ACCEPTING CHECKS

Maybe you do not want to operate as a cash-only business. What do you need to know about accepting checks? If you decide to accept checks ask your banker for pointers on safe and legal ways to accept and verify checks. Things to cover in this conversation include acceptable forms of identification, what might make a check look suspicious, and check verification systems available in your area. You might want to wait and see if you actually have problems with checks before investing in a check verification system.

You will also want to decide if you will accept out-of-town checks. What about out-of-state checks? If you live on a state border as we do, you will probably want to accept checks from both states. Include this in your talk with your banker.

It is a good idea to keep checks in a place not readily visible to customers, such as under the cash tray in the cash register. When you take cash deposits to the bank, take any checks you may have received along with you. Have a special stamp made to endorse the back of your checks. This stamp should include the bank's routing number and your account number. This type of stamp may be ordered from most office supply stores, or your banker should be able to give you information on where to order one.

✂ CREDIT CARDS

But perhaps you want to accept credit cards. Credit cards are a popular way of accepting payment, but you do not just open a new business and start accepting credit cards. You must apply for a merchant account and you must be accepted. Don't be too surprised if you don't qualify right away. When first opening a small business, you may have to deal in cash and checks for a short time, while establishing a credit history for your business.

The best place to start in acquiring credit card merchant status is your current bank. Include credit cards in your talk with your banker.

There will be an application to complete. Be prepared to provide both personal and business financial information and references. It is not a good idea to try to hide past or current financial problems, since the bank has access to this information anyway. You will also be asked to estimate your average sale. This will determine the amount you can accept on a credit card purchase without calling for approval—also known as your "floor limit." This could affect your chances for acceptance, since there is a greater risk with larger amounts being charged.

You will also need to decide if you want to use an electronic verification terminal or a manual card imprinter. The manual route will cost less money but is more inconvenient for both you and the bank. If you are only on the show circuit, however, this option may be necessary.

As with any business transaction, read the contract carefully before you sign. Be sure you are aware of and understand all fees you will be charged for accepting credit cards. Remember, even small per-transaction fees add up.

If you have trouble qualifying for merchant status, wait six months and try again. You may also want to investigate other ways of accepting credit cards. Check with any small business organizations you belong to for information on this.

Accepting credit cards may make certain aspects of your business easier, but remember, they carry their own problems. Not qualifying for merchant status is not the end of the world. It is possible to run a business accepting cash and checks only. We have done it. Deciding what types of payment to accept is totally up to you. Gather information, weigh the positives and negatives of each form of payment, and make an informed decision. Sources of more detailed information on credit cards follow this lesson.

The best time to decide what types of payment you are going to accept is before you start selling. The moment when a customer asks if you will take a check is not the time to decide if and how you will accept checks. If a customer asks if you take credit cards and you are not able to do so, a response such as "No, but I do take checks," may save the sale.

A trip to the bank is an important early step in starting your business. Get to know your banker. She's a good friend to have.

Do Your Homework

1. Gather information on business accounts from three different financial institutions. Compare the benefits, strengths, and weaknesses of each type of account. Make your decision based on what works best for your business.
2. Decide what types of payment you *want* to accept from your customers.
3. Do your research on each type of payment, including paperwork and expenses associated with each. Now decide what types of payment you *can* accept.
4. Develop your own plan for handling cash. Be sure to include counting cash, spotting counterfeit bills, handling cash at craft shows, bank deposits, and so on.
5. Develop your own plan for accepting checks. Include legal forms of identification, check verification systems, accepting out-of-town or out-of-state checks, and other guidelines.
6. Look at the credit card option. Do your research on the various types of credit cards and the procedure for applying for a merchant account. Do you and your business meet the criteria for a merchant account? Are there other ways to be able to accept credit cards?

NEED MORE HELP?

LITERATURE

Casey, Christine. "Q&A: Credit Card Processing." *Sunshine Artist Magazine* (cited: March 2003). Available at: *http://sunshineartist.com/magazine/ccprocess.htm*.

Chypre, Betty. "The Credit Card Wars." Choices (31 October 2000; cited: March 2003). Available at: *www.smartfrogs.com/ccwars.html*.

Hazy, Debbie. "How Would You Like to Pay?" *Sunshine Artist Magazine* (cited: March 2003). Available at: *http://sunshineartist.com/magazine/paymethod.htm*.

Joyner, Jim. "Credit Card Processing in Two Steps." *The Crafts Report* (April 1999).

Lasley, William T. "Accepting Credit Card Payments." *About.com* (cited: July 2002). Available at: *www.artsandcrafts.about.com/library/weekly/aa070600.htm?terms=credit+cards*.

"Public Opinion: What Credit Card Terminal Do You Use? Where Did You Get a Merchant Account?" *The Crafts Report* (August 2001).

Simon, Stacey. "Make Credit Cards Work for You." *The Crafts Report* (September 1999).

Yankee, Steve. "How to Get Credit Card Merchant Status for Your Small Business." *VideoUniversity.com* (cited: March 2003). Available at: *www.videouniversity.com/credcdsy.htm*.

Lesson 10

USING YOUR TAX RETURN AS YOUR ANNUAL REPORT

MOST PEOPLE REALLY DON'T ENJOY doing paperwork. Even those of us who have held jobs where we were paper pushers do not relish the idea of more paperwork. Filing an annual tax return is one of those paperwork jobs everyone complains about, but which we all have to do. So why not make the best of it? While this lesson is not intended to tell you how to keep your books, or how to make out your records, we hope it can give you some useful tips concerning how to make these requirements easier.

When you own a small business, the annual exercise in filing your federal income taxes can do double duty. It can serve as your annual financial report for your business while it satisfies the need to support our government's financial needs. Expenses, profit, and loss—it's all right there in your business tax return; or at least it should be if it is done right.

If you look at your tax return in this light your goal each year should be to pay more taxes. Okay, I heard all those gasps! I think I may have even heard a few people hit the floor when they fainted. Why on earth would anyone want to pay more taxes? Calm down, get back in your chair, and read the rest of this chapter before you throw this book away.

One of the keys to success for anyone going into business is the ability to turn otherwise distasteful duties and situations into useful and profitable ones. Paying taxes, specifically federal income taxes, on an annual basis, is a good example of this. In one sense you can measure your financial success by how big your tax bill is. In other words, if you are paying more taxes, you are also making more money—as long as you are taking advantage of all the allowable exemptions and deductions available to you. Good for you!

✄ GETTING TO KNOW THE IRS

The first unique nuisance that business owners must face, when fulfilling this national responsibility, is that the tax forms for reporting business income are more complicated than those for reporting personal income. Welcome to the brave new world of filing a business return.

Look at it this way. You will have the opportunity to learn many new things. You will learn about new tax forms. Schedule C is the tax form most of you will need to become familiar with since you will most likely own your own businesses and will intentionally keep your business small. However, if you take on partners or become incorporated you will need to use other forms to report your business' income; not-for-profit cooperatives also have their own set of tax rules. It is best to check with either the Internal Revenue Service (IRS) or your local tax expert for advice about these rules.

These various forms, and instructions concerning how to complete them, can be found in an IRS Internet site called *The Digital Daily*. This online magazine is an information service established by the IRS to help change the negative image it had developed in the late twentieth century. *The Digital Daily* has quickly become an excellent method of communication between the people who have to collect the taxes and those having to pay them—much better than having to wait for two or more hours on the phone for a representative to be able to help you as Bob did in the late 1970s. We recommend that everyone, whether you follow your dream of setting up your own business or not, check out *The Digital Daily* as a new way of viewing the IRS.

Doing your own bookkeeping, accounting, and taxes is a wonderful opportunity to learn just how your money works for you. You will need to learn about several simple and not so simple methods, which can either make or break your business. For instance, a business or a self-employed person is expected, in most cases, to pay taxes quarterly. Remember, there is no longer a paycheck from which to withhold your personal income taxes. And if your business hires employees there will be even more new things to learn.

You may consider this bad news, but there is also good news. It's all right there in *The Digital Daily*. The IRS has numerous publications, and even classes, available to help you learn these things. While you're at the IRS Web site, you will also want to visit the IRS Small Business Corner at *www.irs.gov/smallbiz/index.htm*. Spend some time there just looking around. You will find important information that will help you understand your responsibilities as a small business owner.

The IRS offers a number of publications and services to help small business owners. *The Small Business Resource Guide CD-ROM 2001* (Publication s3207), developed jointly by the Internal Revenue Service and the Small Business Administration, is available by calling (800) 829-3676. There is no charge for a single copy.

If you prefer to have your information in hard copy, "Your Business Tax Kit" is an assortment of IRS forms and publications with information for business owners. You will also want to order "Starting a Business and Keeping Records" (Publication 583). Another good publication to have is the "Guide to Free Tax Services" (Publication 910), which is an overview of services available from the IRS.

The IRS has also developed classes for small business owners, which they cosponsor with local organizations. These may be available in your area. For more information, call either your local IRS office or (800) 829-1040 and ask for the Taxpayer Education Coordinator. Ask about the Small Business Tax Education program.

Anytime you are dealing with information or printed documents concerning taxes, be sure it is the most current available. A tax booklet, even from the IRS, that is two or more years old may do you more harm than good. Remember, tax law is in a constant state of change. What was true last year may not be this year. That is why we prefer *The Digital Daily*.

✂ SCHEDULE C

Now that you know how to find information from the IRS, we need to go back to Schedule C, which is designed for small, independent, unincorporated businesses. On the 2002 federal tax forms, the 1040 form (line 12) provides space for business income. This directs you to place here the figure from Schedule C or C-EZ—the forms Uncle Sam provides for you to figure business income. You may think this means you must complete the long form for your personal taxes also, itemizing your deductions on the 1040 form, but this is true only if you choose to do so.

I have already mentioned some IRS publications, but if you have problems with Schedule C you will want to look at some other more specific publications. "Business Expenses" (#535) is as good as any up-to-date college course on understanding how expenses affect business income. It defines what a business expense is, what taxes to figure in your expenses, and insurance you should consider.

This publication also talks about methods of depreciation and which you should use. Depreciation (the wearing out of equipment) is defined as a recovery of the cost of expenses for tangible business expenses. In an article titled "Cost Recovery" in *The Digital Daily*, the IRS explains it as follows:

You can usually "recover" (subtract from income) your cost for capital expenses over a number of years. Each year a part of your basis is recovered through depreciation or amortization. Use depreciation to recover capital expenses for most tangible business assets. Use amortization to recover the cost of intangible assets, such as startup costs. Amortization is discussed in chapter 9 of Publication 535.

Depletion (the using up of supplies) and bad business debts, as well as depreciation, amortization, and other similar topics are covered in this brief, sixty-page booklet along with many other topics. And it is there to help you understand how to use these business expenses to lower your tax debt. You may need professional help to understand these terms. Along with these expenses you can deduct from the cost of producing and selling your products, others like traveling, meals, and entertainment are included in the relatively long list of deductible expenses when figuring your federal income taxes.

You may want to take an introductory tax or bookkeeping course. But how these expenses affect your income is all right there in the IRS information. Don't forget that this help your tax dollars have already paid for is available at the IRS office just a phone call away.

If this booklet does not answer your questions—and since the tax code (laws) fills literally thousands of pages, they very well may not—there are other booklets listed on page 2 of Publication #535 that may help you. These booklets answer questions about things like casualties, disasters, and theft (see Publication #547); travel, entertainment, gift, and car expenses (#463); and just what is defined as income, both taxable and nontaxable (#525). And this is just the beginning of the topics available from the IRS.

The business tax forms (C or C-EZ), if used honestly and properly, while following the IRS guidelines as carefully as possible, are some of the best tools available to determine just how well your business is doing. Remember, the government uses the tax dollars it collects from you and other fellow citizens and business owners around the country to provide a multitude of services. Some of these are very visible, such as our armed services, national parks, and the federal court systems. Others are not so well known but not necessarily any less important. Paying taxes in this country helps provide these otherwise unaffordable services.

✂ DO YOU NEED TO HIRE AN ACCOUNTANT?

The answer to this question is not necessarily yes. There is no reason you as an individual cannot prepare and file your own business tax return.

Whether or not you feel you have the time to do the research and complete the paperwork while also running your business is up to you. However, if you are intimidated by mathematical formulas, by the prospect of addition, subtraction, and even percentage problems—you know who you are—then hiring a person who does do this type of work well could save you hundreds of dollars.

If you do decide to hire someone to help you with this you have choices. Tax preparers, accountants, and tax attorneys are readily available. Be sure they are familiar with the tax code as it pertains to small business and have experience preparing small business returns. Do not forget: Never sign a tax return prepared by someone else without looking it over. If you have questions, do not be afraid to ask. Mistakes, of course, may be made by anyone. However, even though a professional who prepares your tax return signs the return with you and is responsible to go with you if your return is audited, it is you who will ultimately be held responsible for any taxes or penalties if mistakes are made.

It could be helpful if your tax preparer, accountant, or tax attorney knows about arts and crafts, because they may be able to help you think of deductions and other tax-related issues particular to your business that a generalist would not. However, in the eyes of the IRS, business is business. What is most important is that the person who prepares your taxes know about business taxes; it is up to you to know your business well enough to answer the tax preparer's questions adequately.

If you decide to prepare your own business returns there is help. In addition to books, articles, and IRS publications, software packages are available for completing and filing tax returns. If you already do your accounting by computer, you may want to consider buying tax software. Be sure the software you buy fits your needs and is the most current version. This is true anytime you are dealing with information, printed documents, or software concerning taxes. Tax law is in a constant state of change. What was true last year may not be true this year.

✃ BE PREPARED TO PAY QUARTERLY

Remember, you no longer have a paycheck to withhold your taxes from; it is now your responsibility to file and pay quarterly. Do not be caught without the money to pay your taxes. Bob and I recommend keeping a separate tax saving account at your bank or credit union. Estimate your annual tax bill and divide by twelve, putting that amount in your account monthly. This is your tax account. Using the money for other purposes will defeat the goal of the tax account.

Paying your fair share of taxes should never be a major problem if you keep your end goal in sight: increasing your earnings annually. By always being honest, forthright, and sometimes providing a little more information than the government asks for, we have avoided the inconvenience of being called in for an audit. Bob has always done our personal and business income tax returns himself, and he is not an accountant.

✂ ONE LAST TIP

In art work you are required to keep separate records for each project you sell. The easiest way to do this is with a large, nine-by-twelve-inch envelope: Write a description of the project on the outside of the envelope and then place the store receipts inside the envelope as they are received. Although this means that you will have to make separate purchases for each different project, it satisfies the IRS requirement of keeping separate books for the various projects, especially if there is a possibility that the project may need to be worked on between two or more tax years.

DO YOUR HOMEWORK

1. Educate yourself on the tax code as it applies to small business. The following are a few of the ways to do this:

❑ Order the appropriate publications from the IRS
❑ Visit the IRS Web site at *www.irs.gov*
❑ Visit the SBA Web site at *www.sba.gov*
❑ Take a class

2. If you plan to use tax software, go to the computer store and look around. See what is available. Write down the names of the programs you find. Read as much as you can about each program. Internet and computer magazines are good places to start. Make an informed decision as to what is the best software for your business needs. Be sure that the tax software you use is designed for small business. It should also be the most recent version reflecting current tax law.

3. Do you have a tax advisor available if needed?

❑ Tax preparer
❑ Accountant
❑ Tax attorney
❑ Other _____

4. Remember, this needs to be someone who has experience with small business returns. Be sure to place the name and contact information in your rolodex, card file, address book, or computer file for easy reference.

NEED MORE HELP?

LITERATURE

Carter, Gary W. J. K. *Lasser's Taxes Made Easy for Your Home-Based Business: The Ultimate Tax Handbook for Self-Employed Professionals, Consultants and Freelancers.* 4th ed. New York: John Wiley and Sons, 2000.

Battersby, Mark. "Across State Lines Legally: Doing Business in Other States." *Sunshine Artist Magazine* (April 2001).

———. "Goodbye April 15—Hello Tax Return Examination." *Sunshine Artist Magazine* (October 2000).

———. "Snag Tax Deductions in Your Web." *Sunshine Artist Magazine* (cited: March 2003). Available at: *www.sunshineartist.com/magazine/webtax.htm.*

———. "For What It's Worth: Tax Rules Concerning Charitable Donations." *Sunshine Artist Magazine* (February 2001).

Internal Revenue Service, Department of the Treasury. "Cost Recovery." *The Digital Daily* (cited: March 2003). Available at: *www.irs.gov/formspubs/display/0,,i1%3D50%26genericId%3D12761,00.html.*

———. "Publication 535: Business Expenses—When Can I Deduct an Expense?" *The Digital Daily* (cited: July 2002). For use in preparing 2002 tax returns. Available at: *www.irs.gov/formspubs/page/0,,id%3d103918,00.html.*

Kamoroff, Bernard B. *422 Tax Deductions for Businesses and Self-Employed Individuals.* Laytonville, Calif.: Bell Springs Publishing, 2001.

Savage, Michael. *Don't Let the IRS Destroy Your Small Business: 76 Mistakes to Avoid.* 3rd ed. Reading, Mass.: Perseus Publishing, 1998.

Weltman, Barbara. J. K. *Lasser's New Rules for Small Business Taxes.* 5th ed. New York: John Wiley and Sons, 2002.

West, Susan. "33 Bookkeeping Necessities for the Craft Business." (cited: March 2003) Available at: *www.sunshineglassworks.com/bookkeeping.shtml.*

Zobel, Jon. *Minding Her Own Business: The Self-Employed Woman's Guide to Taxes and Record Keeping.* Holbrook, Mass.: Adams Media Corp., 2000.

GO STRAIGHT TO THE SOURCE—
THE INTERNAL REVENUE SERVICE (IRS)
[Up to the first five copies of these CD-ROMs are free. Call 800-829-3676.]
Small Business Tax Calendar,
Publication #1518.

Introduction to Federal Taxes,
Publication #3693.
Small Business Resource Guide,
Publication #3207.
Virtual Small Business Workshop,
Publication #3700.

SOFTWARE

Turbo Tax Business, Turbo Tax Business State, and Turbo Tax Home & Business are released annually by Intuit, Inc. (*www.intuitinc.com*) and are available at most bookstores.

Tax Cut can be purchased from H&R Block Home & Business, H&R Block World Headquarters, 440 Main Street, Kansas City, Missouri 64111.

Lesson 11

GETTING THE BEST PRICE FOR SUPPLIES

WHEN I BEGAN WRITING this lesson my focus was on telling you how to buy your supplies wholesale. Then I realized I might be steering you in the wrong direction. The real issue at hand is getting the best price possible, given your circumstances. You may not use enough of a particular item to qualify for wholesale prices. You may be able to buy some supplies wholesale and not others. The goal is to get the best price you can.

✄ HOW DO YOU FIND THE BEST PRICE?

Know your retail prices. The best way to start looking for the best price is to know what your supplies sell for normally at retail prices. Check you area art, craft, fabric, or other retail stores. Compare various prices among them. Keep this information in a small notebook you can keep with you. Update it from time to time as you shop. This will give you a baseline to compare with other types of pricing you may find. A supplier may say he is offering wholesale prices, but if the price is just a few pennies lower than your local retailer it may not be worth the extra paperwork or any applicable shipping and handling costs.

How do you find a manufacturer or wholesaler? A good place to start is by looking on the packaging of your supplies. There should be at least a name and sometimes an address. Or look through a business directory such as the *Thomas Register,* usually available in the reference or business section of your library. Or, if you are savvy with the Internet, do a search on a good search engine.

Who can buy wholesale? You will be asked to prove that you meet the qualifications for a wholesale buyer. Remember, you are playing with the big boys.

This is the time to put your best professional foot forward. All correspondence should be conducted on letterhead. You will be asked to provide your tax resale number. Other items you may be asked for to verify your business include brochures, business cards, letterhead, catalogs, a business check, or other specific items the supplier may find important. Don't be surprised by their requests. Unless you are a large buyer, most transactions take place by phone, fax, mail, or e-mail. However, don't be surprised if a company representative stops by early in your relationship with the company to see your business.

How much will you have to buy? Minimum orders vary and may be defined by dollar amount or quantity. Read the manufacturer's or distributor's rules for this very carefully.

What Exactly Is Wholesale?

The way the word is used in actual practice by industry varies greatly. Some define wholesale in dollar values. Others define it by quantity. For still other companies, wholesale prices are given only for items intended for resale in a retail store. So when looking for a wholesale supplier the first thing to do is find each company's definition of wholesale. Then discover what you have to do to qualify for wholesale prices from each supplier. Stay within those guidelines and get excellent prices you can make a profit with—simple as that.

✄ ALTERNATIVES TO RETAIL

Now please don't think if you cannot qualify for wholesale pricing, you are doomed to paying retail. That is not necessarily the case. There are other options.

Distributors often offer a form of wholesale pricing somewhere between factory direct and retail. They usually offer deals on hundreds of items per purchase, instead of thousands of items like manufacturers. Ask manufacturers or wholesalers if they can connect you with a distributor in your area.

Buying clubs may charge a yearly membership fee, but then members qualify for discounts for supplies ordered through the club. Rules and membership requirements are going to vary from club to club, so check them out. Don't forget, your membership fee counts as part of the cost of buying this way in your bookkeeping.

Some craft supply retail stores give discounts to professionals. This is, of course, up to the individual retailer, so don't expect it. Keep in mind that they do this as a courtesy. But it never hurts to ask.

Stores going out of business are another way to find bargains on supplies. This is another one not to expect, because it may happen rarely, but if your favorite supply store announces it is going out of business, watch the prices carefully. The longer you are able to wait after the announcement, the better the prices will be, but keep in mind that your selection will dwindle severely when the big price reductions come.

If you simply can't meet minimum purchase requirements on your own, consider starting a *purchasing co-op*. Many health food stores began as co-ops with the members joining together for the purpose of buying products they all use or need. There are a few health food co-ops still around today. I mention this because a buying co-op seems to be a good way for artists or craftspeople who work in the same or similar media to get better prices for their supplies. Together you may be able to reach minimum order requirements. Since a co-op is also a legal business structure, of course you will want to consult an attorney. If you are already a member of a cooperative gallery group, purchasing may be a benefit of your membership.

✂ BUYING SUPPLIES ONLINE

The Internet, of course, offers just about anything for sale, and art and craft supplies are no exception. I recently spent some time surfing the Web to see what I could find in terms of good deals on craft supplies. As with anything, some sites offer better prices than others. This is one of those times when it is especially important to be familiar with retail prices. What I noticed was a large number of suppliers offering prices advertised as wholesale to the public. There were also a number of wholesale suppliers with no minimum purchase requirement, but with incentives for quantity purchases. I also noticed a number of wholesalers with small minimum purchases; some with dollar amounts as low as $25 or $50. This is much lower than the $500 minimum order required by many of the suppliers we have worked with and should be affordable by most craft artists. If you know you can't meet a large minimum order, I suggest looking on the Internet. You might be surprised by what you find. Good keywords for this type of search are *wholesale craft supplies, wholesale art supplies, wholesale pottery supplies, wholesale knitting supplies,* and others. Customize your search to meet your specific needs; just be sure to get the words *wholesale* and *supplies* in there.

As with any purchases you make on the Internet, be sure you are comfortable with the security precautions used by the site before you give out your credit card information. It might also be a good idea to use a card with a low credit limit for Internet transactions to minimize any losses if someone should misuse your account information.

✂ MY STORY

Have I bought craft supplies wholesale? Yes, I have. Rather, I should say Bob bought craft supplies wholesale for me. I have to admit that this was one of those times Bob led me in a direction I was not sure I wanted to go. Bob and I make a great team, but he thinks bigger than I do. I come up with an idea, and he runs with it.

Like most people in the craft business, I started out buying my supplies at the largest local craft supply store. That is until I was banned from the store for asking for itemized receipts. That was before computerized cash register automatically gave one, like most do now. Itemized receipts had to be handwritten by a manager. When the manager became tired of doing this and told me to get out and not come back, we decided to start looking for wholesale suppliers.

Bob did a great job finding our suppliers. He found possible suppliers in the same ways described in this lesson. He looked through business directories as well as advertising in craft industry publications and the information on the packaging of supplies we had already purchased. As our business grew and expanded, we also started buying products for resale in the store. These included craft patterns as well as cards, stationery, and extra craft supplies, which we packaged ourselves for resale.

We were selling our extra craft supplies at prices that were competitive with the large craft supply store that had banned us. We laughed as we realized they saw us as competition. Our little "mom and pop craft store" was making the big boys nervous, and we loved it.

The reason I believe we had success in dealing with wholesale suppliers stems from Bob's attitude. He approached wholesalers as a businessman, and he didn't think small. He did his research and was able to speak the wholesaler's language. He was able to answer questions about our business and provide the required documentation to prove we were indeed in business. If you approach wholesalers projecting the image of a small-time hobby crafter you will not get far, even if you are prepared to meet minimum order requirements.

The work I do now is largely unique, original, and one of a kind. This does not lend itself to buying supplies in quantity. That does not mean I always pay retail for my supplies, however. I still use the other means of getting discounts discussed, and I can smell a sale a mile off. This does require thinking ahead. For instance, if I find a good deal on quilt batting, I buy as much as I can afford. If I had to buy batting for each individual quilt as needed, I would be held hostage by the prevailing retail price at that time.

Always do a price comparison between local retail prices and the prices advertised as wholesale or discounted. Be sure to add any charges for shipping and handling to compare your actual cost to what you are already paying at retail. Remember, the object is not necessarily always to get wholesale prices, but rather to find the best prices possible given your circumstances.

DO YOUR HOMEWORK

1. Get acquainted with the business reference section of your local library. The main library is best for this. Go in, look around, and meet the business librarian. Become familiar with the *Thomas Register.* Ask the librarian if there are other resources that could be helpful in your search.

2. Do an online search. Experiment with keywords till you learn what will bring up the information you need. *Wholesale craft supplies, wholesale beads, wholesale buttons, wholesale fabric paint, wholesale clay,* and others will get you started. Be sure to use the word wholesale and expect many hits. The closest matches will usually be at the top of the list, so you really don't need to look at 45,000 listings. After awhile you will have a sense of when to stop.

3. Consider organizing a buying co-op. Talk to people you know working in the same media. Consult an attorney about the legalities of setting up a cooperative.

4. Practice looking for sales, merchandise close-outs, and store closings. After awhile you will find it comes naturally.

NEED MORE HELP?

PERIODICALS
[Contact information is available in Appendix B.]
Sunshine Artist Magazine
The Crafts Report

WHOLESALE DIRECTORIES AND DATABASES—HARD COPY
[Contact information is available in Appendix B.]
National Craft Association
The Supply Source Book/The National Directory of Suppliers for Artists and Artisans
Thomas Register of American Manufacturers

WHOLESALE DIRECTORIES AND DATABASES—ONLINE
[Contact information is available in Appendix B.]
Craft Web.com
fineArt forum resource Directory: Services
Make-Stuff.com
Top Craft Suppliers

COMPANIES
[Note: The following resources are given only as contact information to begin your search for the best price for your supplies. Suppliers listed here include manufacturers, wholesalers, distributors, buying clubs, and retailers, some of whom give professional discounts. Discounts are totally at the discretion of the individual companies, and you must deal directly with them and meet their terms, including minimum purchase and providing the information requested to prove the legitimacy of your business.]

ART SUPPLIES
[Contact information is available in Appendix B.]
Art Resource.com
The Art Store
Art Supplies Wholesale
DMR Distributors Inc.
Eco-House Inc.
Mister Art
Pearl Paint
Presto
Utrecht

BASKETS
[Contact information is available in Appendix B.]
The Basket Peddler
Baskets 101.com
Best Buy Floral Supply
Creative Containers

BEADS AND JEWELRY SUPPLIES
[Contact information is available in Appendix B.]
Ambush
Ari Imports
Artgems Inc.
Bally Bead Company
Beada Beada
Beads Galore
Beadworks
Caravan Beads
Empyrean Beads
Enterprise Art
Fire Mountain Gems
Frantz Art Glass and Supply
General Bead

Halstead Bead Inc.
Hands of the Hills
Myron Tobac, Inc.
Ornamental Resources Inc.
Rings and Things
Shipwreck Beads
S S Traders

CALLIGRAPHY
[Contact information is available in Appendix B.]
Art Resource.com
Art Supplies Wholesale
Uchida of America Corporation

CERAMICS AND POTTERY
[Contact information is available in Appendix B.]
Aftosa
American Art Clay Company
Bennett's Pottery Supply
Evans Ceramics Supply
Pottery Art Studio
Sheffield Pottery Inc.

DECORATIVE PAINTING
[Contact information is available in Appendix B.]
Cabin Craft
Utrecht Art

DOLL MAKING
[Contact information is available in Appendix B.]
Airtex Consumer Products
Factory Direct Craft Supply
Fairfield Processing Company
Fun-A-Fair Dolls and Supplies
National ArtCraft

FABRIC LABELS
[Contact information is available in Appendix B.]
Charm Woven Labels
General Label Manufacturing
Pacific Coast Bach Label Company
Raynor and Associates
Valley Products Company

FABRIC
[Contact information is available in Appendix B.]
Buny Fleece
Cloth4Less
Fabric.com
Fabric Club
Fashion Fabrics Club
Laceland
Outdoor Fabrics.com

FLORALS
[Contact information is available in Appendix B.]
Afloral.com
Beverly's Crafts and Fabrics
Crafts a Million
Dried Naturals
Mosses Galore
Natures Best Dried Flowers
Santa's Supply

FRAMING MATERIALS
[Contact information is available in Appendix B.]
Art Supplies Wholesale
Mat Shop Wholesale Frames
Presto
Wholesale Frame Service USA

GENERAL CRAFT SUPPLIES

[Contact information is available in Appendix B.]

Art Resource.com
Art Supplies Wholesale
Bolek's Craft Supply Incorporated
Craft Catalog
Crafts Etc.
Craft Stop
Eco-House Inc.
Factory Direct Craft Supply
Marasco's Craft King
National Art Craft Company
Sunshine Discount Crafts

PAINTING

[Contact information is available in Appendix B.]

Aardvark Art Supply
Paints R Us
Utrecht

PAPER CRAFTS

[Contact information is available in Appendix B.]

Create For Less
DMD Industries
Penny Products Inc.
Scrapbook Factory Outlet
Uchida
We Are Paper

QUILTING

[Contact information is available in Appendix B.]

Airtex Consumer Products
Create for Less
Fairfield Processing Company
Hice Sewing
Pine Tree Quiltworks

RUBBER STAMPING

[Contact information is available in Appendix B.]

Clearsnap Inc.
Darcies
STAMPede
Uchida

SCRAPBOOKING

[Contact information is available in Appendix B.]

DMD Industries Incorporated
Pioneer Photo Albums, Inc.
Scrapbook Factory Outlet
Scrapbook Superstore
Uchida

STAINED GLASS

[Contact information is available in Appendix B.]

Glass Crafters Stained Glass Inc.
Stained Glass Warehouse
Warner-Crivellaro
Whittemore-Durgin Glass
Company

WOODCRAFTS

[Contact information is available in Appendix B.]

Woodcrafter.com
Woodcrafts and Supplies
Wood-N-Crafts Incorporated

Lesson 12

PRICING YOUR PRODUCTS

PRICING IS THE MOST DIFFICULT ASPECT of marketing. There is a fine line between underpricing and overpricing. It is somewhere in this area that you must price your work if you expect to sell your product and make a reasonable profit for your efforts.

Pricing is an issue craftspeople seem to agonize over. The main concern I hear is a fear of overpricing. The truth is that craftspeople underprice their work much more often than they overprice. The goal is to find the perfect price where people buy your work and you also make a profit. We all want to make a profit, right? Pricing your work is a gamble, but not a gamble you have to lose.

✂ THE DETAILS OF PRICING

Pricing begins with a little thing called market research. There is nothing at all that should be scary about this. Market research is nothing more than learning who will buy your work, where they are, and how much they are willing to pay.

So, where do you start? You start out by *getting to know your customer base.* Who is going to buy your work? Who buys your work now? Study this carefully. You may be surprised. Are you sure your work cannot attract an upscale clientele? Have you tried? Where do your potential customers live? How much money are you going to have to spend on advertising to attract these people?

The second aspect of market research is *getting to know the market.* How much will the market bear? This means how much are people in your area willing to pay for your product? The best way to discover this is to scout around local stores and find out how much people are paying for similar items of equal quality. A point of pride for many craftspeople is that their work should be worth more because it is handmade. Have you ever compared prices between handmade and mass-produced goods of comparable or even lesser quality? We have noticed that many times the mass-produced work is priced higher. We can also say from experience that some people are quite willing to pay more for handmade items, but the quality has to be there. In fact, it must be close to flawless.

Know your true competition. Your true competition may not be craft fairs and craft malls. Some people who choose to sell their work in this way do not understand pricing, profit, and quality issues, and tend to underprice or overprice their work. If you set your pricing standard at craft fair or craft mall prices, you may find yourself not meeting your expenses. Look around at local retail specialty stores for an idea of prices products similar to yours are bringing.

The next consideration in pricing your work after doing your market research is to be sure you *cover your costs.* Of course you need to cover the cost of the materials used in making your products. Are you still paying retail for your supplies? If so, this will make it difficult for you to charge reasonable prices for your work. Even if you do not qualify for wholesale pricing there are other ways to get the price of your supplies down. Do the best you can.

You also need to be sure that you *cover the costs of producing your work.* This means labor. Legally, if you are the business owner and you are also producing the product yourself, then your salary is the profit from your business. So you are not really making a salary as such. The amount you allow for your labor counts as part of your profit. It is important to figure time and labor expenses into your prices, however. If your business expands to the point of needing to hire employees, you might be faced with the need for major price increases if you have not already figured time into the equation. Be sure to be realistic when determining the amount to allow for your time. What would its cost to hire someone to do what you are doing?

If covering the cost of your time or the time of others really does put your work in an unrealistic price range, you are faced with a choice. Not covering your labor costs does not have to be the first action you take to lower your prices. Are there ways to help reduce the cost of your supplies? Could time- or labor-saving devices or techniques be used to reduce the time it takes to produce a particular work? Are there ways to lower your overhead? Could the amount of time you spend on your work or your attention to detail actually help command a greater price?

✂ ARTISTIC VALUE AND QUALITY

Another important thing to remember when pricing your work is *the artistic value of your work.* Fine artists will understand this one perhaps more easily than will craftspeople. A painter, for instance, does not total up the cost of the canvas and paint to come up with a price for his work. A sculptor does not spend six months on a piece, adding ten dollars to the price of supplies, believing she can't charge for her time. In most cases fine artists don't even think about these things. Perhaps they should, but often they do not. Prices are set based on artistic value. A craftsperson's work may also have artistic value. This especially applies to work that is innovative, creative, and original. Price can also be determined by the artist's experience, reputation, and the demand for the artist's work. The higher the demands for a particular artist's work, the higher price it will bring. The downside is that it takes time to build such a reputation.

People are willing to pay for quality. If you produce high-quality work you do not have to give it away. People will pay for quality handcrafted items. Low prices for poorly made merchandise do not always win customers. Unique, one-of-a-kind designs will command higher prices than mass-produced items.

Most crafts professionals worry about overpricing, but *you can also underprice.* There are dangers in underpricing your work. Many people are underpricing to the point they are either not making a profit or perhaps even taking a loss. Some do not realize they are doing this. Others don't care. If you do not eventually show a profit, you will not stay in business. When you underprice your work, you not only undermine yourself, you also undermine other artists. People who create works of art with both skill and pride are going to have a difficult road as long as the industry standard is substandard work or low prices.

✂ BUSINESS VERSUS HOBBY

Sooner or later you will have to decide if you want to be in business or if you want your craft work to be a hobby. This will have an effect on your pricing decisions. If you truly want to be in business, you must understand that not only the expenses of the business, but your personal living expenses, must eventually come from the income of the business. That means your prices must be high enough to show a profit. If this is simply a hobby, you may not have to be as concerned about this. If you are serious about your business, however, you must recognize that the hobby crafters are out there selling and will often either deliberately or quite unintentionally undercut you in the price department.

The IRS says that the difference between someone who has a hobby and a business/self-employed person is that a business is intentionally done to make a profit, whereas a hobby is not. The following, taken from the IRS article in *The Digital Daily,* can help you determine if you are conducting your work as a business:

1. You carry on the activity in a businesslike manner.
2. The time and effort you put into the activity indicate you intend to make it profitable.
3. You depend on income from the activity for your livelihood.
4. Your losses are due to circumstances beyond your control (or are normal in the startup phase of your type of business).
5. You change your methods of operation in an attempt to improve profitability.
6. You, or your advisors, have the knowledge needed to carry on the activity as a successful business.
7. You were successful in making a profit in similar activities in the past.
8. The activity makes a profit in some years, and how much profit it makes.

And:

9. You can expect to make a future profit from the appreciation of the assets used in the activity.

   . . . An activity is presumed carried on for profit if it produced a profit in at least 3 of the last 5 tax years, including the current year.

   (Note: No one of the items in the above list can cause an activity to be either accepted or denied the classification of either a business or hobby.)

✂ MY PRICING STORY

Now let me tell you my pricing story. When Bob and I decided to sell my original clothing and jewelry designs to other retail stores, we started out selling at wholesale prices to everyone, even the general public. We did this from our own store, which doubled as our wholesale showroom. And we did okay. Not great, but okay.

Our wholesale prices were established after a great deal of research. Bob insisted that we first shop for items similar to what I was making in retail stores. So we shopped. Keeping track of the prices in mainline, moderately priced stores throughout the city where we lived at the time, we came up with an average price for dresses similar to those I was making at that time.

When we cut that amount in half, we had a general idea of what stores were paying for similar items at that time.

After that, Bob had a general concept of what amount we had to work with to pay for my supplies, overhead, and some profit for the items I was making. This may sound like it is working backward from most pricing formulas, but if a person wants to be competitive this is the best way to lay the groundwork.

Then we set out to find the best prices available on my supplies. We bought bandanas by the case lot, making them available to us at $0.27 each. We bought spools of thread by the dozen whenever we could do so on sale, and the same with snaps and elastic for waistbands. Since it took six bandanas to make one of my southwestern-style dresses, this meant my total cost for all of my supplies was only $1.42. Next Bob figured the cost of my time for making such a dress. Since I had minimal cutting to do on this pattern, I estimated to take approximately one hour; at $10 per hour, that meant $10 total. Finally, Bob had figured the overhead to average $3.00 per item, and the additional overhead cost on this item (at 10 percent of wholesale price) was $1.44 per item. This made the total wholesale price equal $15.86. To use scientific pricing, I placed the store price on these dresses at $15.99. We thought, "Great! We'll sell a bundle of these at this price." But the sales were actually quite slow.

Then we were told by the landlord that our store must be a retail business. This was not in our contract, but was an unwritten rule that the antique mall owners insisted on being followed. So, with fear and trembling we raised our prices, and not just a little. Our jump from wholesale to retail was a full 100 percent price increase. That's right, we doubled our prices. We were so upset with our landlord that we quickly decided to start making plans to move our store.

However, we were totally unprepared for the results. We soon noticed that people started showing more interest in my handmade items. Soon I started having to make more, until within two months Bob told me that by doubling our prices we had also doubled our sales. We could have lost our shirt—that's the gamble. But what we discovered was that potential retail customers had been concerned about quality. People often think low prices mean poor quality.

We also discovered that we had been giving unfair competition to our wholesale customers, who needed room to mark up the merchandise to make a profit. So, instead of selling wholesale to everyone, we set retail prices and gave other retailers price breaks for quantity purchases. We later learned this is the way retailers do business. Our wholesale sales increased rapidly.

The moral of this story? Do your research before setting prices and never be surprised by public reaction.

✂ SO, HOW DO YOU COME UP WITH THAT PERFECT PRICE?

Many people use a pricing formula. Do pricing formulas work? Yes, they can, but they are not magic. Even the best formula can't guarantee sales. A pricing formula is nothing more than a tool. A tool that will help ensure that you cover your expenses and make a profit, but still just a tool.

Remember what we said about artistic value. If your work is unique and original as well as being of extremely high quality it may be worth much more than the cost to produce it. Pricing formulas simply do not work in all cases.

There are a variety of methods used by craftspeople to arrive at their prices. First is good old *making it up as you go* pricing. An example of this would be looking at your work and pulling a price out of your head. I hear you laughing, but people actually do this. I did it in the early days, before I met Bob. The only time this is not extremely dangerous is if you are basing your price on a comparable piece of work you have priced more scientifically. What is most dangerous about this practice is that when it comes to being sure your expenses are covered, you do not have a clue.

Another method of pricing is called *comparison pricing*. Comparison pricing means you look at what other people are getting for the same or comparable items. Of course this assumes the other people know what they are doing. What if they don't have a clue? What if your quality is much better? What if the other person is taking a loss on that item? Knowing the market, the prices others are putting on their work, is important, but you want to base your own pricing structure on more than what your competition is doing.

We have all heard about *pricing rules*. They are the clichés of pricing. An example of a pricing rule is: add up the cost of your supplies and double or triple that number. These seldom work because they may not cover all of your expenses.

Pricing formulas sound terribly mathematical and difficult, I know. They really aren't. Pricing formulas are really nothing more than adding together all the costs associated with making an item, including profit, to obtain the minimum price. This will tell you how much you have to get for that particular piece to break even, which is to cover your expenses. Then you go by what the market will bear to set your price.

A pricing formula is only a tool to be sure you are covering your expenses. You will find that most of your prices will require adjustment as you get out and actually sell your work. The formula is only a starting place or a jumping-off point. By not being afraid to play around with different formulas you will find the one that works for you.

✀ EXPENSES YOU NEED TO COVER IN YOUR PRICING FORMULA

The first expense you need to cover is the cost of your raw materials. This is also known as *direct costs* and includes everything you use to make your item, including often-forgotten items such as thread and glue. For materials such as these you don't count the cost of the entire bottle of glue or spool of thread, only what portion you used in your particular project. You do not have to stay up nights trying to figure this out. Simply do your best to come up with a rough estimate. It might only be pennies, but remember, those pennies add up.

Overhead, also known as indirect costs, covers all the other expenses that go into producing your work. Overhead includes things like your studio rent, utilities, any equipment you may use in your work, insurance, and so on.

Your time and the time of others to produce your work are your *labor costs.* It is very difficult to find balance on this one. People seem to think either that they cannot charge for their labor at all or that they should make $20 an hour. This may be possible if your business grows. However, a business owner's income does not come in the form of added labor costs. According to the way income taxes are required to be figured—that is, the way accountants are trained to figure income—a business owner's income is the profit from the business.

Profit is the amount remaining from a sale after both direct and indirect costs are deducted from the total amount of that sale. Some pricing formulas have profit built into them. This is a good idea. Bob allows 10 percent of the amount required to produce an item for profit. The resulting price is the wholesale price. You double the wholesale price to arrive at the retail price, for more profit for you. This is how you build profit into your wholesale prices. Your profit per item will not be great if you sell wholesale, but remember that you are going for volume here.

✀ EXAMPLES OF PRICING FORMULAS

So, what does an actual pricing formula look like? The following are a few examples from other craft professionals. You may recognize the names.

"The cost of making your product + your desired profit = your retail price." From *The Crafter's Guide to Pricing Your Work* by Dan Ramsey.

"Materials + Labor + Overhead + Profit = Wholesale" and "Wholesale x 2 = Retail." From *Handmade for Profit* by Barbara Brabec.

"Cost of goods + indirect costs (overhead expenses like rent, utilities, insurance, phone, etc.) + profit (what you expect to make beyond the cost of your labor) = minimum price." From "The Basic Guide to Pricing Your Craftwork" by James Dillehay, available at Craftmarketer.com.

Now ours:

Cost of materials to make one item
+ labor cost per hour / number of items produced per hour
+ overhead / total number of items to be sold in a year
= Actual cost of produced item

Actual cost of produced item
+ actual cost of produced item x 10 percent = actual profit
= Wholesale price

Wholesale price x 2 = retail

The cost of materials for one item is added to labor cost, overhead, and profit, the sum of which equals the wholesale price. The wholesale price doubled equals the retail price, similar to previous formulas. However our formula allows a little more detail, flexibility, and accuracy. Labor cost per hour is divided by the number of items produced during an hour. Total annual overhead for operating the business is divided by the number of items to be sold in a year.

Your labor cost per item
+ actual profit
= taxable profit

Finally, notice that we separated the amount we paid ourselves for doing the actual work of production and pure profit, but they were added together before figuring income taxes. The reason for this is because a business owner, for tax purposes, is not allowed to pay herself a wage as such. The profit you derive from being in business is your assumed wage, and vice versa, by the Internal Revenue Service. You cannot therefore claim a loss in your business because your salary or wage causes your expenses to be greater than your business income.

However, at the same time, you should determine how much your work is worth in the event that you eventually need to hire someone to do that work to free you to do other things in the business. Otherwise, that person's salary will have to come out of your actual profit with the ultimate possibility of causing you a loss.

NOW YOU TRY IT
Choose one of the formulas mentioned above. Select one item you are currently making. Plug your own numbers into the formula and see what you get. Remember, some additional math may be required to obtain the numbers to

put into the formula. Are you not sure of some of your costs? You may have to project or speculate. That's okay for now; just try to be realistic and do the best you can. This is just a practice run.

What did you come up with? Do you think it is at least in the ball park? Did you come up with a price of $25 for an item everyone else is selling for $2.50? If so, you have a problem. If you really do need to get your prices down, the way to start is by looking at the price you are paying for your supplies.

If your materials costs are down to the bare minimum and your prices are still too high, look at the time it takes to produce your work. Are there ways to cut time without compromising quality? Inferior work is never the way to save money. In the long run it will cost you. There may be times when you simply decide you can't afford to produce certain items for sale. I have done that. Those are the items I reserve for personal use or to give as gifts, if I make them at all.

✂ WHOLESALE PRICING

It is important to always establish a wholesale price first and then double it to find your retail price, even when you are first starting out. Why? Suppose a retailer approaches you about buying your work for his store. He is going to want special price considerations, often a discount of up to 50 percent. Could you do this and still make a profit?

Buyers or merchandisers expect price cuts to be in a tiered-level program based on the quantity purchased. For instance, often you will find catalogs with several levels of discounts arranged according to the amount of product purchased. Thus if a person buys one to six of an item, she would be expected to pay full retail price. However, if she buys seven to twenty-four items, the catalog might offer a 25 percent discount; twenty-five to seventy-five items a 35 percent discount; seventy-six to a hundred items a 45 percent discount; and over a hundred items a 50 percent discount. This type of tiered-level price discounting both encourages larger sales of specific items and increases the profits while decreasing the expenses on sales overall.

A variation of the above tiered-level discounting system is done on the overall purchase cost. This is an excellent simplification method for the business with several products to sell, making it possible not to have to figure the discount on every type of item. For example:

Up to $49 worth of merchandise gets no discount
$59 – $149 = 5 percent discount
$150 – $249 = 10 percent discount
$250 – $349 = 20 percent discount

$350 – $449 = 30 percent discount
$450 – $499 = 40 percent discount
$500 and over = 50 percent discount

The above figures, of course, may be changed to meet your needs. However, presenting a discount chart will help you look like a professional when dealing with buyers. This will also encourage the retailer to save money by buying more. And, of course, do not forget to request these price breaks when you are a wholesale customer buying your supplies.

If you forget everything else about pricing, remember these two things: Your work has value; and when you underprice, you hurt other artists and craftspeople, you hurt the industry, and you hurt yourself.

Scientific Pricing

Why is $22.98 a better price than $23.00? It is better simply because it is less significant to the subconscious mind. Put simply, research has shown that for some yet unknown reason, people simply buy more often at a price marked one or two pennies less than a whole dollar amount. People always seem to go for a lower price, even if the difference is a very small one. If you watch how you buy, you will notice that even you do this.

DO YOUR HOMEWORK

1. Take a field trip to a variety of retail stores, consignment shops, craft malls, and craft fairs selling items comparable to yours. Do not forget department stores if they carry similar items to your work. It does not matter if the items are mass-produced as long as the quality is similar. Get a feel for what people are paying for this type of product. Write down prices along with any notes you want to make about quality. When you get home make a list of the prices from highest to lowest. Is there a large gap between the highest and lowest? Where do you think your work belongs on the price continuum? Do not automatically go to the bottom. Having the lowest prices does not necessarily make your work more salable. The process you have just completed is called market research. Not as scary or difficult as the name sounds, is it?

2. Decide on your target audience. Who do you want to buy your work? If you are already selling, who is buying?

3. Choose three different pricing formulas and play around with them. Plug your numbers into the formulas and see what you get. Remember, pricing formulas are tools to ensure that you cover your expenses and make a profit. You still set your own price using the formula, information gathered from your market research, and your knowledge of your customers or target audience as well as the artistic value of your work.

Need More Help?

Literature

Chypre, Betty. "How Much is that Doggie in the Window? Formulas for Setting your Retail Price."

————. *Choices: The Yellow Pages of Art and Craft Shows* (cited: July 2002). Available at: *www.smartfrogs.com/pricing.html.*

Dillehay, James. *The Basic Guide to Pricing Your Craft Work.* La Vergne, Tenn.: Ingram Books Company, 1997.

————. "How Much Should You Charge for Your Work?" *Craftmarketer.com* (cited: July 2002). Available at: *www.craftmarketer.com/craft_articles/ how_to_price_crafts.htm.*

Landman, Sylvia, and Marilyn Maddalena. *Pricing Guidelines for Arts and Crafts: Successful Professional Crafters Share Their Pricing Strategies to Help You Set Profitable Prices for Your Art.* Lincoln, Nebr.: iUniverse, Inc., 2000.

Landman, Sylvia Ann. *Make Your Quilting Pay for Itself.* Cincinnati, Ohio: Betterway Books, 1997.

"Marketing the Crafts of Missouri Artisans." *Missouri Choice Natural Fibers* (cited: July 2002). Available at: *http://agebb.missouri.edu/mcnf/business.*

"Pricing Crafts Is Part of the Answer to Your Success" *Money Making Crafts* (cited: July 2002). Available at: *www.moneymakingcrafts.com/pricing_ crafts_to_sell.html.*

"Pricing Right." *Sunshine Artist Magazine* (October 1999).

Ramsey, Dan. *The Woodworkers Guide to Pricing Your Work.* Cincinnati, Ohio: Popular Woodworking Books, 2001.

Saylor, Mary. "Pricing Crafts." *Arkansas Small Business Development Center.* Document #7013 (cited: March 2003). Available at: *http://asbdc.ualr.edu/bizfacts/7013.asp.*

Zell, Alan J. "Pricing your work." Alan J. Zell, *Ambassador of Selling* (cited: March 2003). Available at: *http://sellingselling.com/articles/pricing.html.*

Lesson 13

MARKETING DECISIONS

WHEN IT COMES TO MAKING your work available for sale to the public, you have two choices. Sell your work yourself or pay someone else to do it for you. Once you make that choice, there are many different marketing strategies available to you.

In making this decision you must consider things like how selling your work will affect your creativity and production time as well as where your creative inspiration comes from. If your inspiration comes from people and their reactions to your work, you might want to consider selling your work yourself. Your personality will also come into play here. Maybe you are just not a people person and prefer long, solitary hours working in the studio. If this is the case you might prefer to have someone else to do the selling for you.

✂ DIRECT SALES

For this brief introduction to marketing we will begin with the marketing strategies involving direct sales. "Direct sales" means selling your work directly to the public. There are a number of ways to do this.

When most people think of selling art or craft work the first thing that comes to mind is *art or craft shows.* This is a good marketing strategy if you are a people person with lots of energy. If you are not, you may want to consider other ways of getting your work out to the people. Shows may also be used along with other marketing methods as a way of building your reputation and staying in touch with your audience. Remember, though, that craft shows are not your only option.

Another way you can sell you work is to open *your own retail store or gallery.* A retail store or gallery may be owned alone, in partnership with someone else, or with other artists as part of a collective or cooperative. This requires the most financial investment and work, but it also gives you the most independence. Remember, the success of your own store or gallery is up to you.

Selling wholesale belongs here if you are the one representing your work and making your own wholesale sales. What the retailer does with your work is a different matter. The benefit of selling wholesale is that the store-owner accepts ownership and full responsibility for your work with the exception of certain legal issues such as product liability.

Catalog mail order sales allow you to go either way in terms of selling your own work or paying someone else to sell for you. It seems this is something people often start out doing out of their basement so I have included it here. Are you really ready for this? Especially if it gets big, which, of course, you hope it does. Look at catalogs offering similar items. Can you really afford to put out a high-quality catalog with color photos? Could you fill one million orders in one week? One month? One year? I know the idea of mail order sales is an attractive one, but in most circumstances it is not something I would recommend.

Open houses and parties have become popular in recent years. Both involve opening up your home, or that of a friend, for people to come see and buy your work. If you are planning on doing this regularly from the same location, you will want to check with city hall on the legalities. Since you are opening your home for these events, you may also want to consider having these events on an invitation-only basis for your protection.

Garage sales and flea markets are also sometimes used to sell craft items. Before you do this, however, stop and think. Is this really the image you want to project of yourself and your work?

✂ INDIRECT SALES

Maybe you really do not want to sell your own work. After all, you are an artist. You would rather spend your time creating your art than trying to convince other people to buy it. There are ways to get other people to do the selling for you.

You can attempt to hire a good *artist representative or agent*. These are professionals who make their living marketing the work of artists and craftspeople. Turning this responsibility over to someone else can free up your time for the creative aspects of your work; this is why you are an artist, right? However, if you choose this option, be careful. Remember, you are turning your livelihood over to this person. You have the right to interview candidates, and you should do so. Check out credentials and references. Ask to talk to current and past clients. Once you have signed a contract your interest and concern for business details should not stop. Take the time to look over any paperwork including contracts and financial statements on a regular basis. Do this at least once a month. If your agent or representative is handling major financial transactions and banking responsibilities, be sure you know where your money is coming from and where it is going.

Consignment is one of those unique situations where someone else is selling your work in a retail environment, but you retain ownership. You do not receive payment for your work until it is sold. You are also paying someone else to sell your work. In consignment arrangements, the storeowner takes a percentage of the selling price of your products.

Craft malls are large retail stores that are usually, but not always, divided into small booth spaces for individual crafters to display their work. Craft malls will usually require a monthly booth rent or membership fee whether you sell anything or not. The mall may also collect a percentage of your sales and may require you to work in the store without pay. With both consignment and craft malls, there are issues concerning insurance as well as who accepts responsibility for your work while it is in the storeowner's care. For these and other reasons, a contract is absolutely necessary in these types of arrangements.

Now, carefully consider the positive and negative aspects of each marketing strategy. What is the best compromise between your personal preferences and reality? Paying someone else to sell your work through a lower price (wholesale) or a commission or percentage of sales (consignment and agents) may best fit your personal situation.

✂ MY MARKETING STRATEGY

How did I decide which marketing strategy to use in my own business? I guess you could say it evolved over the years. Like most people starting out, I began on the craft show circuit. I can't say I really put a lot of thought into the decision. I just didn't know there was any other way to sell my work. When I first started going to shows, I didn't do well. I think this was largely because I wasn't being terribly creative or original in my work. I was just making more of what I saw at craft shows. This is a common mistake of people just starting out.

I also made several not-so-successful attempts at selling my work on consignment during this time. Every time I tried, I lost product.

It took a lot of encouragement and a little pressure from Bob to convince me that I could do work that was original and uniquely mine and that I could sell to a broader audience. To tell the truth, I was scared to death when we first opened our store. It didn't help that the area we chose to locate our store in turned out to be not especially craft friendly. But we managed to overcome that and build a successful business.

We had several craft designers and retailers stop by our store, and they encouraged us to explore wholesaling. From our retail business we acquired several wholesale customers and began concentrating on that area of marketing.

I didn't stop going to craft shows during this time, I just became more selective. Craft shows became a way of getting my name out and letting people see my work rather than my sole means of selling. Since I no longer had to go to craft shows I could wait for that perfect show to come along. My sales also began improving greatly at the shows I did attend.

There are also marketing strategies I have deliberately avoided over the years for a variety of reasons. Some do not project the image of professionalism I want my business to have. These would include garage sales, flea markets, home shows, and some craft malls. Others, such as mail order, are things I have simply not been ready to handle.

Sometimes a change in your work will make it necessary to change your marketing strategy. That is where I am right now. I stopped doing clothing and jewelry design to concentrate on original fabric art. This is something I choose not to mass-produce and my pieces are one of a kind. I also only manage to complete five or six art pieces a year, which makes having enough finished work to fill a store or show booth difficult. Because of their artistic value, these also command higher prices than the work I did in the past.

Right now, I am still working on perfecting my craft and exploring marketing possibilities, including gallery representation and the Internet. I have given quilts to friends as gifts that are on display in public buildings. I participate in an annual local quilt show and have had my work on display at the public library. Our apartment also serves as an informal gallery with quilts in just about every room. You wouldn't believe what a conversation starter a quilt hanging on the wall can be.

Just as my marketing strategy evolved over the years, so will yours. Nothing is set in stone here. If you find that one marketing strategy doesn't work for you, try another until you come up with the best strategy for you.

✂ PROTECT YOUR HEART

Alex Anderson, one of my favorite television quilting personalities, often talks about protecting your feelings when entering work in judged competitions. She says to "take your heart and put it in a box with lots of batting around it."

Those words also apply when trying to sell your own work. Not everyone is going to like your work. Not everyone is going to be kind. A few unscrupulous merchants may even belittle you and your work, just trying to get the price down.

For me, the most heartbreaking example of this would have to be when I was trying to sell products left over after we closed our store. I approached the owner of a new store with merchandise that had a wholesale value of well over $1,000. Before we could get around to discussing money he said, "It's not bad. Tell you what, I'll take it all off your hands for $100." I cried for a week over that one.

This is why Bob made most of our sales calls. I had too much of a personal investment in the business. You can toughen up a little as time goes on, but I don't think you ever get to the point where it doesn't bother you just a little bit.

The key to not allowing selling your own work to get to you is to minimize the negative and focus on the positive. If you hear the same negative remarks over and over you might want to consider if you have a problem, but if you take every negative comment to heart you will find yourself depressed, discouraged, and not selling much.

You will likely approach many people before you make your first sale. Don't focus on all those who didn't buy. Celebrate the one who did.

Do Your Homework

Use this worksheet to help decide which form of marketing best meets your needs. Go through the checklist for each marketing strategy and read the statements. Place a "+" in the space provided beside the statement if you consider it to be positive, something that would meet your needs or attract you to this type of marketing, or a "−" if you consider this statement a negative.

After you have filled in all of the spaces, go back and look at your +'s and −'s. Remember, it is not simply a matter of counting them up and the one with the most +'s wins. You will also want to consider the following questions. Do some of the statements carry more weight—are they more important than others? Are some of these flexible while others are nonnegotiable? Do your personal values, including your moral and ethical beliefs, come into play here? This checklist can be a valuable tool in decision-making, but remember, it is only a tool.

Marketing Approaches Worksheet

DIRECT SALES

___ Artist retains ownership of work till sold.
___ Artist sets price.
___ Artist is responsible for advertising.
___ Artist sells own work or pays someone else to sell it for them.

CONSIGNMENT

___ Artist retains ownership till work is sold.
___ Artist doesn't have physical possession of work while on consignment.
___ Someone else sells work.
___ Storeowner takes a percentage of sale price of item.
___ Insurance may not cover items on consignment.

WHOLESALE

___ Retailer accepts ownership and responsibility for work.
___ Retailer may require a buy-back clause.
___ Artist receives wholesale price.
___ Retailer may make more on item than artist.
___ Large orders are possible.
___ Someone else sells work and deals with the public.
___ Retailer is responsible for advertising.

CRAFT MALL

___ Artist retains ownership until work is sold.
___ Artist does not have physical possession of work while in craft mall.
___ Someone else sells work.
___ Mall owner takes a percentage of sale price of item.
___ Payment is received after work is sold.
___ Insurance may not cover items in craft mall.
___ Monthly booth rent or membership fees.
___ Members may be required to work without pay.

ARTISTS AGENTS OR REPRESENTATIVES

___ Another person makes business decisions for the artist.
___ Artist does not have to go out and sell own work.
___ Agent receives a commission that is a percentage of sale price for items sold.
___ Artist retains ownership of work until it is sold.

NEED MORE HELP?

LITERATURE

Arena, Barbara, and Phillip L. Reed. *The Complete Idiot's Guide to Making Money with Your Hobby.* Indianapolis, Ind.: Alpha Books, 2001.

Better Homes and Gardens. *Crafts to Make and Sell.* Edited by Carol Field-Dahlstrom. Des Moines, Iowa: Better Homes and Gardens Books, 2000.

Bongiovanni, Marie. *How to Sell Your Carvings: Advice from the Pros.* Mechanicsburg, Pa.: Stackpole Books, 1998.

Brabec, Barbara. *Handmade for Profit.* New York: M. Evans, 1996.

Casey, Christine. "Marketing Helps." *Sunshine Artist Magazine* (May 2000).

Gerhards, Paul. *How to Sell What You Make: The Business of Marketing Crafts.* Mechanicsburg, Pa.: Stackpole Books, 1996.

Hiam, Alexander, and Al Reis. *Marketing for Dummies.* New York: John Wiley and Sons, 1997.

Kohl, Susan. *Getting Attention: Leading Edge Lessons for Publicity and Marketing.* Boston: Butterworth-Heinemann, 2000.

Lasley, William. "Sales Representative Tips for Crafters." *About.com* (cited: March 2003). Available at: *www.artsandcrafts.about.com/library/weekly/aa051100.htm.*

———. "The Story Behind Your Crafts." About.com (cited: March 2003). Available at: *www.artsandcrafts.about.com/library/weekly/aa041300.htm.*

Sager, Susan Joy. *Selling Your Crafts.* New York: Allworth Press, 1998.

WEB SITES AND WEB ARTICLES

[Contact information is available in Appendix B.]

"Craft Business" @ About.com

"Selling Your Arts and Crafts" @ National Craft Association

The Professional Crafter

Tips and Business Information for Craftsmen and Artists

Lesson 14

CHOOSING A RETAIL LOCATION

WE'VE ALL HEARD that the three most important things to consider when looking for real estate are location, location, location. This is especially important if you are planning a retail store or gallery. This does not necessarily apply if your studio is a work space only and you do not expect the general public to come in to buy. Even if this is the case, your location can effect your work attitude.

✄ CHOOSING YOUR LOCATION

When it come to choosing a retail location there are questions you need to ask yourself. *First, you need to think about the image you want your store, studio, or gallery to have.* Is there an area in your city that would help project that image, such as an old town or gallery district? How can the exterior or interior of your building help project this image?

You also need to ask yourself if the location is easy to find. Can you give directions to the location that are not too complicated? Being hard to find works only if you have already built a reputation as an artist.

Will this location attract the type of people who buy your work? Do they already frequent the area? Are there stores in the area that draw your potential customers? Competition is not always a bad thing. Friendly competition is a wonderful marketing tool used very effectively by gas stations, grocery stores, and others. Have you ever wondered why certain streets are lined with fast food restaurants and other streets have none? This same concept can work for artists and craftspeople.

Is the location zoned for the intended use? Check with your city or county government as well as your local zoning board. You may need to have the zoning changed or request a variance. This will usually require a public hearing to give neighbors and other interested parties a chance to voice any concerns they may have about the zoning change.

Does the building have any unique or interesting qualities that could help create the image or atmosphere you want your business to have? Maybe you are looking for an historic building, or an ultramodern one. Our store was located in a re-creation of an old-time western town complete with wooden sidewalks.

Are there any potential structural or environmental problems with the building? This could include crumbling front steps, ancient electrical wiring or plumbing, mold, or other problems with the building itself. Who would bear the responsibility for repair—you or the landlord? Purely practical stuff here; but very important.

Are you prepared to deal with the special problems of older or historic buildings? One such problem you may want to consider is mold. Yes, that green stuff that grows on trees and wants to grow in your bathroom, on your hair-brush, shoes, clothes, and sometimes even between your toes. There are two problems with mold. First, many people have allergy problems that are aggravated by the pesky green and brown stuff. Having customers pass out because they can't breathe is probably not the best advertising for your business. The second problem with mold is that it likes to get on anything in its way and cause as much damage as possible. If you have mold problems, you probably also have a moisture problem. Do you really want your artwork in this environment?

Is a prime location worth prime rent? Can you really afford to be in your local shopping mall? How much will you have to sell just to pay the rent? If you do sell well in a busy location, will you have time to keep producing work to sell? Keep in mind that hiring employees increases your expenses.

Can you live with any restrictions the landlord or management company may place on your business? Are you allowed to set your own store hours? Are there any extra charges, such as advertising or building maintenance fees? Are their limitations on what you can sell or how you are allowed to advertise? Any restrictions should be detailed in the contract. It is not a good thing to learn these things after you have been open several months.

If you are considering locating in a shopping mall or strip mall, how many empty stores are there? Why did people leave? Was there a sudden mass exodus? Do you know why?

Once you have narrowed your list of possible locations down to one or two serious contenders, *make several visits to the area from the point of view of a consumer.* Is this an area where you would like to go? Then go back and look the area over from the point of view of a businessperson. Talk to storeowners. Gently lead the conversation to their business. How are they doing? What do they like about their location? If you see a major potential problem you can tactfully try to see if the storeowner sees this as a problem. For instance, if the street in front of the store is closed for major repairs you could say something like, "I am sure you'll be glad when that road construction in front of your store is finished." Be cordial and try to gain your information from a casual, relaxed conversation. Don't turn it into an inquisition. Remember, these people could be your neighbors.

✂ COMMERCIAL LEASES

Is the contract something you can live with? Any time you sign any type of lease or rental agreement you are making a contract. A building lease for a business is often more complicated than for a house or apartment. Your attorney will be mainly looking at the legalities of the contract. It is still up to you to determine if the lease is something you are able to live with. Malls, strip malls, and shopping centers often have very strict rules. These often dictate your store hours, the type of sign you can have, where and how you advertise, and other issues. If a leasing agent indicates there are these types of rules and conditions, don't sign that lease without taking the contract and any accompanying rules home and looking them over. Have your attorney look them over. Are there other fees that are not optional, fees that you are required to pay? These could be for advertising, maintenance, and so on. If the landlord makes any promises not in the lease, ask that they be included. The lease should carefully spell out the responsibilities of each party, including details such as who is going to pay the utilities, shovel the snow, pick up trash outside the building, and any other details.

A commercial lease should also define your responsibility for preparing the building for your use. Sometimes your building will be ready for occupancy and you will not be allowed to make major changes. In other cases you will be leasing only a shell, and finishing the interior to meet your needs will be up to you.

Never assume that because a contract looks legal or is written in legalese that it complies with the laws of your state. *Take it to your attorney for at least a quick look over.* It doesn't matter how much you like the landlord or leasing agent. Even the sweetest little old lady can have a dark side. It doesn't matter if you are afraid the person will be offended. It doesn't even matter if the landlord says the contract was drawn up by an attorney. This is business. Take the contract to your attorney—*before you sign it.* This could save major problems and expense in the future.

Victorian Treasures

A friend of mine opened a small shop selling handmade gifts in an old Victorian home. She did a lot of work restoring the building, paying great attention to detail, including decorating the interior to complete the Victorian theme. She also did a great job of arranging her merchandise by room to give her store an intimate, homey feeling. Her location on a major street in town encourages drop-in business from people curious about her building. She made her building work for her, and her business is very successful.

✂ MY STORY

Now, do you want to hear the story about my retail lease? Are you sure? This is an area where we had a few problems, to say the least.

We tried to do things right, it just didn't quite work out that way. We were thinking about opening a retail store somewhere in the future. One day we went out to a nearby suburb looking for antiques. This was a quaint little community with several retail areas with antique and craft stores. When we got there, lo and behold, there was a building for rent. Try to imagine our excitement as we thought the perfect location had fallen in our laps.

We rushed to talk to the owner and signed the lease right there on the spot, totally ignoring the advice I just gave you. Why should we pay to have an attorney look at the lease when the owner was such a sweet little grandma? This is definitely a situation where the old saying, "do as I say, not as I do" applies.

It didn't take us long to learn that what we thought was a high-traffic tourist area was only wishful thinking. Initially this was a major disappointment, but in reality it was not a bad thing since we just weren't ready for constant crowds.

It also didn't take long for the sweet little old lady to start telling us how to run our business. All sorts of rules not stated in the lease started appearing out of nowhere. Our electricity was turned off for nonpayment (the landlord's responsibility). We were also concerned about liability issues surrounding a hazardous sidewalk.

When we finally took the contract to our attorney, we learned the contract contained clauses that were not even legal in our state. His guess was it had come from a book of prepared contract forms. He didn't have any better luck dealing with the owner than we did. His advice was to just wait out our lease, going on with business as best we could until the year was up, and then relocate. Which is what we did.

This does not mean our first retail experience was a failure. Far from it. In fact, financially we were very pleased. We worked very hard at drawing customers to our store, and we broke even the first year. Not bad at all. But our first year was full of legal and interpersonal headaches that could have been avoided if we had slowed down, done more research, and taken the contract to our attorney.

Choosing a location for a retail store, studio, or gallery is one of the most exciting experiences you can have. Once you have a location the dream starts becoming real, something you can actually see. Just be sure you choose a location that is right for you, your business, and your customers.

Do Your Homework

1. *Creative Exercise.* What does your perfect retail space look like? Close your eyes and try to see your perfect store, studio, or gallery. Spend as much time as you need envisioning your perfect space. Walk around and take a good look. When you come back from your visit take some time to write about what you saw. Make sketches if you desire.
2. *Creative Planning.* Get started making that ideal store a reality. Start thinking about the practical, concrete steps you need to take to make your ideal store happen for you.
3. *Creative Action.* Take that important first step toward making your retail dream come true.

Lesson 15

SELLING WHOLESALE

MANY ARTISTS AND CRAFTSPEOPLE would love to sell their work wholesale, that is to another business for resale, but don't know how to make it happen. This is a different type of sale. It is not necessarily difficult, but it is different. Storeowners and buyers have their own language and their own rules. At first, trying to sell wholesale is like going to a foreign country, but the way you learn to sell wholesale is by doing it.

✄ THE RULES FOR SELLING TO RETAILERS

The first thing you need to do is learn the rules. These are a few of the basics of dealing with retailers. Following these should help you at least get in the front door.

First, make an appointment. Never just drop in. Call ahead and ask to speak to the buyer. Sometimes this will be the owner, but not necessarily.

Once you've made your appointment, keep it. Not only keep it, but be on time. This is important, even if the buyer does not remember you had an appointment, and he may not. Buyers and storeowners are busy people and are notorious for forgetting appointments. If this happens, don't see it as a personal rejection; it isn't. Remind the buyer whom you are, that you have spoken before, and that you have an appointment. This courtesy will help present you in a professional light.

Be professional in your personal appearance, attitude, the whole package. Be sure to take along your business cards, brochures, sample case or photo book, order pads, and any other professional sales tools you may need. Don't forget your pen.

Take either good quality photos in a nicely arranged presentation book, or better yet, samples of your product. In fact, if your product lends itself to this, make it possible to close the agreement and leave a small quantity of the item.

Unsolicited mass mailings of pictures or products usually do not work and are expensive. When I was a retailer all unsolicited submissions either went in the trash or were returned to the sender at their expense. Business owners usually do not want to take the time to deal with this stuff.

Please do not send a box of handmade pot holders to a business picked out of the phone book with a letter saying, please sell these for me. Don't laugh, I have received such packages. Without a contract the business owner is not obligated to sell, return, protect, or pay for your items. So you might lose your items altogether doing this. It is dangerous, unwise, and unprofessional.

Remember, you are playing the numbers game. Not everyone will buy. If you talk to one hundred storeowners by phone, feel fortunate if ten take the time to see you. Of those ten buyers, one may show enough interest to want your work in his store if it meets his needs at the time.

Don't take rejection personally. This is easier said than done. I have been known to go home and have a good cry after a buyer said no. After all, these rejected items are my babies. But for the storeowner this is business. She may like your work, but not have room. In that case, leave the door open to come back later. My experience has been that if a buyer or storeowner really attacks the work or the quality but is still interested in buying, she is often trying to get the price down. She may actually like your work. This is where your negotiation skills are tested.

Have prices set before you go in, and be confident about them. When it comes to talking money, never say, "whatever you think is fair." Have a printed price sheet with quantity price breaks for the buyer to keep. Be sure your business name and phone number are on any materials you leave with the buyer.

When pricing for wholesale, set your retail price, then give several levels of price breaks for quantity purchases. This is what the buyer will be accustomed to and expect.

Don't expect, but be prepared for, the possibility of very large orders. If you accept large orders, be sure you can realistically fill them. You don't want the legal headaches or the damage to your reputation that could result from taking orders you are not prepared to fill.

✄ PAYMENT AND SALES TAX ISSUES

If you are selling your work to a business outright, payment must be received before the store receives the merchandise. Some merchants require a repurchase or buy-back agreement. This means that if the store cannot sell your work, you will buy it back. Could you come up with the money to do this? What would you do with the product if you had to buy a large quantity back?

When you sell wholesale to a business, you must be given the resale tax number for that business. It is a good idea to have a special form made up with the business name, address, contact name, and tax number. Keep it on file. You do not charge tax on wholesale purchases by businesses. The tax is collected by the merchant actually selling the item to the public. When you sell your work directly to retail customers you must collect the tax.

Most buyers will expect you to contact them concerning reorders or future purchases. They will generally not contact you. Keep records of your wholesale customers, including a list of past purchases. You may use our Tracking Sheet for Wholesale Customers at the end of the lesson for this. Write down callbacks on your calendar so you won't forget them.

✄ TRADE SHOWS

Trade shows are another way to sell your work wholesale. Trade shows will enable you to reach many retailers at one time. Be sure you are ready for the possibility of very large orders before even considering this. This is really playing with the big boys.

Wholesale trade shows typically involve a major financial investment, so careful planning is essential. *Is your business ready to make the transition from retail to wholesale?* Notice that I didn't ask if you want to sell millions of items and make some major money. I asked if your business is ready. Are you realistically able to fill orders for hundreds or thousands of one item?

If you still think this is something you want to do, contact the company that produces the trade show by mail or phone. Ask for printed information to be mailed to you. Read this information carefully. When we requested trade show information we received a large packet of materials including a program book from a previous show.

Pay careful attention to the rules concerning displays. This is not just another craft show. You will be taking wholesale orders, not selling single items. Take samples of the items you wish to sell and printed information. Some wholesalers will include a pictorial display of the way in which their product is produced. *If possible, try to get into the trade show as a nonbuying visitor before going as a vendor* to get a feel for what the show is like.

✄ MY STORY

Bob and I looked at trade shows at one point in the development of our business. At the time I was designing and making original clothing and jewelry with a country or southwestern flair. Since we were located in the Midwestern United States, the closest major clothing markets were Chicago and Dallas. There was a Western-wear market in Dallas, so that is where we chose to focus our attention. The woman Bob spoke with on the phone was very helpful and sent a packet of information. Next we asked ourselves what items we were ready to take to market. We decided on several jewelry items we could produce easily and inexpensively. We could also train others to help make these items and had one trained jewelry maker already working with us.

We seriously considered going to a wholesale market, but we didn't. Why? We were already having some success approaching local and regional retailers and decided to explore that option more. We did not rule out the wholesale market entirely, we just decided it was somewhere down the road for us. What we did not know was that as we went down that road I would make major changes in my work. I now do one-of-a-kind original fabric art that does not lend itself to mass-production and therefore needs to be marketed in a different way.

✄ HIRING A SALES REPRESENTATIVE

Now, one final thought about selling wholesale that many people don't think about. Most people start out in any new business doing the work themselves. The craft business is no exception. When you start out wholesaling your work you may be representing yourself. If you do this, keep in mind there may come a time when you need to turn this part of your work over to someone else. *Do not build your wholesale business around your own personality* to the point that it is difficult or impossible for someone else to sell your work. When making this type of transition it is a good idea to take the new representative with you and introduce her to your wholesale buyers, explaining that she will be taking over the account. Careful training and screening is also important to be sure the person representing your work understands your work, your business philosophy, and any special deals you may have made with your wholesale clients.

Selling your work wholesale is not impossible. It can be done. But it is important to do your homework and go in at least looking like you know what you are doing. If you don't, you will either not be taken seriously or, even worse, you might be taken advantage of—and I mean cheated. Don't allow yourself to be forced into an arrangement you are not comfortable with just to sell your merchandise. Be confident, be professional, and go out there and sell!

SELLING WHOLESALE **121**

DO YOUR HOMEWORK

1. Make a list of retail stores that might be interested in carrying your work.
2. Do a little research and find out who does the buying for the store. Is it the storeowner or is there a central corporate buying office in another city or state that buys for all the stores in a chain? Or do they buy at market exclusively?
3. Make a plan. Which retailers are you going to target? How are you going to make the approach? How are you going to make the sale? Are you able to fill orders comfortably and in a reasonable time?
4. Decide what method you will use to keep track of your wholesale customers and use it.

Tracking Sheet for Wholesale Customers

Make a separate sheet for each store or company you deal with. Keep these on file for your records. Enter this information into your computer if that is your record-keeping system.

GENERAL INFORMATION

Store or Company Name: _____

Buyer's Name and Title: _____

Address: _____

Phone: _____

Tax ID Number: _____

Notes on this buyer: _____

_____

_____

_____

_____

_____

_____

_____

_____

_____

_____

_____

_____

_____

_____

_____

	PURCHASE RECORD		
Date	Items Purchased	Quantity	Call Back

NEED MORE HELP?

LITERATURE

Brabec, Barbara. *Creative Cash*. Rocklin, Calif.: Prima Publishing Inc, 1998.
Caputo, Kathryn. *How to Produce a Successful Craft Show*. Mechanicsburg, Pa.: Stackpole Books, 1997.
Gray, Madeline. *Selling Your Crafts at Craft Shows: The Basics for Beginners*. North Adams, Mass.: Storey Communications Inc., 1997.
Sedestrom-Ross, Carol. "Wholesaling 101 with Carol Sedestrom-Ross." *Sunshine Artist Magazine* (cited: March 2003). Available at: *http://sunshineartist.com/magazine/wholesale101.htm*.

TRADE SHOW ORGANIZERS

[Contact information is available in Appendix B.]
Advancestar Communications
American Craft Council
The Boston Gift Show
Dallas Market Center
The Denver Merchandise Mart
Kansas City Gift Mart Inc.
Offinger Management
Rosen Group
Trade Shows Inc.
Western Exhibitors LLC

LISTINGS OF TRADE SHOWS

[Contact information is available in Appendix B.]
National Craft Association

Lesson 16

THE CRAFT SHOW EXPERIENCE

I LOVE FOLLOWING the creative flow of things and spending hours or even days at a time working in the studio. But I also love to get out and meet people. That is where some of my best ideas come from. Comments from customers have helped me refine designs and make them better, more than once. I have even given small prizes for the best ideas. Bob has also received vital marketing information from craft shows.

But craft shows are also a lot of very hard work. Another thing to remember is that art and craft shows involve direct contact with people—lots of people. If you are not a people person you may want to consider another way of marketing your work. There is absolutely nothing wrong with that. You are not doomed to failure because you choose not to go out on the show circuit.

✂ WHERE ARE THE CRAFT SHOWS?

When you are first starting out, finding shows to enter may be a problem, especially if you live in a rural area. I live in a city and this is not a problem here. There are small shows, large shows, juried shows, open entry shows, neighborhood shows, fundraising shows, shows that are part of summer festivals, national shows, and professionally promoted shows. You name it, we seem to have it. But how do you find a show if this is not the case where you live?

Before you get started, *decide how far you are willing to travel.* Determine your maximum travel distance. Take out a map. Beginning with your city use a compass to draw a circle the distance you are willing to travel. This is your target area. Are you looking only at local shows? Are you able to travel to another city or state? This will give direction to your search.

Believe it or not *a good place to start looking for craft shows is your local newspaper.* Pay careful attention to the want ads and the entertainment section. Don't just look for shows that are accepting applications. Also look for advertising for scheduled events. Unless the show is tomorrow, they may still be accepting vendors. If there is contact information it doesn't hurt to check it out.

Commercial directories, in hard copy or online, list upcoming craft shows. Keep in mind that these are usually national or regional, so coverage of your area may not be adequate, but it's still worth a try. Listings in some directories are considered advertising and are not free. Keep this in mind if you wonder why a certain show is not included.

Trade magazines sometimes list shows. *Sunshine Artist Magazine* specializes in this. Also try *The Crafts Report.* Magazines for your specific media may also be helpful.

One of the best ways to find craft shows is through *word of mouth.* Talk to people. When you go to your local craft supply store ask if they keep a list of upcoming shows. Check the bulletin board if there is one.

Put yourself on *mailing lists* for show announcements. When you see an announcement for a show you may be interested in ask if there is a mailing list (regular mail or e-mail). Once you start entering shows you may find yourself automatically receiving show announcements.

✂ CHOOSING A SHOW

How do you choose a craft show? There are many things to consider.

What type of show is it? Is the show an event in itself or part of a larger festival or celebration? The latter can be lots of fun. We had a blast when we took my country-style clothing to the Walnut Valley Festival. In case you don't know, this is a music festival, bluegrass to be exact.

You will also want to know if the show is a *fundraiser.* In this type of show booth rents, admission fees, and sometimes a percentage of sales go to the sponsoring organization. This is often good exposure. It also just makes you feel good, especially if the show is for a cause you believe in. Just be clear on the terms and conditions. We have done fundraising shows and probably would still consider doing one for the right cause.

There are also *shows run by professional promoters or management companies.* Professionally organized shows are often national shows and are usually juried, so you will have more competition. It will cost more to get into this type of show, but remember to balance that against sales potential, exposure, typically large attendance, and money spent on advertising.

Where is the location of the show? Is it easy to find? If you have trouble finding it, chances are customers will as well.

How many exhibitors are expected? Large shows tend to attract large crowds, but not always. Any show must be well promoted to draw big numbers. A small, high-quality, juried, and well-promoted show could draw just as well.

How much publicity is there about this show? Common sense says a well-advertised and promoted show should generate better attendance. People have to know about the show to be able to attend. Keep in mind that someone has to pay for advertising, so expect to pay more by way of entry fees. There could also be an admission charge to the public.

How much is booth rent? Deciding how much you are willing or able to spend on booth rental fees needs to be done on a case-by-case basis. Quality, reputation, location, drawing ability for crowds, sales potential, and any services provided by the organizers must all be considered for each show.

Will an admission fee be charged? As a consumer I have trouble paying to go shopping, so I try to stay away from shows that charge admission fees. One exception is if the fee is for a larger event such as a rodeo, music festival, or holiday celebration, and the art or craft show is simply a part of the larger event.

Finally, don't forget those not quite so often thought about but no less important things like the image you want your business to project and even how your own financial, moral, and ethical values will come into play here. Are there certain days you will not go out to a show? These might include your days of religious observance, certain holidays, your birthday, or anniversary. Does the sponsoring organization make a difference to you? Would you not choose to participate in a show if alcoholic beverages were sold on the premises? It is important to have these in mind before you start looking for shows.

Choosing a show is not always easy. There are many factors to consider. Take your time. It is best to book shows well in advance so you are not rushed by deadlines. As with everything we have covered in this book, do your homework, prepare, keep a good attitude, and expect the best.

✂ MAKING APPLICATION

Now that you have chosen a show, how do you go about getting in? The application process will vary and depends on whether the show is open entry or juried.

Open entry shows are pretty much open to anyone. The organizers may limit the types of work represented at the show and they may have rules. Getting into such a show, however, is usually just a matter of completing the application and paying your fees. This is the type of show that most of us start out with, and there is nothing wrong with that.

Juried shows mean participation is competitive. You will usually be asked to provide slides, but in some cases color photos or actual product samples, for judging by a committee known as a jury. The jury will determine if you will be selected for the show. Juries usually judge slides of your work, not the work itself, which makes quality photography vital. If you cannot do this yourself, hire someone. If you don't trust your own photography skills and you just can't afford a professional, do you have a friend or family member who is a talented amateur? If not, try calling the art department of a local high school or college and ask if they could recommend a student.

Bob and I do our own photography. We do this because we enjoy taking photographs and own a good camera. This is something we do largely for fun. We enjoy setting up displays and situations to make my work look its best. For instance, when photographing a barbecue apron that is an original design of mine, we took one of the aprons and our camera along with food and charcoal to our favorite park and had a barbecue. We took turns snapping photos of each other wearing the apron and cooking on the grill. We have also arranged nice displays of jewelry on a neutral background, as well as photographing me wearing my original clothing designs. We couldn't afford models back then, so we had to use ourselves.

When doing your own photography, it is a good idea to take more than one photo of each item. Then you can choose your favorite. I make sure that between the two of us, we take at least four or five shots of each item. Bob says this is probably overkill, but I am still a bit unsure of my photography skills and want to be sure I get at least one usable photo.

Now that my work has changed and I am making original fabric art, there is not as much room for creativity in our photography. Sometimes living in an apartment with blank, dull, white walls can be a good thing. It gives us lots of display space as well as providing a nice neutral background for photography.

As important as good photography is to remember that juries judge not only the quality of your work as seen in your slides, but also things such as the originality and creativity of your work. If the show has a theme, they will also consider how well your work fits that theme.

Rejection is never a pleasant experience, but *rejection from a juried show does not necessarily mean your work was not good enough.* Juried shows often limit the number of artists working in each medium to provide good variety. So your rejection might simply mean the quota for artists in your medium is full.

Don't let the jury process intimidate or overwhelm you. My first jury experience was much more frightening in my imagination than in reality. This was my ideal show. I wanted into this show so bad I could taste it. Qualifying for the show represented success for me in a big way. Looking back, I can now say I was putting way too much importance on that one show. Because of this I turned the jury process into more of an ordeal than it needed to be. The most difficult part of the process was the waiting.

We filled out the application and decided which items we wanted to take to the show. For this particular show specific products were juried and nothing else was allowed to be exhibited. This is not always the case, but for this show it was. Next we took photos of those items. We are basically amateur photographers, so it took several tries to get good quality photographs.

Then we put the application in the mail and the waiting began. Every day I wondered what was going on. Was this the day the jury was meeting? I wished I could be present to hear what they had to say about my work, but at the same time I was glad that I wasn't. What were they saying about my work? They hated it. I knew they hated it.

By the time the letter actually arrived I had worked myself into quite a frenzy. It took a couple of days to work up the courage to actually open it. Then I made Bob read it first so he could soften the bad news for me. But it wasn't the bad news I was afraid it would be. I did get into that show. In fact, it turned into one of my most successful show experiences.

If you don't make it into that ideal show on your first try, learn from the experience and try again. By all means, don't let fear of the unknown keep you from entering juried shows. You might be missing out on a wonderful and profitable experience.

✄ GETTING READY

A successful art or craft show experience takes preparation. This means more than just having your product ready to go. Being prepared will help make your craft show experience a good one.

One of the most important points I can make about preparation is *don't leave everything till the night before.* If you are a person who gets obsessed about details, like I do, this won't be a problem for you. I know you start packing a full month before the show, hand out assignments to family members, and walk around with a checklist faithfully checking off each item as it is completed. If, on the other hand, you believe that the details will take care of themselves and tend to leave things to the last minute, like Bob, you might need to do some work in this area. Have a designated place for all display equipment, product, marketing materials, and other items that are going to the show, and start collecting them there. Remember, you don't want to wear yourself out before you even get to the show. And if that doesn't convince you, packing your car or van the night before means you get to sleep a little bit later in the morning, not to mention starting out on the road rested instead of after two or three hours of hard manual labor. That extra hour of sleep gets Bob every time.

Make sure your night-before preparations don't keep you up all night. *Go to bed as early as possible.* You will be leaving early in the morning for setup and things will go smoother if you start out rested.

Allow adequate time for setup. Set up the night before if allowed. Setting up a booth on the morning of a show is when Murphy's Law—anything that can go wrong will—kicks in. Be familiar with your display equipment and how it goes together. Try out new equipment or booth design by actually setting your booth up at home first. Give yourself a chance to work out any problems before the day of the show.

If you are going to an outdoor show, go prepared to be outdoors. Take along a tent or canopy to protect your work as well as to help define your space—and don't forget the sunscreen. Be prepared for unforeseen weather conditions such as rain or high wind. I went to one outdoor show where it was so windy we had to tape the clothing hangers to the racks to keep them from flying away. Thank God for duct tape!

Take a small product repair kit. There will be wear and tear on your merchandise. It is a good idea to repair minor damage on site.

Don't forget to take change. One ten-dollar bill, one five, five ones, one roll each of quarters and dimes, and two rolls each of nickels and pennies will get you started. This gives you an even $40 worth of change to begin your selling day, making it easy to know how much to subtract at the end of the day to determine what you brought in during the day. If your prices are in even dollar amounts with the tax included, replace the coins with more bills.

You may think $40 doesn't sound like much, but all you really need is enough to get started; as change is going out more will be coming in from sales. If a customer hands you a $20 bill for a $2 purchase you can politely ask if the customer has a smaller bill. People are often just looking to break a large bill. If you get a reputation as a place to get change you will be giving out a lot of change. Keeping too much cash on hand is also a safety concern. If you think you may need more than $40, keep it in a separate, safe place until needed. You will also need a *cash register or a receipt book, calculator, and a secure place to keep your money.*

Take a guest book and encourage people who are interested in your work to sign their names, along with their address, phone number, or e-mail. This is a good way to start a mailing list of prospective customers.

Pack drinking water, snacks, and a lunch. You may not always know the availability of these at a show until you get there.

Take along plenty of helpers. During times of heavy traffic, this helps with theft control. You will also need someone to cover for your lunch and bathroom breaks. Trade off during slow times so no one gets stuck in the booth all day.

Be sure to take your paperwork. This includes a copy of your application and any written verification of your entry. If you already have your booth assignment, take that. It's also a good idea to take along a copy of your tax resale certificate.

It's a good idea to take something to sit on—such as a folding chair or, better yet, a bar stool—because you will get tired standing all day, often on concrete floors. Why a bar stool? It puts you at your customer's eye level. Take advantage of slow times to sit down for a minute and rest your feet. However, unless you have a physical problem that prevents standing or makes it difficult, please don't just park yourself in that chair all day long and not move. You know what I'm talking about. We've all seen it and most of us have done it. Even if you cannot stand you can still interact with the visitors to your booth by talking to them. One of the best artist/saleswomen I've ever seen works her booth from a wheelchair. She still moves around her booth and actively engages her customers.

A Tool Kit Can Save the Day

Take a small tool kit with you, even if you think you don't need it. Include any tools needed to put your booth together or to repair it. A good basic show kit would include a lightweight hammer with nails, two screwdrivers (flat head and Phillips) with screws, a pair of pliers, a lightweight battery-operated drill, one roll each of electricians tape and masking tape, and a heavy duty extension cord (be sure to check show rules before using). You may be able to combine some tools to cut down on weight and bulk. I have a lightweight hammer with a screwdriver set in the handle that is very useful at shows.

✄ DESIGNING AND SETTING UP A CRAFT BOOTH

Booth design is one of the most important things to consider when preparing for a craft show. If you sell your work through shows only, having an attractive and functional show booth is vital. First impressions of your work will be based on how your work is displayed. Believe it or not, your booth design and display equipment will affect your sales. Items that are well displayed will grab the attention of potential customers, possibly leading to sales.

We've all been to shows where *everyone lays her work out on a long table,* then sits behind the table collecting money (hopefully). There are shows where this is expected. I had this type of booth at my first shows, simply because I didn't know there was any other way. But most booth spaces are square, usually six by six feet, eight by eight feet, or ten by ten feet. Tables often are not. The tables used at craft shows are usually long and narrow, right? So, what happens to the extra space? Too often it is wasted.

Another choice you have is to set up a booth *that uses the entire space and invites people to come in and look around.* My name for these is mini-galleries, and they are my preference. Bob and I enjoy talking to our customers, and this type of booth encourages that. This is a type of booth you will often see at professional shows.

Keep in mind that there is more of a financial investment in this type of booth than in a folding table. It takes both money and time to create a unique and exciting booth display, but there is room for compromise. If you have more time or skill than money, you can build certain elements of the display yourself. Or you can spend time looking for display equipment at store close-outs, auctions, garage sales, and flea markets. This will not be an ongoing expense. Once your display is satisfactory, you will use it over and over.

Always use display equipment that makes your work look its best. For instance, hang paintings and other framed works on lattice screens, ply-wood, or particle board walls constructed for your booth. Small sculptures or pottery are quite impressive displayed on fabric-draped pedestals or wooden boxes. It doesn't really matter what you use here as long as it's sturdy and works in your space. Display clothing and jewelry on racks. Stores going out of business and auction houses are good sources of display equipment. You may need to go a little bit outside your geographic area to find these, but the drive could end up saving you a lot of money.

When we were setting up our retail store Bob and I drove an hour to attend an auction for a women's clothing store that had recently gone out of business. We were able to buy several clothing racks, many jewelry racks, and a three-way mirror for our dressing room for a fraction of the cost of new items. Think about how you are going to transport large items before you go to an auction. I still laugh when I think about all the times we brought things home tied to the roof of our little red car. But we got them home.

There is room for creativity here; after all, you are an artist. If a flea mar-ket find works for you, by all means use it. Your display equipment doesn't have to be made for your intended purpose as long as it gets the job done.

Properly displaying your work will also cut down on damage from con-stant handling by people visiting your booth. Of course there will still be the impulse to touch, but if your work doesn't have to be handled to be seen there will be much less wear and tear on it.

✂ LIGHTING FOR YOUR BOOTH

One final thing you might want to consider in your booth design is light-ing. Many people believe lighting is vital to a good display. However, proper lighting equipment can be expensive, and you will need to have an electric hookup available at all shows to use lighting. I would suggest that you try out your booth for awhile and take time to determine where lighting is needed before making this investment. If you go to outdoor shows that will be open at night, you will definitely want to invest in lighting.

Before you do anything with lighting do your research. Advances in technology have greatly changed the types of lighting now available. In addition to incandescent and fluorescent bulbs, we now have halogen and other low-voltage bulbs. Lighting fixtures no longer have to be big and bulky. If you choose a low-voltage system, be aware that you will need a transformer to be able to plug your system into a conventional outlet.

You will also want to determine your lighting needs. Do you want to illuminate specific items or do you want to create an overall effect with your lighting? Know where and how you will attach light fixtures.

Finally, remember that your lighting system must also be easily portable. So be sure your system will travel well and withstand being set up and torn down over and over and over. Be sure that anyone who helps you design your lighting understands your intended use of the system.

I never actually went out on the craft show circuit, going out every week. Instead, I used craft shows for advertising and to familiarize people with my work. It was not my main way of marketing my work, so it did not seem to be worthwhile to invest in lighting for shows. In my store, however, I did use spotlights on certain items. I also used lighting in my front window as a form of advertising at night when the store was closed. We always kept a nice display in our front window, which we changed every month. Many people told us that they watched our window to see what we would do next. Several of our customers said they had enjoyed driving by our window on the way to work and made the effort to come back when we were open. We also used a timer to turn various lights on and off throughout the night for security reasons. The literature section following this lesson will help you find more information on lighting.

✂ STILL COMMITTED TO TABLES?

If you still firmly believe you must use tables to display your work and nothing else will do, then let me make a few suggestions. *Try moving your table to the back of your space,* instead of across the front. This still requires people to come into your space. It also gives people a chance to escape the crowd for a few minutes.

Consider using other display equipment along with your table. With your table along the back of your space you now have room for other displays in front of your table or along the sides. Lattice screens along the sides of your booth would be an example of this, as would a hanging rack for wearable art or a Christmas tree with ornaments in the area in front of the table.

Could you use more tables? Placing two tables in an "L" or three tables in a "U" shape also takes better advantage of the square shape of your space as well as giving you more display room.

Take some time to create a well thought out and attractive booth. Your efforts will pay off.

✄ COMMON PROBLEMS WITH BOOTH DESIGN

What are some of the common problems crafters seem to have with booth design? The major problem I see is *overcrowding* in craft booths. You want to show as much of your work as possible, but trying to pack too much into your booth won't make your booth design effective. Unless the rules of a particular show state otherwise, you don't have to start out with everything in your booth when the show opens. As you sell, you can bring in more.

Worked displayed too low is a problem. Work displayed at eye level will be noticed by your customers more readily than work displayed lower. That does not mean all your work must be at eye level. In fact, that might be a strange-looking booth. But I suggest having your best work hung at eye level to draw people in. Once they are in your booth they will look around at your other work. If you have to display your work low enough that customers need to bend, squat, or stoop to look at it, offer to bring the item out for the customer to look at up close.

There She Blows!

Famous whalers used to say, "There she blows!" when they spotted a whale some distance from their ship. Don't let those words be said about your booth. When going to outdoor shows be sure your tent is sturdy and well-stabilized. You will need extra weight to hold the tent down. Over the years I have seen everything from metal tubes filled with sand or concrete to ten-gallon jugs filled with water hanging at the corners as weight. One woman who told me she hangs sixty-pound weights in each of the four corners said, "My tent isn't going anywhere." Added stability may be given to display surfaces for hanging paintings, photographs, and other items by tying them together with metal rods. This is something that seems to be learned from experience, so talking to other artists could be helpful.

✂ MY BOOTH DESIGN PROCESS

It has been awhile since I have been to a craft fair. However, some very good shows have been tempting me to get back out there. So, I am going to let you in on my booth design process as I come up with a new booth design for these shows. First, I need to have a rough idea of the type of work I want to display. Okay, let me think. I have large, bed-sized quilts, wall quilts, small framed pieces, purses, and jewelry. I also need a place for my guest book, business cards, and other promotional literature. How am I going to display this stuff?

First I would start out with my lattice screens across the back of the booth space. We had these screens custom-made to be sturdy and to fit in the back of our vehicle. They cost us quite a bit, so I try to use them whenever possible. The framed work and wall hangings would hang here. I would fill in empty spots with jewelry on cards, investing in good, sturdy metal or PVC framework for the sides. I would cover the railing with acid-free paper and hang my quilts from these. I have four wooden coat racks, which I would place near the front and back corners. Two of these coat racks would be borrowed from our living room and bedroom, the other two are in storage. I would hang from these the purses and necklaces. Another item borrowed from our bedroom would be a small table with removable legs for the guest book and literature. The last final touch would be to choose my most spectacular, flashy, and generally wonderful quilt to hang on a quilt rack (also borrowed from my bedroom) at the entry to my booth. Of course I would arrange the quilt on the rack to make it look its best. That's it. Most of my work is displayed around the outside edges of the booth allowing plenty of room for people to move around. If I needed more display space for jewelry, instead of a table I would probably borrow Bob's display rack, which he uses for his bird collection. It is a wrought iron and wicker baker's rack with four shelves. The advantage of this rack is that is collapses for easy transport. Bob and I work shows together, with one of us at the front of the booth and the other inside, toward the back. We are able to keep a close eye on things this way. If you work alone, I would not place small items that could walk away easily at the front of your booth.

✂ TAKING IT ON THE ROAD

How easy is it going to be to travel with your booth? Remember you will be putting this booth up and taking it down, over and over and over. How difficult is that going to be? How much time does it take to set up your booth? If your answer is in terms of days or weeks, you have a problem.

Do you have room in your vehicle to transport everything to a show? Do you have access to an additional vehicle and driver if needed? If you go to national or out-of-state shows, could you transport everything a long distance comfortably?

When you design your booth, remember that you are going to be moving it often. Making your booth easy to transport can save wear and tear on your vehicle, your back, and your temper.

✂ THE ART OF SALES

When you take your work out to a show you enter the world of sales. A scary thought for most artists, but it doesn't have to be.

When you sell your own work you have a built-in sales technique. You are the artist, the creator. People are going to be curious about you. Who are you? How is your work created? Why? Be prepared to answer questions. If your work is portable, consider working in your booth. This will generate interest from passersby and encourage people to stop and watch. If you do this, take along someone to sell for you.

A FEW SALES BASICS

To make sales there must be someone present to take the money. Now this may sound like a silly statement. Most of you are probably thinking that's a given. But you don't know how many times I have seen booths left totally unattended, or with the artist hiding behind her booth, even at kiosks in major shopping malls.

You can hire or draft someone to make sales for you. If you are absolutely convinced you can't sell your own work, you can hire someone or take a family member along to do that for you.

The artist's presence can encourage sales. Even if you have someone else selling for you, hang out in the general area of your booth and at least pop in from time to time. As was said earlier, people are curious about you as the artist. They want to meet you. They want to be able to tell their friends they have met you. This is your chance for your fifteen minutes of fame. Don't blow it! By all means don't be rude. Don't behave as though you would rather be anywhere else but at the show. Your presence can make sales, but it can also destroy them.

Talk to people. Make small talk if you can't think of anything else to say. It will get easier with practice.

Watch people. Take note of those items that seem to draw people to them. If a customer seems to really want to buy but hesitates or puts the item back and walks away, ask yourself why. You may want to ask the customer a few gentle questions to find out. Is the size, color, or price wrong? Is there something you could do to save the sale or direct the customer to another item?

Listen to people. Listen not only as people engage in conversation with you, but as they talk to each other while in your booth. I have learned ways of improving my work and my sales numbers by listening to comments people make while looking at my work.

Work on your closing technique. Remember, a sale is not made until the person indicates that he wants an item and actually hands you the money. Closing a deal or actually getting a customer to part with the money is one of the most difficult parts of sales. Even the best salesperson has had sales fall through at the last minute. There are a few ways you can subtly encourage people to go ahead and buy. High-pressure sales rarely work so balance is important here.

One way to close a sale is to give the customer a choice that does not involve a yes or no answer. For instance, instead of asking, " Would you like to buy that today?" to which the customer could respond, "No, not today," try "Would you like that in blue or green?" Or you could ask, "Would you like that gift-wrapped?" You will find that this technique works. Sometimes all a customer needs is a gentle nudge to go ahead and buy.

Sometimes a customer will ask your opinion. After all you are the artist. This can help close a sale. If, for instance, a customer asks if you think a certain piece will fit with her home decor and you really don't think it will, your choices are not limited to telling a small fib or being truthful and losing the sale. Perhaps you could say something like, "I have something over here that would be perfect in your living room."

You can also use this technique to make additional sales. For example, if you sell clothing and jewelry you could tell the customer who just selected a dress, "I have a pair of earrings that would be lovely with that dress." Or better yet, go get the earrings and show the customer how nicely they go with the dress. Can you see how this is better than asking, "Do you need earrings to go with that?" When you ask that question you are giving the customer an easy way to say no.

Selling is not really difficult, but it does require practice. It may also require a change in your thinking as well as your behavior. Remember, the way you interact with the people who visit your booth will have an effect on our sales. That is a given. It cannot be changed. You can, however, influence whether that effect will be positive or negative.

The Artist Knows

I was drawn to his booth by a particular painting that really caught my eye. As we were approaching the painting for a closer look, the artist said, "Now, which one do you want that you can't have?" I replied, "How could you tell?" His response, with a twinkle in his eye was, "I've been in this business a long time, I can tell. It's a look in the eyes." How are you at reading your customers?

✂ EVALUATING THE EXPERIENCE

The show is over. Was it a success? That depends on your idea of success. Do you think of craft show success only in terms of the amount of money taken in, or the number of items sold? Is exposure, or getting your name out to the public just as important? Do you use a craft show as a way to make contact with potential customers and collect contact information? Do you use craft shows to test drive new products and see how the public reacts to them?

What determines whether a particular show experience is successful or not is based on what you need and want to accomplish. This may change from show to show.

The first thing most people think about in terms of craft show success is how much money they made. It is important to remember that your profit doesn't begin until you have covered all of your expenses. In this case your expenses include not only the cost of the products themselves, but also the cost of the craft show to you. This includes travel expense, motel and food while at the show, in addition to booth rent and any other fees the promoters may charge. If the show was held in connection with a larger event and you considered this a family vacation as well as work, then your definition of success for that particular show may be making enough to cover the expenses of that family vacation. If, however, your purpose was to go sell product and make lots of money, you would probably not be happy if you only covered your travel expenses. Only you can determine if you are happy with the amount of money you make at a craft show.

Another measure of craft show success might be how many items you sold. If your goal was to sell fifty items at a particular show and you sold one hundred, then your idea of success was not only met, it was exceeded. If you only sold twenty-five you may want to come up with a new sales plan.

Or perhaps you are more concerned about attendance numbers. How many people attended the show? Are you happy with that? These people are potential customers, even if they did not buy at that particular show. They will remember you and your work when they see you at other events, and sooner or later, some of them will buy. Did you remember to give visitors a chance to sign a guest book? This gives you a list of people interested in your work. Some artists send out a newsletter, which includes their show schedule, so their regular customers will know when and where to find them.

What factors might have influenced low attendance? Was the location hard to find? Were there other problems with the location? Was there an admission fee? Was it too high or too low? (Have you ever wondered why shows charging a fifty-cent admission fee even bother collecting such a small amount?)

Weather that is either too bad or too good can also keep people away. Was the date or time a problem? Was there another major event in town that might have drawn your audience away?

Was the show well-organized or did confusion reign? If the event was poorly run, did you sell enough or make enough contacts to make it worth enduring?

✂ LESSONS LEARNED

What did you learn from this show? A show that does not produce the desired number of sales or cash flow is not a failure if you learned something. I can say from experience that we learned more from the bad shows than we ever did from the great ones.

The following are a few of the lessons from our on-the-job-training file. *First, never take a new booth design out to a show without setting it up at home first.* Not following that one probably contributed to my greatest craft show disaster. This was the first time I tried to take quilts to a show. Since I had never done this before I needed a way to display the quilts. After much thought and discussion we came up with the idea to turn the entire booth into a giant quilt rack. We built a six-by-six-foot wooden frame (the size of an average booth space) and strung heavy gage wire to fill in the frame. The quilts would then be hung on the wire. The actual building of this new display took longer than expected (there were complications) and we found ourselves applying the final coat of stain at midnight the night before the show. There was no time to try out the display to see if it would actually work. The show was getting ready to open and we were still trying to put the thing together. People were walking in the door as I was literally throwing quilts over the wires. Our first customers were in the booth when to my horror I noticed that the entire booth was leaning noticeably to the left. This is the show where Bob spent the entire day standing at the front of the booth greeting customers. People probably thought he was leaning on the booth because he was tired, but the truth is he was holding it up.

The second, but equally important real life lesson is you can't do anything about the weather. The year we chose to go to a major local craft show in eastern Colorado it was snowing lightly when we left for setup early in the morning. As we were unloading at the auditorium, it started snowing more heavily. By midmorning we were in the middle of a full-fledged blizzard. Needless to say it wasn't the most well-attended craft show ever held. Who could have predicted that the first severe winter storm of the year was going to occur in October that year?

Don't go to an outdoor show without sunscreen. If you forget once you won't do that again. A serious sunburn is something you don't want to take home from a show. I couldn't sit down for a week after my first outdoor show. I can look back on it now and laugh, but there was nothing funny about it at the time.

And finally, *attitudes are contagious.* A negative artist in the next booth can spell disaster if you catch the negativity. I spent one of the longest days of my career in a booth next to a woman who felt the need to complain about everything. Whenever I looked—to her—as if I weren't busy, she would come over to complain. As the day went on I learned to find busy work to do when there were no customers and she eventually got the idea that I didn't have time to talk. When I finally got home, I felt like I had been slimed with negativity.

Would you be willing to try this show again? Keep a list of shows you have attended with notes on the experience. Identify the shows you want to go back to as well as the "never again" ones. After awhile they all start to blur together. If this was a first year for a show would you be willing to give them another chance to get the "bugs" out? Would you go back the next year or would you wait longer? Only you can determine if a craft show was successful for you. Setting clear goals will help you make this decision.

✄ GOING HOME

If you still have your day job, you may have to be at work the Monday morning after a big weekend show. But if you are traveling out of town to a show, I highly recommend staying overnight after the show is over and driving home the next day. This is a safety concern and comes from my own terrifying experience driving home from a show behind Bob, watching in horror as he was obviously falling asleep at the wheel. After what seemed like miles of honking my horn and flashing my lights I was finally able to get him to pull over. We did make it home safely, but this experience made us aware of just how tired one can be after finishing a craft show and that getting behind the wheel in that condition may not be a good idea.

A word of caution about shows. Marketing your work in this way is a very hard road. Bob and I learned this early on. Packing up and taking your work across town, your state, or the country involves a lot of wear and tear on your work, not to mention you. It is exhausting, especially if you have to get up the next day and go to your other job. Only you can decide if craft shows are for you.

DO YOUR HOMEWORK

FINDING AND ENTERING SHOWS

1. Learn where to look for art or craft shows. Keep your eyes and ears open for shows in your area. Explore the Internet for national show schedules.

2. Make a list of your three most important criteria for choosing a craft show, starting with the most important. If you will only consider juried shows, this might be number one. Then perhaps location is crucial to your decision. Your third criteria might be the reputation or past attendance numbers of a particular show. Keep this list, keeping in mind that you will be applying these three criteria to all shows you even think about entering. This will help you make a good decision.

3. Find three shows in your area you might be interested in entering. Call or write for show information. Be sure to take notes when inquiring by phone. After you have received any application materials, compare the three shows. What are the strengths and weaknesses of each? Which one best meets your needs?

4. If you are planning to enter a juried show you will need clear, good quality photographs or slides of your work. How are you as a photographer? Are you prepared to hire a professional photographer if needed? Do you know a talented amateur photographer, or perhaps a photography student who could help you with this?

GETTING READY

1. Use our checklist or develop your own to be sure you have everything you will need for the show. Designate a special place to start collecting everything that will be going with you. This makes packing a lot easier.

2. Develop your own plan for packing, travel, and booth set-up to help minimize stress. Make plans to start packing well in advance of your departure time if possible. Try to start out well rested. If booth setup is allowed the night before, take advantage of that if possible. Remember, the best laid plans can still go awry, so be as flexible as you can.

EFFECTIVE BOOTH DESIGN: A CREATIVITY EXERCISE

1. What do you want your booth to look like? Sit down in your comfortable chair, relax, and do a little daydreaming. Think about your perfect booth space. Can you close your eyes and see it? What does it look like? When you are finished and like what you see, take a few minutes to write or draw what you came up with.

2. Develop an action plan for crafting that perfect booth. How easy will your booth be to put together and take down? Will it go up in the allotted time? Will you be able to transport your display equipment comfortably? Make a list of what you will need to buy, including prices. Make a list of items you can make yourself, along with costs.

DEVELOPING YOUR SALES SKILLS

1. Practice your people watching skills. You can do this while walking through the shopping mall, at work, in the grocery store, at church, anywhere people gather. Pay special attention to body language. What can body language tell you about the person?

2. Develop your own sales strategy. Come up with a brief but informative and entertaining way of telling the story behind your work. *Be prepared to answer any questions about your work.* Write down a list of possible questions and think about what your answer would be. Take the time to actually write down your answer if this is helpful for you.

   Make a list of three ice breakers. These are nonthreatening ways to approach a customer and get them talking. How difficult would it be to have an actual project-in-progress in your booth? Are you comfortable giving demonstrations of your technique to the public? Do you have a helper who could be on hand both to encourage people to buy and to take the money if you are working on your art while in the booth? If working in your booth is not practical, *develop a photo display* showing how your work is done.

   Practice closing. This is where you actually ask for the sale. Make a list of three possible closing statements to encourage the customer to actually buy. Ask a friend or family member to role-play closing with you.

3. Sit down with a group and brainstorm ways to get your name out at shows and make contacts for future sales. Write down any and all ideas that come up, no matter how silly or impossible they may seem. Later you will decide which ones are workable for you and come up with your strategy for making them happen. Here are a few of my ideas to get you started. I actually use these.

4. Have a *nice, professional quality sign made to display at the entrance* to your booth. This helps get your business name in front of people. *Take a guest book or sign-up sheet* for your mailing list to shows. This gives you a list of prospective customers for advertising purposes. *Make your brochures and business cards work for you.* Keep them out where customers can just take one. Don't make them ask. Drop a brochure or business card in the bag when a customer buys something.

5. Now it's your turn. Get your creative juices flowing and think about ways to keep people thinking about your work after they leave the craft show. Try out at least one new idea at your next show.

EVALUATING SHOW SUCCESS

How are you going to judge craft show success? Keep in mind that the definition of success may vary from show to show.

❏ Number of items sold
❏ Amount of money taken in
❏ Number of contacts with potential customers
❏ You were able to combine this show with a family vacation and a good time was had by all
❏ Lessons learned
❏ Other _____

No show experience is a failure. Even a miserable day is not time or money wasted if a lesson is learned.

GOING HOME
What arrangements do you need to make to have an extra day for rest, relaxation, and recuperation after a major show, especially if you are traveling out of town? How far in advance do you need to start thinking about this?

CHECKLIST OF IMPORTANT THINGS TO TAKE TO A CRAFT SHOW

❏ A copy of your show registration or receipt
❏ Your space number, if already made
❏ Display equipment
❏ Helpers
❏ A copy of your tax license
❏ A good tool kit
❏ An extension cord, if allowed, and electrical tape
❏ A folding chair or bar stool
❏ Change
❏ Cash register or calculator and receipt book
❏ A secure place to keep money
❏ A guest book
❏ Snacks and drinking water
❏ Lunch, especially when working alone
❏ Business cards
❏ Promotional materials such as brochures, newsletters, catalogs
❏ Extra product labels and price tags
❏ A small product repair kit
❏ A good selection of your work—go prepared to sell
❏ A positive attitude
❏ A smile

NEED MORE HELP?

LITERATURE

Baker, Bruce. "Busy-ness Means Business." Booth Business column. *Crafts Report* (September 2001).

———. "Prices, People, . . . Prices." *Show Business Crafts Report* (February 2002).

———. "What You See Is What You Sell." *Crafts Report* (June 2001).

———. "Why, Oh, Why Won't the Craftspeople Sell?" *Crafts Report* (March 2001).

Backer, Noelle. "Behind Closed Doors: Inside the Final Jury Session for the Smithsonian Craft Show." *The Crafts Report* (April 1998).

———. "Getting Ready For Juried Exhibitions." *The Crafts Report* (June 1998).

Butland, Grace. "Show and Sell Tips for Creating Displays That Attract Customers and Increase Sales." *The Crafts Report* (May 2001).

Caputo, Kathryn. *How to Show and Sell Your Crafts.* Cincinnati: Betterway Books, 1997.

Coughlin, Kirsten (compiler). "Public Opinion: How Do You Feel about Having Non-Artists On Juries?" *The Crafts Report* (July 1998).

Detwiler, Amy. "Display Tips: Light Right." *Sunshine Artist* (August 1999).

Fleishman, Rich. "Where Do I Fit In: The Non-Traditional Crafts Person vs. The Establishment." *The Crafts Report* (December 1996).

Gordon, Molly. "Up Close and Personal: Make the Most of Craft Shows." *Coach Lady Bug* (cited: March 2003). Available at: *www.mollygordon.com/ resources/marketingresources/knit/artsandcrafts.html.*

Gray, Madeline. *Selling Your Crafts at Craft Shows: The Basics for Beginners.* North Adams, Mass.: Storey Publishing Bulletin, 1997.

Kadubec, Philip. *Crafts and Craft Shows: How to Make Money.* New York: Allworth Press, 2000.

Kelley, Lisa. "Wooing the Customer." *Sunshine Artist Magazine* (August 2000).

Lasley, William. "How to Attend a Craft Show." *About.com.* (cited: March 2003). Available at: *www.artsandcrafts.about.com/library/howto/ htattendshows.htm.*

Marquand, Barbara. "Words Can't Hurt You: How to Take the Sting Out of Criticism and Rejection." *The Crafts Report* (October 1996).

Meltzer, Steve. "18 Tips for Photographing Your Work Outdoors." *The Crafts Report* (August 1999).

———. "11 Foolproof Tips for Great Photos." *The Crafts Report* (December 1998).

Richardson, Loretta. "The Application Process: Rejection, Tenure, Slide Requirements, Cancellation Fees." *The Crafts Report* (June 1997).

"The Sales Primer." *Sunshine Artist Magazine* (February 2000).

"21 Sample Closes." *Sunshine Artist Magazine* (February 2000).

CRAFT SHOW LISTINGS AND DIRECTORIES—HARD COPY
[Contact information is available in Appendix B.]
The Art Fair Source Book
The Arts and Crafts Society
Artrider Productions Inc.
Craftmaster News
The Crafts Report
Festival Network Online
The Ronay Guide
Sunshine Artist Magazine
Art and Craft Show Yellow Pages™

CRAFT SHOW LISTINGS AND DIRECTORIES—ONLINE
Art and Craft Shows.net *(sponsored by Sunshine Artist)*
The Art Deadlines List
Artnet
Crafts Fair Online
Netcrafts Show Guide
Wildlife Art Industry Exhibition and Trade Shows
Worldwide Quilting Page—Quilt Exhibitions and Museums

DISPLAY EQUIPMENT
[Contact information is available in Appendix B.]
Art Fixtures
Brightman Design
Cover Me Inc.
Craft Canopy
Dealers Supply Inc.
Eclectic Lighting and Electric
Fetpak
Flourish Company
Fred's Studio Tents and Canopies Inc.
International E-ZUP Inc.
Jenkins Crafted Canopies
New Venture Products and Awning Works Inc.
Newton Display Products Inc.
USA Light

Lesson 17

SELLING ON CONSIGNMENT

PLACING WORK FOR SALE on consignment simply means you leave your work with a business owner to sell for you; then you are paid a percentage of the retail price after your work is sold. No money changes hands until the item is sold.

✄ THE CONTRACT

Just as in any business relationship, there are good consignment agreements and not so good ones. The most important step to having a good consignment relationship is setting the ground rules early in the game.

Done correctly, consignment is not a bad way to sell your work, but be aware of the pitfalls that go along with this type of arrangement. Never leave your merchandise on consignment without a written contract. If you do, you could never prove ownership of an item if the storeowner decided to claim the item for his own without paying you for it.

These are the major details that should be included in any consignment contract. You or your attorney may think of others that fit your particular situation.

The length of time the retailer will try to sell your work should be specified in the contract. Including exact dates will ensure sure there is no doubt. What will happen if your work is not sold during the specified length of time? Will you be required to remove your work from the store? Could you renew the contract for extra time? Would the storeowner lower the price on your work? Will you still make a profit, after the storeowner takes her percentage, if this happens?

147

The retail price to be placed on the item and the percentage you will receive should also be in the contract. This is up to the individual retailer and will often, but not always, yield you a return of somewhere around 50 to 70 percent of the retail price with the retailer taking 30 to 50 percent. Don't assume anything. Know what your percentage will be. Get it in writing.

Specify whether or not the retailer has your permission to mark the price of your work down, either because it is not selling or to be included in a storewide sale. The lowest price you will accept should be specified. Don't forget, you still have to make a profit, and of course, the storeowner still gets her percentage.

Who will bear the loss or responsibility for product lost due to theft, fire, or wear and tear while in the store? Most retailers will not take responsibility for any loss incurred while your work is in their care, and their insurance usually will not cover your work. Be sure to talk to your own insurance agent. Your insurance may not cover your work while not under your immediate control. In light of this, our suggestion is not to place anything on consignment you cannot afford to take a loss on, unless the issue of loss is adequately addressed in the contract.

Include when and how payment will be made. Most consignors will write checks once a month on a set day, such as the fifteenth of each month. Be sure to find out if you are to pick up your check at the store or if it will be sent to you in the mail. Be sure this is part of the contract.

Make an inventory sheet and attach it to the contract. Be sure this is updated as things are sold, at least quarterly. Always check the storeowner's records against your records to be sure all items are accounted for, either as sold or still in the store.

Be sure the contract is signed and dated by both you and the storeowner. Both you and the retailer keep a copy of the agreement. If problems come up, always refer to the contract.

Hang on to that contract for dear life. Why are we so insistent on having a contract? Well, I left work on consignment without a contract and lost product. And not just once; oh no, I did it twice. The first time the storeowner insisted nothing had been sold, even though I had been present in the store when the items were sold, to a friend of mine no less. Then the storeowner promised to send a check in the mail. Payment was never received. The second time, several years later, with a different storeowner I was told the items were stolen. Indeed they were, but I was never sure by whom.

I did go on to have successful consignments, with contracts. Also when we opened our own store we accepted the work of others on consignment, using what we had learned to try to create a positive experience for our consignees.

✂ FAIRNESS

While you are certain to be concerned that the storeowner is being fair to you it is also a good idea to ask yourself if you are being fair to the storeowner. I monitor the Internet for what's going on in the art and craft world, and many of the complaints I hear online about consignment sound to me as if the person complaining may be just a tad unrealistic.

Sales take time, and trashing a merchant for not selling your work in two weeks is not just unrealistic, it is extremely rude. If you signed a contract saying you would leave your work with a merchant for a certain length of time, you need to honor that contract and give him that time to try to sell your work.

Another complaint I hear about consignment is, "I demanded she send my work back to me and I haven't received it yet." Here again, allow a reasonable amount of time for your work to be returned. Two or three days or even one week is probably not long enough. I would allow at least one month and put this expectation in writing to the merchant. From Nebraska to California by United Parcel Service (UPS) standard delivery can take up to six business days, plus you need to add time for your request to get to the consignor and for her to pack and ship your items. That is if everything goes well.

Many consignment problems I hear about seem to come from dealing with out-of-town or out-of-state merchants. It is certainly easier to deal with local merchants. You have a chance to visit the store and see what type of business you are dealing with. You can also talk to the owner in person or via a local phone call if problems arise.

If you choose a consignment with an out-of-town or out-of-state merchant, my advice would be to start out small. Just send a few items, not your entire stock. Don't count on this business to supply your entire income. Then, if the arrangement seems satisfactory, consider adding more items.

When entering into a long-distance consignment agreement, it is important to do your homework. Check the business out with the appropriate authorities in the state where the business is located. Try to find other artists who have consigned work there and see if they are satisfied with the arrangement.

Be careful about taking action against a consignor. Be sure you have your facts straight. Getting an attorney involved is not a bad idea. At least get a legal opinion on whether you have cause for action. Going out and trashing the merchant verbally, or in writing—even on the Internet—can damage your professional reputation as well as leaving you open to a lawsuit.

DO YOUR HOMEWORK

1. Write down the names of three businesses that you know, or think might, work on consignment.
2. Go to each business, in person if possible, and ask about the details of the consignment agreement. Be sure important points, such as the time period of the contract, percentages, and time and method of payment are covered. Ask for any printed information they may have. This includes things such as brochures and a copy of the actual contract, if they have one.
3. Don't make a decision on the spot. In other words, don't sign a contract on your information-gathering visit. Go home and think about it. Talk to friends, your spouse, and other family members and ask their advice. Have your attorney take a quick look at the contract. Compare the agreements of the different stores. Which is best for you?

Monthly Consignment Tracking Sheet

Wholesale price per item _____

Name of Item	JAN	FEB	MAR	APR	MAY	JUN	JUL	AUG	SEP	OCT	NOV	DEC
Previous Month's Balance												
Number Missing This Month												
Total Items Sold												
Number of This Item Added This Month												
Month Ending Total												
Store Owner/ Manager Initials & Date												

NEED MORE HELP?

LITERATURE

Crawford, Tad, et. al. *The Artist-Gallery Partnership: A Practical Guide to Consigning Art.* New York: Allworth Press, 1998.

Chypre, Bettye. "Considering a Consignment Relationship?" *Art and Craft Show Yellow Pages™* (2000). Available at: *www.smartfrogs.com/consign.html.*

Haddock, Cindy Lee. "Selling Your Crafts on Consignment." *Craftbits.com* (cited: August 2002). Available at: www.craftbits.com/html/articles/sellingcrafts/consignment.htm.

Skelley, Heather (compiler). "Public Opinion Gallery Owners: What Percentage Do You Charge on Consignment Sales?" *Crafts Report Magazine* (cited: March 2003).

Zell, Alan J. "Some comments on consignments." Alan J. Zell, *Ambassador of Selling* (2000). Available at: *http://sellingselling.com/articles/consign.html.*

Lesson 18

CRAFT MALLS

MANY PEOPLE WHO PLACE their work for sale in craft malls are pleased with the arrangement. There are also people who have craft mall horror stories. As with most major decisions we make in life, there are both positives and negatives associated with this type of marketing.

I have said over and over in this book, do your research, and it is especially important here. Always shop around and talk to more than one place before deciding. Ask questions and write down the answers. Ask for printed information, including a copy of the contract. What are some of the questions you need to ask?

⚓ GATHERING INFORMATION

In this type of situation I think it's best to start with the obvious. What is the name of the craft mall? Who is the owner? How long has the mall been in existence? Has it changed name or location recently? If so, do you know why?

Next you will want to know if there is a contract. There should be. Before you sign anything, ask for a copy to take home with you. Read it. Have your spouse, partner, parent, or adult child read it. Spend the money to have your attorney look it over. This could prevent major problems. Is there anything about the contract that bothers you? Be sure the important details of the agreement are specified in the contract. Never leave anything at a craft mall without a written contract. If there is not a contract you can ask the owner if she will sign a contract you provide. The owner may not agree to this, but it's worth a try.

What will happen to your work if the mall closes or changes locations? This is something no one wants to think about, but unfortunately it does happen

153

and should be spelled out in the contract. Does the contract state that you will be given ample notice and opportunity to collect your work if the mall goes out of business? Will you be given the choice of continuing or voiding the contract if the mall moves to a new location that is not satisfactory to you?

What is this actually going to cost? Add together all costs, fees, extra charges, and so on. Is there a membership fee? What is the monthly booth rent? Does the mall also take a percentage of your sales? If there is a work requirement, place an hourly value on your time and determine how much it will cost you in time to have the booth.

How are fees collected? Are they withheld from your earnings? If there are no sales or your sales do not cover the expenses, by what day of each month are you required to make payment? Is payment required up front in advance?

How will you be paid for any sales you make? Are checks automatically generated on a certain day of each month? Are they mailed, or do you pick them up?

How much will have to be sold per month to meet your financial obligation to the mall owner, that is, to pay your fees? How much to break even and cover all your expenses? How much to make a profit?

Does the mall owner accept responsibility for your work while it is on her premises? A craft mall agreement may include a non-responsibility clause saying that the business owner bears no responsibility for damage to your work while on her premises. If the storeowner or manager says her insurance does cover your items, be sure this is stated in the agreement. If it is not, assume your items are not covered, even if the storeowner says differently. Are you willing to accept the risk of loss? Don't assume your insurance will cover your work when it is outside your control. Check with your agent.

Check for liability clauses. Know who will bear the legal responsibility if a customer is injured in your booth.

Talk to current and past exhibitors, if possible. How much did they sell? Did they make or lose money? Are or were they happy with the arrangement?

Is there a work requirement? Are you required to actually work in the store for no pay as part of your membership requirements? How many hours? Can you afford to do this? Do you want to do this? Remember, for the most part this could be considered nonproductive time. This may also not be legal in your state, so check it out.

Is this mall a cooperative (co-op)? Please understand that there is more to a co-op than having a work requirement for the exhibitors. What sets a true co-op apart from other forms of business is that a co-op is member-owned. In the case of an artists cooperative, the owners would be artists. There are membership requirements, which may include attendance at membership meetings, time worked in the gallery or store, jurying of the work of prospective members, and a membership fee. The members share both the financial responsibilities and rewards of business ownership. That is, they share the bills and the profits. *A co-op is not a privately owned business requiring unpaid labor from the people who display their work.* If the other qualifications are not in place, chances are you are dealing with a privately owned business looking for free labor.

Some craft malls offer classes. Will you be paid if you teach classes? Does the store charge for these classes? If you don't get paid, does teaching classes fulfill your work requirement?

Are you required to set up and maintain your own booth? What hours are you allowed to do this? Are these hours adequate? Are they reasonable? Do they fit in your personal schedule? Remember, you sure don't want to have to do this during busy times in the store.

Who makes pricing decisions? Do you set your own prices? Does the mall reserve the right to mark down your merchandise if it does not sell during a set time period? Can you live with that? Can you still make a profit?

Another thing to remember is that craft malls are selling two different types of products. Of course they sell craft work, but they also sell space in their stores. A certain amount of money is coming in every month even if they do not sell anything other than booth space.

So what is the motivation for selling your work? You are still obligated to keep your contract; that is, paying for and perhaps occupying your booth, even if you sell nothing. Now if you don't sell, you may leave at the end of the contract, but the storeowner still has the money you paid during the duration of your contract. There will also always be other people waiting to get in.

There is another problem associated with craft malls that no one ever wants to think about. (This is also a problem with work on consignments.) What if the store goes out of business? We have talked to several people with horror stories about this. One woman had a sad story about a craft mall that had closed with her work still inside. She had been given no warning about the closing; she found the doors locked and a closed sign on the door when she tried to check her inventory. Repeated phone calls yielded first no answer, then a recorded message. She finally reported the business owners to the local police and the better business bureau, but was given little hope of recovering her merchandise or the money she was owed. So, please be careful when placing work in a craft mall. It is important to remember that anytime you allow someone else to sell your work without first paying you for it, you are taking a risk. It is up to you to decide if the possible profits are worth such a risk.

✂ KEEP ALL OF YOUR OWN PAPERWORK

Paperwork is always important, but especially so when you have work placed with anyone else while you retain ownership. Keep a copy of your contract in a safe place where you will be able to find it if needed.

You will also want to use some sort of tracking system, such as our Monthly Craft Mall Tracking Sheet. Don't rely on the storeowner to do this for you.

As in any type of marketing there are both positive and negative aspects to selling work through a craft mall. Before making any marketing decisions do your homework and go into it with your eyes wide open.

DO YOUR HOMEWORK

1. Write down the names of the craft malls in your area.
2. Go to each business on your list and look around. If you like what you see, ask about the details of the craft mall agreement. Be sure important points such as length of the contract, booth rent and other fees, time and method of payment, and other issues are covered. It is also important to be clear on things such as work requirements, times set aside for you to set up or stock your booth, and paperwork. Ask for any printed information they may have. This includes things such as brochures and a copy of the actual contract, if they have one. You may want to consider having a basic craft mall contract drawn up for occasions when the owner of the mall does not have one of his own. Keep in mind, however, that the owner may not be willing to sign it.
3. Don't make a decision on the spot. In other words, don't sign a contract on your information-gathering visit. Go home and think about it. Talk to friends, your spouse, and other family members. Have your attorney take a quick look at the contract. Compare the agreements of the different stores. Which is best for you?

Monthly Craft Mall Tracking Sheet

Wholesale price per item _____

Name of Item	JAN	FEB	MAR	APR	MAY	JUN	JUL	AUG	SEP	OCT	NOV	DEC
Previous Month's Balance												
Number Missing This Month												
Total Items Sold												
Number of This Item Added This Month												
Month Ending Total												
Store Owner/ Manager Initials & Date												

NEED MORE HELP?

LITERATURE

Butland, Grace. "How to Run a Successful Co-Op." *Crafts Report* (March 2002).

Stim, Richard. "The Legal Considerations for Starting a Co-Op." *Crafts Report* (April 2002).

ORGANIZATIONS OF BUSINESSES

[Contact information is available in Appendix B.]

University of Wisconsin Center for Cooperatives

International Cooperative Alliance

Lesson 19

BUILDING, PROMOTING, AND
SELLING FROM YOUR OWN WEB SITE

BUILDING AND MAINTAINING A WEB SITE can cost a small fortune, but it doesn't have to. It all comes down to if you have more time or more money. You can have the whole thing done for you. This can be costly but may be worth the money spent if you have little or no computer knowledge or experience and don't have the time to learn. If however you have lots of time and very little money, there are free and low-cost options available.

However, as I am rewriting this lesson (for the third time) due to changes occurring in the current "Internet crisis," free Web-hosting services are vanishing. Who knows if they will still exist when this book is published? Things will be different for sure. Services that were once free may begin charging, but the cost may still be less than if you had to provide the services they offer for yourself. For this reason, I am not removing the information on free Web hosting.

✂ FREE WEB HOSTING

One option for creating a low-cost Web site is to use a *Web hosting service.* This means you are borrowing Web space, site-building tools, and a domain name from someone else. These vary greatly in terms of the amount of space you are allowed and the ease or complexity of actually creating a site. If you are a novice look for Web hosting services that provide templates to help you build your site. These are often as simple as point and click or just typing in your information. Once you get into sites where you must build your own html code, things start getting complicated. You can create an attractive site using templates and these often include clip art and ways to include your own photographs.

One drawback to using a Web hosting service is that you do not have your own domain name, at least not in most free services. Instead of your address being *www.jeansjunque.com* it will be something like *www.jeansjunque. sitebuilder.com* or *www.sitebuilder.com/jeansjunque,* or it could be even more complicated.

If you do choose to register your own domain keep in mind that selecting your domain name is just as important as when you named your business. This will be your identity on the Internet. This will also be the way people get to your site, so you want to make it as easy as possible. A domain name should be short, easy to remember as well as spell, and not easily confused with other names. For most business sites your choice of suffix will be .com. Your domain name also can't be longer that 67 characters (letters, numbers, and dashes only), including the suffix.

So, where to start? Your business name is a good place to start. If that is already taken you can try using parts of your name or a variation on your name. If that still doesn't work, try thinking about what you do or what makes your business unique. You will also want to be sure your domain name will attract your target audience. For instance, if you are selling craft supplies online you probably don't want *www.xyztools* for your domain name. Of course it is a good idea to avoid trademarked names. See lesson 2, "Presenting Yourself as a Professional," for information on trademark and choosing your business name.

All free Web hosting services are going to have additional services available for purchase. One of these could be your own domain name. It might be a good idea to pay the fee to go ahead and do this. The staff of *Jumpline.com* recommends going ahead and registering a domain name, even if you don't have a Web site yet. This is because the good names are going fast, and when you decide you want to register a name the best ones may be taken. Other for-fee services could include things like the use of certain site-building tools, or the purchase of additional space.

A drawback of free Web hosting, for some people, is the advertising. In exchange for the free Web site you allow advertising to be placed on your site. You usually will have no control over the advertising on your site. Ad-free sites are available—for a small fee, of course.

Another potential problem with free Web hosting is that in the world of the Internet things change, often at a blinding rate. Your Web hosting service might be here today and gone tomorrow. Or it might change the rules, or start deleting services, or start charging for its basic services. These changes often happen with little or no warning. I have had all of these things happen using free Web hosting services. The most important thing is to decide how flexible you can be. If stability is the most important thing to you then you should, by all means, consider registering your own domain name (there is a fee for this) and acquiring the software and knowledge to build your own site or hiring someone to do this for you.

✂ CREATING AN ATTRACTIVE WEB SITE

Remember, the Internet is a print medium. You have photos for people to look at and words for them to read. To be effective, a Web site must be not only attractive and pleasing to look at, but also easy to navigate, moving from page to page and location to location on those pages. It must also be readable.

Before you start building your own Web site, do a little surfing. Look at Web sites. Look at lots of Web sites. What works? What doesn't work? Make notes on what you like and what you don't like.

READABLE SITES

Let's start out by talking about what makes a Web site readable. As with printed documents the *size and style of type (font) is important*. Please look ahead to lesson 20, "Quality Printed Materials," for more information.

Carefully choose the background for your pages. In the computer world this is also known as wallpaper. Don't choose a background that is too busy. This can be distracting as well as difficult to read. Remember, you must be able to read any print you put on the background. Can you really read black print on a dark purple background? We have seen this on the Internet. If you use a dark background consider using white or another light color for the print.

CONTENT

Your site will attract more visitors if it is not purely commercial. That is, if your site is about more than selling something. People who use the Internet are often looking for information—usually free information. Providing this will draw people to your site. Once they are there it is up to your sales presentation on the site to sell them your product.

There are different types of content as well as sources of free content. *Articles are a common type of Web site content* and may be used as an effective sales tool. If you sell glues, adhesives, and glue guns, for instance, an article describing different types of adhesives and their uses in various crafts could help you sell your products. Be sure you position buttons to allow readers to order your products in strategic places either within the article or close by.

If you are a writer you may want to write these articles yourself, or use articles written by someone else. The easiest way to find articles is through syndication. Syndication is a way writers make their articles available for use on Web sites, and it may be done in several different ways. Some syndicates will offer articles on an auto-feed system. This means that you simply put a small bit of html code on your site and articles change automatically at intervals determined by the syndicate. For articles this is usually weekly or monthly. It is still a good idea to keep an eye on what type of articles come to your site to make sure nothing objectionable slips in. Some free Web hosting services do not allow auto feeds, so check it out first.

There are also sites where you can sign up, usually free, and choose individual articles for yourself. This allows you to find individual articles that fit your needs. There are also sites where you may sign up to receive e-mail either with full articles or announcements of new articles.

Individuals will also sometimes offer articles for use which you can find on their own Web pages. As you are surfing, make note of anything like this you find. Do this even if the articles don't fit your immediate needs. There may be a time when the articles will work for you and your chances of remembering when you found them and how to get there are slim to none. If you use one of these articles be sure to send the author a short e-mail letting her know that you are using her article and inviting her to visit your site. Many times this will be required, but it is just common courtesy. Many times a link from your site back to the author's site will also be requested.

Search engines, especially ones related to the subject matter of your site, are always a good idea. For instance, a link to a search engine just for crafts-related subjects, or that search engine's box located directly on your site, could be a nice addition.

Polls and quizzes allow you to include information that is interactive, but in a small, controlled way. They also allow you to collect demographic information and get to know your audience.

Message boards and live chat may draw people to your site, but they are also very time and labor intensive. Take some time to look at various sites with message boards and live chat. You will see that message boards that are not monitored quickly fill up with off-topic posts, advertising, and sometimes obscenity. The best message boards and live chat are usually moderated. This means that an actual person is participating either regularly or as a drop-in and is monitoring content. The moderator has the ability to delete inappropriate messages or intervene in heated discussions at his discretion. If you do not have the time to do this, I suggest you stay away from the interactive stuff.

Every Web site should have a guest book. This is where your visitors make comments and suggestions about your Web site or just let you know they stopped by. The comments left on guest books are often positive and may just make you feel good. Sometimes visitors will leave their e-mail or Web site address. This is a good way to start building your contacts.

Content Boxes Add Variety to Your Web Site

Content boxes are just that, small boxes containing content. They are a good way to catch the attention of your readers. The exact type of content may be anything from recipes to helpful hints to inspirational quotes to the local weather forecast to games and puzzles. As with articles these are often available on an auto feed. Many change daily so this is a good source of consistent fresh content. Of course you can also create your own. This can be really fun.

IS YOUR SITE EASY TO NAVIGATE?

When people come to your site they will usually come to your front page, also known as a homepage. This is the front door to your site. If you have additional pages, you must find ways to get people to go beyond the front door, to step inside, and look around.

One way to do this is to make your site easy to navigate. That means having buttons or text links to go easily from page to page. It doesn't hurt to have both. Be sure you do this on all pages, not just the front page. The button for your front page should be labeled home. This is what people will be looking for.

If you have introductory text on your homepage you can include text links there. For instance, if you say, "We have a new line of craft patterns available," making the words *craft patterns* into a link would encourage people to go take a look, and possibly buy.

Creating a good-looking, readable Web site that is easy to navigate can be a daunting task. But it is also very rewarding. When you are finished you have tangible evidence of your hard work. Your work is not finished once your site is built, however.

✄ SITE PROMOTION

Now, you have your Web site. How are you going to get people to come to it? This is not a case where the line from the movie *Field of Dreams* "if you build it, they will come" works. It takes intentional effort, and a lot of it, to get your site noticed.

One way to get your site noticed is to *create a site people will talk about.* Word of mouth still works, even on the Internet.

Submit your site to the search engines and Web directories. Doing this is very important if you want your site to be noticed. You can do this yourself or pay someone to do it for you. This is too complicated to give all the details here. Do your homework and visit the sites listed in the resource section of this lesson for help with the process.

When people sign your guest book at craft shows include a place for their e-mail address if they wish to give it. Send out e-mail invitations for people to visit your Web site. It is a good idea to mention that they asked to be on your e-mail list so you won't be accused of spam. In addition to being canned luncheon meat, spam is also unsolicited e-mail and is really frowned on.

Create a signature file to use when sending out e-mail or participating in mailing lists and message boards. This means including your site address, often as a link, after your user name at the bottom of an e-mail or online posting. Get as creative as you want, including your logo or other artwork if desired.

Web rings and banner exchange programs are a good way to draw a targeted audience to your Web site. Banner exchanges are pretty self-explanatory: You exchange advertising banners with other Web sites. Your banner is displayed on another Web site, and a banner for that site is placed on yours—an even trade. These banners are also direct links. Before you even consider entering into this type of agreement, however, you should be sure you have a high-quality banner to exchange. If you do not have the ability to create one yourself, there are people who will do this for you, for a fee, of course.

Web rings are chains or rings of links that will take people from site to site throughout the Web ring. Web rings are usually made up of sites with something in common. There are Web rings made up of sites ranging from angels, to crafts, to working at home. Once you join a Web ring, you will be given permission to add a Web ring banner to your site and to become part of the chain or ring of Web sites.

The downside of banner exchanges and Web rings is that they take people away from your site. Once someone clicks on that banner or decides to follow the Web ring, they are gone and they may or may not ever find their way back to your site. Of course the sites you exchange banners with and the other members of your Web ring will also be sending people to you. But too many banners also clutter up a Web site, so be selective.

Contests and giveaways draw numbers, but be certain you have something to encourage people to look *around while they are there. You don't want them to just sign up for the contest and leave.*

Put your Web site address and e-mail on your offline advertising and promotional materials. This includes your business card, brochures, and letterhead.

Another way to attract people to your Web site is by *sharing links with other Web sites.* Be selective here. Don't forget the specific audience you are trying to attract. Try to place your link on sites that attract your audience.

You may be asked to place a link back to the other site on your site. This is known as a reciprocal link and is only fair. In the early days of the Internet, many sites tried to charge for links. This slowly disappeared, but lately it has started to surface again. I have seen several sites charging for links recently. It is up to you to decide if this is something you want to pay for, but we make it a practice not to pay for links. Even small charges add up if you link to several sites. This is also extremely difficult to enforce because it is so simple and can be easily done without the permission of the site owner.

The methods of site promotion I have mentioned will get you started. As you get into the world of site promotions you will find others.

✂ MY WEB SITE

Bob and I decided to build a Web site to give me a professional presence on the Internet. After much thought and discussion and a few arguments (*shush*), we settled on a magazine format. We also decided to try to reach a broader audience than just quilters or other craft professionals. I wanted to have a chance to show the rest of the world that life can be more fulfilling, not to mention fun, if lived creatively. So *The Creative Life MagE-zine* was born.

We worked on it for months. I spent long, exhausting hours searching the Internet for just the right content. By the time it was ready to receive visitors, it was magnificent, even if I do say so myself. A friend of mine, Del, who is not easily impressed, still goes on about what a great Web site it was. But, yes, unfortunately, the operative word here is *was*.

About a month after the site officially opened we started getting bad news about our affiliate programs. Many programs were being discontinued all together. Others were changing their terms, making payments smaller and based on sales only. No more money just for sending traffic to a Web site. Some companies were leaving large affiliate networks such as Commission Junction to start running their own independent programs. To sum up the situation, it was a mess!

We were still trying to sort out the affiliate disaster when the *really bad news* came. The Web hosting service was going to start charging! This wouldn't have been so bad if it weren't also discontinuing many of the services we had enjoyed while the site was free. It just didn't make good business sense to pay more for less, especially since the site had not started earning money in other ways yet.

During this time it appeared as if the Internet was crashing down around us. During a one-month time period I lost my business Web site, my business e-mail, my personal Web site, the replacement Web site for my personal site, and three different personal e-mail accounts. Some were gone altogether. Some were beginning to charge for their services, but when we did the math we realized we were being asked to pay over $100 a month to replace everything. So, bye-bye beautiful Web site.

And the losses weren't over. I went on to lose another personal Web site and yet another e-mail account. So for awhile I chose to "lay low" and wait for the dust to clear to see what would be left when the crisis was over.

After a year of waiting I finally decided to try again. This time on Geocities, sponsored by Yahoo!; they have a proven track record, and I figured that if they go down, we're all in trouble. I'm still not selling my work on the Internet. I'm also not getting into affiliate programs or syndicated articles this time. For now, I just have a nice, friendly little personal site where you can come and meet our family, see photos of my work and read articles written by me. In case you are interested I may be found at *www. geocities.com/quiltnart.*

Now for a word from the learning-through-experience department. Nothing is lost if lessons are learned, and we learned a lot from the most recent Internet crash. We learned how to build a "killer" Web site, and we had already acquired several regular visitors. My guess is that the Internet will change and evolve over the years, but it will be with us for a long time to come. And I am ready. Not bad for someone who was afraid to even turn on a computer just ten years ago.

✄ SELLING ON THE INTERNET

We are hearing a lot about using the Internet for sales and marketing purposes. The Internet is being used both as a way of advertising to reach a broader audience and as a way of selling merchandise. Many artists and crafters are rushing out to try this new way of marketing and many more are thinking about it. But there is one important thing to remember about the Internet. It is just a tool. It is not magic. Nothing sells itself.

There is still effort involved in Internet sales. No matter what you may have heard, you don't just put your item up for sale on the Web and sit back and rake in the money.

There are different ways the Internet is used for sales and marketing. You can of course set up your own Web site and sell your work from there. This is time-consuming and requires certain computer skills. Setting up an online store is different than a basic Web site. You must be able to accept credit cards, and you will need to learn about secure servers, a way of protecting your customer's credit card information. There are companies who will take care of this for you—for a small fee, of course.

We are all familiar with craft malls and consignment shops in our communities, but did you know they are also on the Internet? Yes, you can rent space on someone else's site to sell your work. They will usually handle the sales as well as the promotion of the site. Sometimes it will be up to you to set up your own booth space on the Web site using their format. Some sites will charge a fee to design a booth for you.

IS ANYONE ACTUALLY SELLING ON THE WEB?

Are people buying art or craft work from the Internet? To tell the truth, I'm not sure. There are articles, complete with statistics, which go both ways. I spend time on the Internet checking out art and craft sites as well as talking to artists and craft professionals, and I hear a lot of discouragement. Many people seem to want to sell more and sell it quicker than they are doing currently. Some of this may be due to unrealistic expectations or lack of understanding about the finer points of Internet commerce. Or it might be the economy. Who knows?

This is not a way I have chosen to sell my work. I have had photographs of my quilts on a personal Web site. All of my work, except my personal collection—actually, Bob's personal collection—is always for sale. If someone made an acceptable offer I would not say no, but I do not actively try to sell online.

I am not sure art or craft items are something people would feel comfortable buying from a photograph, often a small one at that. It would seem that they would rather see and possibly touch the work before buying.

The Internet is definitely something worth watching. As time goes by and the Internet matures and comes into its own, I may regret not jumping in there and selling online in the early stages. But right now, I need more evidence that people are actually selling enough to make it worthwhile.

✂ ADVERTISING ON THE WEB

Reputation and name recognition are vital to an artist. The Internet is one way of getting your name and your work out there in front of an international audience. This is one of the reasons I put photos of my work on my personal site. If you go out on the show circuit or if you have a gallery, you may find people who heard of you first online showing up to meet you in person, take a closer look at your work, and maybe even buy.

There are several ways to get your name in front of people on the Internet. We have already talked about online craft malls where craft work is actually sold. However, there are also online craft malls where individuals and some businesses are allowed to post advertisements for their work. Sometimes these will be free, sometimes there is a charge.

Another way for artists to gain exposure on the Internet is through their own Web site, whether they offer their work for sale or not. Some artists include photos of themselves, their work, or their studio. An artist's statement and exhibition, teaching, or lecture schedules are also often included. Two of my favorite examples of this are the Web sites of David Walker (*www.davidwalker.us*) and Karen Combs (*www.karencombs.com*).

You may also display photos of your work in an online gallery, either on your own site or the site of another individual or an organization. The work may be for display purposes only or may be sold directly for the Web gallery. Examples of online galleries may be seen at *www.passion4art.com* and *www.americancraftsonline.com*.

One of the benefits of membership in an art- or craft-related organization is often publicity. Many such organizations often include profiles of individual members on their Web sites. They may also make exhibition opportunities available through online galleries or member pages on the site.

The Internet is being used by artists and craftspeople to gain recognition as well as to sell their work. We are only seeing the beginning of what the Internet will mean in our lives, and the direction this valuable tool will take is still uncertain. If you decide to try to sell your work on the Internet it is wise to continue what you are already doing in terms of sales and marketing while you test the Internet. Do not risk everything on Internet sales. Used in conjunction with your other marketing strategies, the Internet could increase your exposure worldwide as well as gain recognition for your name and your work.

Do Your Homework

1. Why do you want a Web site? Take a few minutes to think about this and write your answer. This will be important as you decide what features and tools you will need to build your Web site.
2. Make a list of Web site features necessary to meet your needs. This could include things like a guest book, the ability to post photographs, or interactive features such as a message board or chat room. If you are planning to sell from your site your list will need to include access to a secure server for credit card orders and a shopping cart.
3. A free Web hosting service is perhaps the easiest and least expensive way to get started, but may afford less security. If you decide you want a Web site but can't afford to pay for one, do a Web search using the keywords *free Web sites or free Web hosting* and see what you get. Do a comparison of the positive and negative aspects of each before making your decision. Making a chart is the easiest way to do this.
4. Before you start building your site, spend some time online just looking at your Web sites. Make notes about what works as well as things to avoid.
5. Make a plan to draw visitors to your site. Think about the following methods of Web site promotion:

   ❑ Search engines
   ❑ Web directories
   ❑ Online advertising on other sites (free or paid)
   ❑ Links from other sites
   ❑ News groups, message boards, chat rooms
   ❑ Off-line advertising
   ❑ Other _____

6. Another option for advertising or selling your work online is to become involved in an online craft mall. Do a search using the keywords *online craft mall* and see what you come up with. Take the time to look at some of the sites. Write down the particulars and do a comparison of the different sites you find before making a decision. Some of these may not be free, so keep this in mind when making your comparison. Are the extra features or services worth the cost?

NEED MORE HELP?

LITERATURE

Backer, Noelle. "Are Craftspeople Making Money on the Internet?" *The Crafts Report* (January 2001).

———. "Will the Web Deliver on Its Promise of Fortune?" *The Crafts Report* (April 2001).

Campanelli, Melissa. "Dot.common sense." *Entrepreneur Magazine* (May 2002).

Casey, Christine. "Walk into the Web: Easy Steps to Online Marketing." *Sunshine Artist Magazine* (July 2000).

Crabe, Genevieve. *Crafter's Internet Handbook: Research, Connect and Sell Your Crafts Online.* Cincinnati, Ohio: Musai and Lipman Publishing, 2002.

Dillehay, James. *The Basic Guide to Selling Crafts on the Internet.* Torreon, N. Mex.: Warm Snow Publishing, 2000.

Gordon, Molly. "Selling in Cyberspace." *MollyGordon.com* (cited: March 2003). Available at: *www.mollygordon.com/resources/marketingresources/ knit/cyberspace.html.*

Ridgway, Peggi. *Web Savvy for Small Business: The Basics of Planning and Promoting Your Website.* Buena Park, Calif.: Wordpix Solutions, 2001.

Silver, Judith. "The ABC's of Web Site Law." *Entrepreneur Magazine* (13 May 2002).

Strauss, Ted. "Answers to Your Questions about Going Online." *Crafts Report* (February 2002).

Van Dyne, Douglas, James Landay, and Jason I. Hong. *The Design of Sites Patterns, Principles and Processes for Crafting a Customer-Centered Web Experience.* Boston: Addison Wesley Longman Inc., 2002.

INFORMATION ON WEB SITE BUILDING

[Contact information is available in Appendix B.]

Craftmarketer.com
Craftsite Medic
Passion 4art
Scot Style Web Design
Selling Your Art Online
Web Builder 101
Wilson Internet
Creating Killer Websites

CONTENT

[Contact information is available in Appendix B.]

ARA Content
Candlemart.com
EzineArticles.com
Idea Marketers
Insta Coach
Mommy Tips
Motivational Quotes.com
Surfnet Kids
Tipztime
World Wide Information Outlet
World Wide Recipes

SITE PROMOTION
[Contact information is available in Appendix B.]
Art Promote.com
Zen and the Art of Website Promotion

ONLINE CLASSIFIEDS
[Contact information is available in Appendix B.]
Arthby's
Craftfinder.com
Craftersnet.com
Craftown
Dolls by Patricia

Mary's Craft Classifieds
My Free

LINKS
[Contact information is available in Appendix B.]
All Crafts
Craft Marketer
Crafters Catalogs
Crafters Delight
Crafty Links Malls
My Internet Craft Show
Pinehollow Handcrafts
St. Nick Studios
Val Handmade Crafts

Lesson 20

QUALITY PRINTED MATERIALS

ANY PRINTED MATERIALS related to your business should be of professional quality. This includes your business cards, letterhead, advertising fliers, brochures, product labels, hang tags, catalogs, and post cards.

✂ PREPARING PROFESSIONAL MATERIALS

Technology now allows quality materials to be typeset or even printed at home on a personal computer. If you have the equipment and skills to design your own, you can save yourself some money by doing so. If you do not have the equipment or skills, may we suggest taking this work to your local print shop? Shop around and get estimates first, but this is an expense that we think you will find well worth it.

Why is this so important? This is the first glimpse of your business potential customers will get. Don't you want to make a good first impression? Now we are artists and craftspeople and it is perfectly okay to approach this with creativity. Just be sure you are projecting the image you really want people to have of both you and your work.

The first consideration in preparing quality printed materials is that the paper should be appropriate for the document. This includes the weight of the paper. Our suggestions for appropriate papers would be card stock for business cards, good quality résumé paper for letterhead and brochures, and special glossy paper for catalogs. The staff at your copy center is trained to help you with these decisions so don't be afraid to ask their advice. There are now special papers designed for the printers of personal computers. You can get these for business cards, brochures, letterhead, and postcards that all coordinate. These are usually available at your copy center also, which can be a good place to start.

✂ MAKING YOUR MATERIALS READABLE

Now, for the actual printed documents themselves, there should be *good contrast between color of paper and ink*. Black ink on white, cream, or very light tan paper is an example of good contrast. Black ink on dark green paper is an example of poor contrast. Why is this important? Since you are going to the trouble to design and print this material you want people to be able to read it. When using any combinations other than black ink on white paper it is a good idea to run a sample first. Look at it. Is this color combination easy to read? Readability is your first concern. Using patterned paper can also detract from the printed words, so here again run a sample first to be sure you like it. Have a friend read the document. Does he think it is easy to read?

Is the size of type easy to read comfortably? You don't want your potential customers to have to use a magnifying glass to read your brochure. You also want the type size to be appropriate for the type of document. A flier or poster that is going to be posted in a public place and read from a distance should use fewer words and a larger type size. Part of the purpose of this kind of document is to draw attention. The font you choose will also affect the type size, so remember to make the decision of type size separately for each font you choose. If you have a document with a large amount of print, such as a brochure, we suggest 12 or 14 point type for readability. Here again, have your friend look at the document. Does he think this size type is readable?

Is the font (style of type) easy to read? Educate yourself on fonts (style of lettering), colors, type sizes, and other print design elements, but the best way to choose a font is to audition several. Print out a sample (plain paper will do for this) of your document in each font and take a look. You can make the decision based on liking the looks of a certain font, but remember that it is important that your printed materials be easy to read. *A font that looks like handwriting may be nice, but is it easy to read?* Can you read black print on dark blue paper? Is nine-point type really large enough for most people to read without a magnifying glass?

We do not recommend using fonts that look like handwriting for long passages or for important information. As attractive as these fonts look, they are difficult to read. A small amount of such a font, maybe for your name to give a hint of a signature, can, however, work well for you.

Are your logos and other graphics appropriate? Are they tasteful? Get the opinions of other people on this. Is the artwork an appropriate size for the use? The most important thing to remember here is that the logo and other graphics should not overshadow the rest of the document. If this is not your original artwork, is your intended use permissible? Remember, if the work is not in the public domain—another term for copyright free— then you must obtain permission from the creator or copyright owner for its use.

If you plan to use photographs are they clear and of good quality? Adding photographs to your documents will increase printing costs. Compare the cost of your document with and without photographs. Does the intended use make the photos necessary? Can the extra cost be justified? How are you going to pay for it?

First impressions count. Your printed materials will often help people form their first impression of you and your work. Make that first impression a good one.

The Do's and Don'ts of Promotional Materials

When we go to art or craft shows we make a point of picking up artists' promotional materials. Here are a few practical do's and don'ts based on what we have seen.

Do try to make the design of your business card relate to your work. The best example we have seen was from an artist who did pencil sketches. Her cards were on yellow card stock and shaped like a pencil.

Don't give out handwritten business cards or brochures unless you are a calligrapher.

Do use a heavier weight of paper for brochures than regular typing or photocopier paper. Go to your copy center and ask to look at résumé papers. Recycled résumé papers are also available.

Don't keep brochures or other printed documents around that are dirty or wrinkled. Yes, I have been give brochures that looked like they had been wadded up into a ball, then thrown down on the ground and walked on.

Do consider using the blanks for business documents available at your copy center if you do not have a unique idea in mind. You can get coordinating business cards, brochures, letterhead, and even postcards. This is any easy way to produce nice printed documents.

DO YOUR HOMEWORK

1. Collect samples of business cards, brochures, gallery opening announcements, and other printed matter from a variety of artists and non–art-related businesses. Make notes on what you like and don't like as well as what works and what doesn't.
2. Educate yourself on the elements of good printed documents. This includes paper weight, font, type size, paper and ink color, logos and other artwork, and so on. The staff at your local copy center may be able to help with this.
3. Obtain price quotes from three different printers before having your documents printed. Be sure to consider the quality of each before making your decision.

Printed Materials Checklist

Go through the following list of printed materials. Place a check mark in the have column for each item you currently have in finished printed form and, hopefully, are using. For any items that you need now place a check mark in the need column. And finally, put any items that you would just love to have, but that are too expensive or just not a high priority right now, in the wish column.

	Have	Need	Wish
1. A good letterhead	❏	❏	❏
2. Business cards	❏	❏	❏
3. Product labels	❏	❏	❏
4. A simple brochure	❏	❏	❏
5. A full color catalog	❏	❏	❏
6. An artist's résumé	❏	❏	❏
7. An artist's statement	❏	❏	❏
8. Newsletters	❏	❏	❏
9. One-page fliers	❏	❏	❏
10. Printed postcards	❏	❏	❏

Lesson 21

ADVERTISING ON A BUDGET

THE BEST OR WORST ADVERTISING any business can have is word of mouth. That is people telling each other about you. The best way to facilitate word of mouth is to sell quality merchandise at reasonable prices. Always attempt to sell something people will want to talk about, positively.

✄ FREE AND LOW-COST ADVERTISING

But there are other ways of advertising your business that do not have to cost a fortune. As mentioned before, one of the least expensive forms of advertising is to have *good quality business cards* made. This is the first thing you should do when you start your own business. Don't be afraid to give out business cards. If you are talking to someone who shows the slightest in interest in your business, give her a card. Slip a handful in the bag with purchases.

If you have brochures, give them out. Keep the information simple, professional, and readable. Of course, don't forget to mention where you are located and how to contact you.

A monthly or quarterly newsletter can be very effective advertising. A newsletter will be more effective if the content is not all obvious advertising. Talk about yourself, your skills, and any new skills or techniques you are learning. If you have employees, mention any particular skills they bring to the business. Talk about possible gift ideas. Talk about new merchandise you are selling and any specialized services you offer. People who receive your newsletter may pass it on to others. We gained several new customers this way.

Ads in neighborhood newspapers or shopper's papers are often less expensive than those in major newspapers. Your computer can save you money here, if you provide advertising copy that is camera-ready or ready for publication.

Look at other newspaper ads for ideas. Readability is important, and marketing studies show that white space sells, so don't clutter up your ad. Be sure your business name and contact information are in a prominent place.

Sometimes laundromats, grocery stores, and libraries allow small ads to be placed on their *community bulletin boards*. Be sure to ask first. If you are told no commercial advertising is allowed, don't do it. Simple as that.

Networking is that big scary word for talking to people. Let people know about your business. Give them a business card. If your line includes clothing and jewelry, wear them. Have your family wear them. When people comment on them, whip out those business cards. This works.

There may be free calendar listings available for certain types of events. If you own a gallery, advertise special exhibitions or openings by submitting your information to your local newspaper, radio, cable TV, and other media to be included in their community calendar. Be sure to learn the rules before doing this. Some allow only non-profits. Others have separate calendars for non-profit news and business announcements.

✂ PUBLIC SPEAKING

Public speaking is one way to become known in your community. If you make your talk just one long advertisement for your business, however, you may not be asked back. The details of who you are and what you do should be covered when you are introduced. Try to make your talk fit the interests of the group. I am a big believer in audiovisual materials, and they can be very helpful when speaking before a group. If your subject lends itself to slides or a PowerPoint presentation and you have the equipment available, go for it. If your work is unique you may want to include a demonstration in your talk. Props and displays of your work are also helpful. And don't forget to have handouts available. These could be an outline of your talk, a reading list, instructions for a craft project, or your brochure. Just be sure your name and contact information is somewhere on any printed materials you give out.

Now a word from the voice of experience on public speaking. Many years ago, when I still worked for someone else, one of my job responsibilities was to give informational public presentations about the agency I worked for to civic groups and churches. The director of the agency had already put a scripted slide presentation together, so it was just a matter of learning the script so the presentation would sound conversational. I have to say that slides are very helpful. If you forget what you are supposed to say the slides can help remind you. If you rely on technology however, you must be sure you take all needed equipment with you, including an extension cord. I don't think you need to hear the story behind that one. Use your imagination. Also, if you have a set amount of time to fill, don't rely on questions from the audience to fill the time for you. In other words, if you have an hour, don't go in with a twenty-minute presentation and expect forty minutes of questions, especially from a group of thirty teenagers. That was the longest hour of my life. Go with an hour's worth of material with possible stopping points at twenty, thirty, and forty-five minutes.

✂ THE MEDIA

Media coverage—yes, television, radio, newspapers—is available if you have information that is newsworthy. I put this last not because it isn't important, but because I don't want you to get caught up in this form of advertising and forget everything else. First, you need to send out a press release. The who, what, when, where, and why of the event you are announcing should be covered in a basic release. Keep it brief. No more than one page. Short sentences are best. Be sure to follow the rules of spelling, punctuation, and grammar, editing carefully. Most important, please use plain, easy-to-understand language.

Send your press release by first class mail or hand deliver it. Do your homework and find the specific person who handles this type of story and direct your information to that person. Press releases should be in the hands of the editor no later than twenty-four hours before the event, preferably a week before if you want to increase your chances of coverage.

When is a press release appropriate? Whenever you do something that is newsworthy. For instance, when opening a new store, especially in a smaller town, winning an award or other honor, or having a gallery showing.

Don't forget your local cable access television channel. In my city there are several local arts-related programs on cable access. These range from one-on-one interviews to panel discussions. Before agreeing to appear on any television show, even the local news, be sure to familiarize yourself with the specific program you will be appearing on. Watch it for at least one week if possible.

It is a good idea to have a way of tracking the effectiveness of the various forms of advertising you try. One way is with coupons and discounts. Include a coupon in newspaper ads and newsletters. Then be sure to keep track of how many coupons you get back from each source. You can also ask customers, "Where did you hear about me?" Be sure to write down the response. You certainly don't want to waste your money on advertising that isn't working for you.

Advertising doesn't have to cost a small fortune. The keys to advertising on a budget are having a product worth talking about and finding ways to get people talking.

Business Card Referral Discounts

Encourage your customers to give your business cards to their friends by placing a notice on the back similar to this. "Present this card and receive 10 percent off your purchase. The person who gave you this card will receive a discount of the same dollar value." Make sure you have a place on the back of the card for your referring customer's name, phone number, and date. Call the referring customer shortly after you have a card returned and thank them. The problem will be tracking all those cards. If you don't have a computer, try an envelope filing system. The growth of your business will be worth the extra effort. Remember to make certain your prices can afford the discounts and awards.

DO YOUR HOMEWORK

1. Think of three types of paid advertising you would like to use. Get price quotes for each of these. If you can only afford one, which one will you choose?

2. Think of three types of free advertising available to you. How much time or effort from you is involved? Is it worth it? If you could only do one, which one would you choose?

CREATIVE EXERCISE

Design your own newspaper ad or advertising. Get out a blank piece of paper or feel free to use your computer if you are more comfortable doing that. Decide if you will advertise a particular product, a special event (such as an open house or sale), or your business in general. Do you want to include photos and graphics or just words? How will you track the success of the ad? If you plan to use a coupon include that in your ad design. Play around with your design till you come up with something you really like. Do this even if you don't have anything to advertise now. The practice will come in handy when the need does arise.

NEED MORE HELP?

LITERATURE

Butland, Grace. "21 Tips for Creating Effective Advertising." *Crafts Report* (October 2000).

Dahl, Gary R. *Advertising for Dummies.* New York: John Wiley and Sons, 2001.

Davis, Robert, and Ivan R. Misner. *Business by Referral.* Austin, Tex.: Bard Press, 1998.

Edwards, Paul, Sarah Edwards, and Laura Clampitt Douglas. *Getting Business to Come to You.* 2nd ed. New York: Putnam Publishing Group, 1998.

Fletcher, Tana, and Julia Rockler. *Getting Publicity.* Bellingham, Wash.: Self Counsel Press Inc, 2001.

Misner, Ivan R., Virginia Devine, and Sarah Edwards. *The World's Best Known Marketing Secret.* 2nd ed. Austin, Tex.: Bard Press, 1999.

Pinsky, Raleigh. *101 Ways to Promote Yourself.* New York: William Morrow & Co., 1997.

Skelly, Heather. "A Direct Route to More Sales." *Crafts Report* (November 2001).

Timms, Paul R. *50 Powerful Ways to Win New Customers.* Franklin Lakes, New Jersey: Career Press Inc., 1997.

Lesson 22

A BUSINESS PLAN FOR A CRAFT BUSINESS?

A BUSINESS PLAN is the last thing most people wanting to go into the craft business think about. When I was first starting out, if you had asked me about a business plan, I wouldn't have known what you were talking about. However, after years of experience, including many lessons learned the hard way, I can say that a business plan is one of the first things we should think about. That's why I took the time to write this book.

✂ BUSINESS IS BUSINESS

One of the greatest weaknesses I have seen in the craft business is that we seem to believe that our business is so different from other types of business that regular, time-tested business principles do not apply. As someone who has tried it both ways, I can tell you those principles certainly do apply.

A business plan is a tool—simple as that. There is nothing magical, mystical, or even difficult about it. Writing a business plan forces you to do your homework, ask yourself the hard questions, and come up with your own answers. A business plan also requires you to look into the future for possible problems. This is something many people starting out in business don't want to do, but anticipating possible problems can often prevent them.

There is another reason for writing a business plan. If you are looking to other people, such as banks or private investors, for your startup money, then you do not have a choice. They will require a plan, and a good one. Investors want some assurance that you have done adequate planning and research to help ensure a return on their investment. They want to know that you know what you are doing.

You may be asking, "If the business plan is so important, why is this lesson at the back of the book?" To be honest, this lesson has been in various locations throughout this book. It finally located itself in the back of the book for a very important reason. The business plan is actually the major focus of this book. Each individual chapter gives you information that is very important to the creation of your business plan. If you have been reading the lessons and completing the homework assignments, you already have most of the research for your business plan completed. All that is left is to organize your information and put it in writing. To help you do this, I have put the chapter numbers for the lesson where the information can be found in parentheses in this lesson.

✂ WHERE DO YOU START?

So, you need a business plan. How do you write one? The good news is that there is help out there. There are books and software designed to take you step by step through writing your business plan.

There is also free help available from the Small Business Administration (SBA). The SBA's small business startup kit, available online, contains a good, basic business plan outline. In-depth help on developing a sound business plan can be found on the SBA Web site. I have mentioned the SBA before, but if you have not already been to the Web site, please take the time to go there now. The SBA may be found at *www.sba.gov.*

✂ THE ESSENTIALS

No matter what format you choose for your business plan you will want to be sure you cover the basics. *Start your business plan with an introduction.* This is where you introduce yourself and your business idea. Be sure to mention your qualifications to operate this type of business. You will also want to emphasize what will make your business different than similar businesses already out there. What is unique about your idea that makes it stand out from all the others?

Next you will want to discuss how you are going to obtain the product you plan to sell. For you this will usually be called production. Are you going to make every item by hand yourself? Do you plan to sell the work of others? Are you going to hire others to make your designs? Will they work from their homes or will you set up a factory? Would you consider selling a few high-quality commercially produced items that might be of interest to your customers (23)? Think about how you will cover seasonal demand or large orders. Before you decide to sell your work wholesale, make a plan for fill-ing large wholesale orders (15).

Marketing can be a scary word, but it simply means the method you choose to get your product out to the public. In other words, how are you going to sell and advertise your work (13 and 21)? Before you even start making these deci-sions take the time to do a little market research (11). Remember this from lesson 12, on pricing? First, decide what products or services you are going to sell. Then determine if there is a demand for your product or service. In other words, do people want or need your product? Next, identify your market. Who is going to buy your work? Where do they live? Where do they already shop? Is there a certain area these people frequent?

Now that you know what you are going to sell and who you are going to sell it to, you must decide where and how you are going to sell your work. Marketing is more than just advertising. It also involves where and how you are going to sell your product. In this section discuss whether you are going to sell your work yourself or through someone else (13 and 15). Discuss plans for a retail store or the show circuit or list possible, or actual retail outlets or consignment stores to carry your work (15–19). If you plan to be a wholesaler, discuss potential or actual wholesale customers. If you plan to sell your work yourself, how do you plan to advertise (21)? Do you have an advertising budget? Are you aware of free or low-cost advertising that may be available to you? Review lesson 21, "Advertising on a Budget," if you need help with this one.

Another element of marketing is pricing. Explain your pricing strategy (12). Please do not talk about your fear of overpricing or your desire for everyone to be able to afford your work. These are common traps crafts-people fall into, but this just won't fly with a seasoned business person, banker, or investor. Are you going to use a pricing formula? If so, which one? Is the price you obtain using the formula going to be your retail price, wholesale price, or minimum price? What other factors might figure into your pricing? Do you plan to have sales where you reduce the prices on cer-tain items? If so, when?

A major concern for any business owner is financial management. Where is the money to start your business coming from, and how are you going to keep your financial records (10)? Begin this section with a discussion of your startup capital. How much money will you have to start your business, and where will it come from? Next, *develop a monthly operating budget for the first year.* You are going to forget a few things. It just happens, especially if you have never run a business before, so build a cushion into your budget to cover the forgotten and the unexpected.

In addition to spending money you also hope to be bringing in money. *Do your best to come up with an estimated monthly cash flow statement for your first year.* How well do you expect to do the first year? How much money do you anticipate bringing in each month? Base this on the economy, your market, location, and your product. Try to be realistic. Indicate the times of year that you expect bigger sales if your work tends to be seasonal. When do you expect to start getting your initial investment back?

Go on to discuss your *break even point.* When will you stop losing money? When will the business pay for itself? This does not mean that you are showing a profit yet, but that you are covering expenses. Try to define this in terms of how much money you will need to bring in to reach this point. How many items will you need to sell to reach this point? Project an approximate time that you expect to break even. Explain your personal balance sheet and method of compensation. How are you going to pay yourself?

Who is going to keep the books? Are you going to hire an accountant or do this yourself (6 and 10)? Do you have adequate knowledge to do this yourself? How are you going to keep your accounting records? Are you going to use a ledger, or perhaps a computer? If using a computer, describe the particular software you plan to use.

Provide "what if" statements that address alternative approaches to any problem that may develop (1). You are starting a new business, and you don't want to think about what could go wrong, but you must. This won't be the big downer that you may think, because while you are thinking about what could possibly go wrong, you are also developing strategies for dealing with the problems. It will be much easier to come up with workable solutions now, than in the middle of a crisis.

The day-to-day tasks of operating any business falls under the heading of operations. If you anticipate hiring employees, discuss hiring and personnel procedures. If you plan to run the business by yourself, do you ever anticipate needing to hire employees? What would make this necessary (2 and 10)?

Be sure to include insurance, lease or rent agreements, and issues pertinent to your business in this section (7 and 14). Do you have adequate insurance coverage for your business? What types of insurance might you need? If you are renting your business space, what type of lease agreement do you have? If you are going to buy your building, who will be the lender? What are your mortgage payments? If you own the building outright, explain this. What will you pay in property taxes? Account for the equipment necessary to produce your product or services. What do you already have? Is it paid for? If not, who made the loan? How much are your payments? What equipment do you need? How much will it cost?

Account for production and delivery of products and services. Are you going to do everything yourself? Are you going to hire people to make your products either at your location or from their own homes?

Finally, make a concluding statement. This is where you summarize your whole business in a few words. Make those few words count. Summarize your business goals and objectives and express your commitment to the success of your business. This is your last chance to sell your idea. Give it everything you've got!

Good Advisors Are Important

Having a team of good advisors is important in all aspects of starting a business, but especially when developing your business plan. It is a good idea to have people who can be impartial look over your business plan. Have you missed anything? People who have been there may be able to give you the best input here. If you don't know anyone who has started their own business, you can always go to SCORE (Service Corps of Retired Executives). One of their volunteers will be glad to look over your business plan. Small Business Development Centers, which are often affiliated with colleges or universities and of course the SBA, may also be able to help.

When we were planning a major expansion of our business, we took our business plan to our local Small Business Development Center. We were thinking big on this one, and it was reassuring to us that the person we spoke with caught our vision. He was excited about it and thought it was a workable idea.

✂ HOW DO YOU PUT THIS THING TOGETHER?

What should the finished document look like? The most important thing to remember is that this is a business document. That means it should look as professional as possible. What does that mean? First, no handwritten business plans. Longhand is acceptable for a first draft, but the final copy should be typed or printed from your inkjet or laser printer.

Use a computer if you have one or can gain access to one. Save your work on disk. As the SBA says, "The business plan is a flexible document." Changes will be needed as time goes by. Having your business plan on disk makes these changes easier.

It is important that the document itself look its best. Print your business plan on good quality paper. Twenty-pound paper with a watermark is recommended. Use one-and-one-half-inch margins and double space. This allows room for your lenders or business advisors to make notes. These notes may give you valuable information, so be sure to make room for them.

Your business plan should have a cover sheet. Be sure to include the following information on your cover sheet: your name, the name of your business, contact information (addresses and phone numbers), and the date.

If you desire, put your business plan in a cover for protection. A plain two-pocketed folder works well for this. Add a label to the front of the folder with your business name, your name, and contact information. Put your business plan where it will be seen when the folder is opened. If there are already slots on one of the pockets to hold a business card, put your card there. If not, cut your own or glue or tape a card to the pocket. The other pocket may be used for supplemental information such as your business brochure, projected profit and loss statements, a history of the business, or any other printed materials you may have. This makes a nice package to present to lenders or business advisors.

Take the time to write a business plan, even if you do not plan to apply for a business loan. It will be time well spent.

DO YOUR HOMEWORK

1. Do research on business plan formats. Read books on writing a business plan. Look at the various software programs available. Go to the SBA Web site for information on writing a business plan, including their format.
2. Review the homework assignments you have already completed as you have read this book. You may find that you have already done most of the preliminary work. All that is left is to organize your information and put it into written form.
3. Write your business plan.
4. Have a trusted friend who understands business or your business advisor read your business plan. Make any needed changes or adjustments and finalize your formal plan. Congratulations!

NEED MORE HELP?

LITERATURE

Covell, Joseph and Brian J. Hazelgreen. *Your First Business Plan: A Simple Question and Answer Format Designed to Help You Write Your Own Plan.* 3rd ed. Naperville, Ill.: Sourcebooks Trade, 1998.

Hynes, William G. *Start and Run a Craft Business: A Step-by-Step Business Plan.* 7th ed. Bellingham, Wash.: Self Counsel Press, 2002.

McKeever, Mike P. *How to Write a Business Plan.* 5th ed. Berkeley, Calif.: Nolo Press, 2000.

Peterson, Steven and Peter Jaret. *Business Plan Kit for Dummies* (with CD-ROM). New York: John Wiley and Sons, 2001.

Robbins, Stever. *Creating a Business Plan That's You.* Entrepreneur Magazine (6 August 2001).

SOFTWARE

[Note: Your local computer store should have a selection of business plan software. Take some time to go in and look it over. Ask questions and look in computer magazines for more suggestions. The following are a few of the business plan software programs available, but, of course, there are others.]

Business Plan Pro 2003, Business Plan Toolkit for Mac, and Plan Magic Business are available at *www.paloalto.com.*

Plan Write® for Business is available at *www.businessplansoftware.org.*

Ultimate Business Planner, from Atlas Business Solutions Inc., is available at *www.bptools.com.*

ORGANIZATIONS AND BUSINESSES

[Contact information is available in Appendix B.]

Small Business Administration

WEB SITES

Bplans.com

Business Plan Center

Small Business Plan Guides

Small Business Assistance Center Network

Lesson 23

BRANCHING OUT—
EXPANDING YOUR BUSINESS

AFTER YOU HAVE BEEN IN BUSINESS awhile and are firmly established, you may want to look at ways to expand your product or service. There are many ways to do this. I will discuss a few here, but I encourage you to be creative and come up with ideas of your own.

✂ TEACHING CLASSES

Teaching classes is a good way to branch out and expand your business. It can also be good advertising. But before you decide to teach craft classes consider whether or not this is a good thing for you. This is something you must enjoy to be effective. You need to be comfortable talking in front of a group. You must be able to explain craft techniques in a concise and understandable manner as well as demonstrate the actual techniques with your own hands. You can't be easily rattled. When teaching, always expect the unexpected.

The following are a few things to consider when making the decision whether or not to teach. First, *do you have any previous teaching experience?* Have you taught a Sunday School class or Vacation Church School? Have you every been a Boy Scout or Girl Scout Leader? Do you volunteer at your local Senior Center, Community Center, or Boys and Girls Club? If you have never done any of these things, or something similar, you might want to think about trying one of them on a volunteer basis first. This will give you an idea of what is involved in teaching.

What age group or groups do you prefer? Do you prefer to teach children, teenagers, young adults, adults, or senior adults? Are you comfortable with all age groups?

192

What kinds of classes are you able to teach? While teaching craft classes usually will not require special training such as a college degree, you must be proficient in the skill you are going to teach. What has prepared you to teach this class? Have you taken classes in the media or project you are teaching? Are you self-taught? This is not necessarily a negative, especially if you are teaching something unique or original you developed yourself. Do you practice a craft that has been passed down through your family for generations? This could be a selling point for your classes.

Where will your classes be held? If you have your own retail store or studio you have the perfect place to hold classes. Be sure to have someone available to "mind the store" if you have classes during store hours. A special room is not absolutely necessary to hold classes. They may be held right out in the store if space permits.

If you do not have a retail store there are other options for offering classes. If no other space is available you can always teach from your home. If you decide to do this, use a family room, basement, or other area where it is okay to make a mess.

Art and craft supply stores as well as fabric stores often offer classes. Check with specific stores for details. Your community college may offer non-credit community service classes. Some communities have programs known as free universities or "communiversities." These are classes taught by people with expertise in their field, but they are simply for fun or knowledge—they are usually not affiliated with an actual school or college. I started out teaching my first craft class through a free university.

Your local community center, senior center, or public library may have meeting space. Learn the rules for using such rooms before you schedule your class. Some of these may not allow you to charge for your class or collect money on the premises, so find out first.

That brings us to the question, *do you have to make money from teaching?* Not always. I have been known to teach "freebies." When I do this, however, I require the students to bring their own supplies and any special equipment such as scissors. While it is nice to be paid $15 per hour to teach a class, there are other benefits from teaching besides the money. You might think of it as free advertising or even better, advertising you get paid for. Be sure your students leave with your business card and brochure. Once people get to know you they will look for your classes and hopefully your products.

Are there any special skills students must have prior to class? Never assume students will have these skills. Spell it out in your course description. I didn't think about this once and ended up with all non-sewers for a class that required machine sewing several short straight seams. It took four hours to complete a very simple necklace, but all was not lost. A good time was had by all and the non-sewers were so proud of their finished project.

Is any special equipment needed for your class? This includes things like sewing machines, a kiln, soldering irons, and so on. Will you be able to provide these yourself? Are you able to provide one for each person if needed? Could the location of the class provide special equipment? This could be one advantage to holding class at a school building or a store. Could the students bring their own?

If students are going to provide their own materials and supplies, you will need to make up a detailed list for each class. If you want your students to have their materials and supplies at the first meeting, find a way to distribute your list in advance.

If you are providing materials or even handouts, be sure to have more than enough for the number enrolled. You may have a few extras show up the day of class. Your handouts will reflect on you as a teacher, so be sure they are easy to read and understand.

If you are a people person and enjoy sharing your skills with others, teaching may be for you. This can be a fun and exciting way of increasing your income as well as becoming known as an artist in your community.

An Extra Set of Hands

When working with young children it is a good idea to have plenty of adult or teenage helpers. If you are offering classes for preschoolers, ask parents to stay with their children. Concentrate on crafts a parent and child can do together. For school-aged children having a helper who can assist in maintaining a little order, as well as providing an extra set of hands as needed, can save the day. If a child or an adult with special needs signs up for a class, don't assume you know what they need to be able to participate. Always ask.

✂ CUSTOM WORK AND SPECIAL ORDERS

In the fine art world, this type of work is known as a commission. A *major problem* with custom work or special orders is that in most cases the client has an idea or vision, if you will, of what the finished work will look like. Your job as an artist or craftsperson is to get into that person's head and see the finished item in the same way. Not an easy task. Even if a commission is very open-ended, there may be a theme or purpose to guide your work. Sitting down with the individual for a brainstorming session and having a written agreement will help prevent serious misunderstandings.

Start out by getting in the client's head. The most important thing to remember about a commissioned work is that you are selling your skills to make a specific piece of art for someone else. This is not something you decided to make on your own on spec, hoping it will sell. This makes it very important for you to have a clear idea of what the client wants. Get the person to talk about what she sees when she thinks of the finished project. Try to get as many specifics as possible. Listen for words about color, size, shape, intended use, and other elements. Try to make the client comfortable and your manner conversational. Ask for a phone number where she can be reached if you have any questions.

It is a good idea to keep a record on your custom clients. Record their name, address, phone number, sizes, if applicable, color preferences, and any other pertinent information. Keep track of all special orders you do for each client along with any problems that may have come up along the way. Use my tracking sheet, included at the end of this lesson, or come up with your own.

Always have a written agreement or contract. The following are the three basic components of this type of contract.

What is the person asking you to do? Include any specific details gained from your visit with the client that she feels she absolutely must have. For instance, if the work is for a specific place or location, the physical dimensions of the finished work may be vital. If this is the case, it is best to go out on location and take measurements yourself—don't rely on measurements taken by someone else. Color is another thing that may be very important to the client and needs to be specified in writing.

When does she want it done? Be realistic here. You know what your time constraints and other limitations are. Do not agree to a completion date that you know starting out you can't meet. If, once you are into the work, problems arise that could delay completion, such as difficulty in obtaining materials, notify the client explaining the problem. Also discuss any changes in the agreed-upon design or materials with the client before implementing them.

How much will the client pay you for doing it? Include when and how payment is to be made. At least an estimate of the cost should be made and if possible an actual price set before work is begun. Partial payment, usually 50 percent at the time of the order with the balance due on completion, is the standard business way of doing this, and I strongly suggest you follow this standard. If the work is to be personalized to the point that no one else would want to buy it if the client defaults on the agreement, you might want to ask for payment in full up front. Do not even begin work on the project until you have money in the bank—that is, until the check clears. No, I don't want to hear, "But this is different." I also don't want to hear, "But my clients will think I don't trust them." This is not about trust; this is about business and protecting both your interests and the interest of the client.

Sometimes I hear questions like the following. "I am making a set of bedroom curtains for a client. I am about finished and have no idea what to charge. What do you think about $50?" Does that make you shudder? It should. Let's analyze this. What's the problem here? If your first thought is, "I don't have enough information," you are correct. You don't know the size of the panels, how many, lined or unlined, type and cost of fabric, who provided fabric and other materials, and other important information for figuring cost.

But is there a bigger problem here? She is almost finished and hasn't discussed price with the client? What happens if the client has a figure in mind that is much lower than the seamstress wants or needs to cover expenses? What if the client decides not to pay and the seamstress is stuck with the curtains? Or perhaps the seamstress allows the client to take the curtains with a promise to pay next week and the client decides not to pay? I have heard true stories with all of these outcomes.

Other things the commission agreement should contain include the need for special work space or equipment to enable you to get the work done. If you need to work on the customer's premises, have times clearly specified. If you are a clothing designer, make sure the contract makes it clear that the customer must come in for fittings before the work can be completed. In short, think of all the possible circumstances that could cause problems in getting your work completed and make sure they're covered in the agreement. And be fair. If you damage something owned by a customer, state your liability to replace, repair, or pay for it.

✄ MY STORY

I am going to close this discussion with my own sad story about special orders. I had some very good luck with special orders, but once I found myself stuck with twenty-five extra, extra large T-shirts with a company name and phone number on them because I didn't wait until the check cleared before I began work. In fact, by the time I was aware that payment was a major problem, the shirts were done. The customer tried to talk us into leaving the shirts at his business with promise of payment later, which of course we did not do. We finally turned this over to an attorney, but even he could never get payment for us. Worse than that, we were stuck with twenty-five huge T-shirts with custom printing. We finally gave them to charity. Please learn from my mistake and remember that work on special orders does not begin until the deposit check clears the bank and ownership of the article does not change hands before payment is received in full.

Creative Ways to Increase an Artist's Income

Do you only have one way of bringing in money from your art? Let this story help inspire you to come up with new ideas. A local artist is a great example of the many ways an artist can make money. This artist is wonderfully diversified. First she owns a gallery where she sells her work as well as the work of other artists, for which she charges a commission. Even though she has her own gallery, you will still find her at major shows in our area. She also illustrates children's books as well as selling prints and greeting cards made from her original paintings. One of the more unique moneymakers for this artist is custom paintings of people's homes. Not being one to waste space, the back room of her gallery is used for teaching classes. She also actively seeks commissions, and her work is a part of several public buildings.

Does this give you ideas for ways you can diversify?

✂ WRITING AND PUBLISHING

You might want to consider writing a book or magazine article or publishing your own patterns if you have an original art or craft idea or pattern, a unique or unusual technique, or a simple and clear way of teaching your art form or craft to others. You may also want to share your experience or research with others.

Before we delve into the fine points of writing and publishing I need to say a little about copyright. There is much misinformation going around about copyright—what it is, what it does, and how it is obtained. When it comes to finding current, accurate information I always say go to the source. This is especially important when it comes to copyright. Don't rely on information from friends or an Internet chat room. Go to the source, in this case the United States Copyright Office.

Copyright law has changed in recent years, so if you think you are familiar with the idea of copyright, but your information is from ten years ago, you are not current. *Now*, after these new laws were established, all written work is copyrighted as soon as it is put to paper. It is still a good idea to put your copyright notice on all written work. A copyright notice includes the name of your book, article, or pattern followed by the copyright symbol or the word copyright, the year, and your name. We usually put this information in the form of a header at the top of each page along with the page number. Why put this information on every page? Pages sometimes get separated. Having each page clearly marked will help avoid confusion if this happens. You may also register your copyright for added protection. The copyright office can tell you how to do this. My editor tells me that registering your copyright with the Copyright office is the best way to ensure copyright, should a court case arise. If you are published by a press (such as Allworth Press, my publisher), the publisher registers copyright in your name.

Another thing to remember is that you cannot copyright an idea. You can only copyright your tangible expression of that idea. You can copyright your words, illustrations, and photos used to convey that idea, but you cannot copyright the idea itself. If you have an original idea for a tangible product that you think might be able to earn you money, then you might want to consider obtaining a patent.

The copyright office has a wonderful and very thorough Web site at *www.copyright.gov.* Answers to many of your questions will be found there. Don't rely on stories, myths, and urban legends when it comes to copyright. Go to the source.

WRITING AND PUBLISHING DETAILS

Now, let's get down to the details of writing and publishing. First, I must say writing is not as easy as most people think. Putting your ideas on paper or in a computer requires practice, discipline, and time. Sitting at a computer for hours at a time can cause physical pain. Believe me, my massage therapist loves my need to sit at a computer for hours at a time. I keep him in business.

Getting work accepted for publication is also not easy. It often doesn't matter if you have the most timely, fresh, creative presentation of your subject matter. You will still find yourself playing the "numbers game" when it comes to submitting your idea to a publisher, especially if you are a first-time author who has never been published before.

Most publishers will expect a book proposal that includes a cover letter, a table of contents of proposed chapters, and the first two or three chapters of the book. For patterns and magazine articles it is best to ask for submission guidelines. This is also a good idea for books.

If you need help with the format for a book proposal or article query see the *Writer's Market.* It should be available at your local library, but if you are serious about writing and getting your work published go to your local book store and buy a copy.

Okay, so you have a wonderful, unique, and creative idea. *How do you find a publisher?* To start, go to your local major bookstore or library and browse the sections containing books in your general subject area. Who is publishing your type of book? Write down names and addresses.

The *Writer's Market* and writers' publications such as *Writer's Digest* and *The Writer* include listings of publishers with the subject areas they publish.

Your favorite art or craft magazine may also give you some ideas. It also doesn't hurt to try the Internet. Some publishers will include information for authors on their Web site.

If you are trying to publish a pattern, become familiar with the major craft pattern companies and the type of patterns published by each. Take a walk through the pattern section of your local craft store for ideas.

With today's computer technology there is another way to publish without going through an established publishing company. *You can always self-publish your work.* There are certain advantages to self-publishing. You can probably get the book out on the market more quickly. When you self-publish you also retain full editorial control. A publisher will often make suggestions or request or require that you make changes in your manuscript.

But there is also a downside. When you self-publish, you take on full responsibility for all aspects of publishing your work. You do not have an editor to catch those little mistakes you are too close to see. When you self-publish you are also responsible for marketing. You are the one who must find retail outlets for your book, arrange for your own publicity, and arrange for delivery of your books after they have been sold to bookstores. You also take on full responsibility for typesetting and printing your book. It is important to make every effort to make a self-published book look good. You don't want it to look like something that was turned out in your basement, even if it was.

Another part of the downside of self-publishing is that having a book printed can be quite expensive. If it costs $25 just to print your book can you really compete with similar books on the market selling for $19.95?

Having your craft patterns or books published is not impossible. This is an area where research and quality are very important, however. Be familiar with the work put out by each publisher you approach. Be familiar with accepted writing styles and formats. And finally, be sure that any work you send out is the very best it can be.

MAGAZINE ARTICLES

Writing articles and sending them to every publication you can think of will usually not produce the results you desire. There is a procedure to be followed. It is slow, tedious, and frustrating. But it is the way things are done. Learning the rules of the game is necessary if you hope to see your words in print.

Become familiar with magazines that publish articles related to what you do. Browse the newsstands or magazine section of your public library. If you find one you are really interested in submitting an article to, buy it. Take it home and study it. Become familiar with the kind of articles the magazine publishes, as well as the writing style and format. Look through the *Writer's Market* and other writing periodicals for information on specific publications.

After you have narrowed down your choices, *send for the writer's guidelines.* This is important. This will tell you how to write your article for a specific publication, including content and format. If you send an article to a publication on spec you will usually receive a response telling you to send for the writer's guidelines. When you receive the guidelines, study them carefully.

It is best to write an article with a specific publication in mind rather than writing, then trying to find a magazine to publish what you have written. *Send a query letter to the editor* of the publication. This is where you pitch your idea to the editor. Please refer to the *Writer's Market* if you need help writing a query letter. Address correspondence to the editor of the publication or the department you are interested in, by name if possible. Ms. is considered to be proper for addressing a woman in business correspondence unless she expresses a preference for Miss or Mrs. Avoid "Dear Editor" letters if possible.

Look the contract over carefully. Have your attorney take a look at it. Be sure you understand the concept of rights. Know what rights you are selling. It is important to understand that if you sell all rights you cannot use the article again. It does not belong to you. Money may be a factor here. If you have a really hot new craft idea you may not want to sell all rights for $25, but you might consider $725.

Find a way to track your submissions. It is important to keep a record of where you have sent an article and the response received. Use a notebook, file cards, computer, or whatever is most comfortable for you. You may make copies of the Tracking Sheet for Article Submissions at the end of this lesson and use them if you desire. Remember, permission is granted for copying the worksheets in this book for your use only.

WRITING FOR THE INTERNET

There are differences when publishing articles on the Internet. *Articles for use on Web sites are known as content and the people who write them are content providers.*

A few Web sites follow the traditional form of article submission used in print articles. Most, however, do not. If you want to write for publication on the Internet the best way to get started is by doing it. Put your articles on your own site, or the sites of friends or family members. When Web surfing if you find sites looking for articles, contact the Web master. If you see a new site going up, make contact early—they will most likely be looking for content. Once Web masters start seeing your work out there, they will contact you.

Unfortunately, most Web sites are not paying for articles. This may change in time, but as long as people are giving away quality articles it will be difficult. Make sure there is something in the arrangement that benefits you, even if it's only a link to your site. If you have affiliate programs or other moneymakers on your site, the free advertising might be valuable.

If you write for Web sites, insist on being given credit for your work whether you are being paid or not. Never allow your work to be used on a Web site belonging to someone else without your name and copyright notice.

There are Web sites where you can list articles you are willing to make available for Web use. This is known as *syndication*. Sometimes permission is given for Web masters to copy and paste or download articles directly from the site. Others require permission of the author.

If you put your original articles, craft designs, or patterns on your Web site or someone else's do not be surprised if they show up other places without your permission. The Internet is still new. Rules are still being written. Some people do not seem to realize that some of the old rules still apply on the Web, such as copyright. Enforcement on the Web is difficult at this time, so be careful.

Writing articles for magazines or Web sites can be a rewarding experience both emotionally and financially if approached in the right way. Do your homework, use your own good judgment, and ask for advice when needed.

✂ EXPANDING YOUR RETAIL BUSINESS

Is your retail store doing well? Are there ways you could expand your retail business? If you want to start out small, you might *consider carrying impulse items*. These are small, inexpensive items that people will buy without even thinking, such as greeting cards, key chains, craft patterns, or books. Display these close to the cash register. Why do you think candy and magazines are in the checkout lines at grocery stores? Try to keep small items where you or an employee can keep an eye on them since these can walk away.

Another way to expand your retail business is to *add variety to your product line*. Carry other people's craft work or buy tasteful manufactured products that might fit in with your business. One way to increase your variety, as well as to get a price break on your supplies, is to sell craft supplies as well. For example, if you are a jewelry maker, order extra jewelry findings from the manufacturer. Sell what you do not need for your immediate work at retail prices.

If you insist on not carrying *commercially produced items* stop and think about this. Quality items that fit in with the image you want your store to have can help increase your customer base as well as your income.

Be sure you have a *range of prices.* Lower cost items will sell more easily than very high-priced items; have a balance of prices, ranging from low-end to high-end as well as somewhere in the middle.

Are you capitalizing on anything unique about your location? If your store is in an old Victorian house, carry out a Victorian theme inside. If you are located in an area that has many antique stores, think about having antiques for sale. These may be used as store fixtures, so your store does not have to look like an antique store. If you do this, be prepared to replace your store fixtures and display equipment as it sells.

✂ MY STORY

Our store was located in an area that had obtained official designation as the "antique capital" of our state. We were not an antique store, but we did use antiques as store fixtures, which were also for sale. Clothing was displayed on coat racks and in a wardrobe closet. Quilts and other needlework could be seen peeking out of trunks and drawers. My favorite piece was the antique printer's cabinet that I used to store my beads and jewelry findings.

Bob went to estate sales and auctions to buy the antiques and often came back with boxes of odds and ends thrown in with the items he actually wanted. We put these items in a bargain basket along with my "seconds" (jewelry items with "boo-boos"). You wouldn't believe how much of this odd assortment of stuff we actually sold. People love to rummage through things looking for bargains.

We also sold commercial products such as craft patterns, books, picture postcards, and greeting cards. We used these items along with handmade beaded key chains as impulse items that we kept close to the cash register at the front door.

I also took quality art and craft work on consignment, but it had to be quality work, and it had to fit in with the country and western style of the store. Special orders were also important for me, and I had several regular customers.

Another way we chose to expand our business also helped me get my supplies at wholesale prices. We sold the extra supplies that I did not need for my production work in our store. Most of my work was made from bandannas, and we ordered large quantities. By making the extra bandannas available for sale in the store we were able to have a very impressive display of the largest assortment of bandannas in our area at the lowest price. We also repackaged extra beads, jewelry findings, and other craft supplies for retail sale. As mentioned earlier, it was a great surprise when we realized that a large craft supply store in our area saw us as competition.

Offering my extra supplies for sale had a surprising effect on my business. I also bought unusual beads and they started selling quickly. These really sold. The people who bought our beads were often young teenage boys in the twelve-to-fifteen-year-old age group. Selling items that appeal to children and teenagers does not have to be a problem as long as you stay in control. These kids have money and they will buy. But please treat them with the respect you would give any customer. They will really appreciate it. The kids started buying the beads. Then they started asking for classes. Then they realized that girls would buy the jewelry they made and they started asking for business advice. Bob even worked it out so they could get a small discount on supplies they bought from us. These young men became an important part of our customer base and were valued customers. All of this started when we decided to sell our extra beads.

We sometimes had people react with anger and disgust when they realized we were not an antique store. It took awhile for me not to fall apart when I heard angry or vulgar words about crafts. And I cannot say I ever got to the point where it did not hurt. But I did learn that if I could get those people to actually come into the store they might buy something. Sometimes these people would buy antiques. We were the only store in our area that carried tourist postcards, and sometimes the angry ones would buy those. We also sold a line of unique greeting cards that did well.

There are many ways to expand your business. These are just a few suggestions and possibilities. You are the only one who can determine what works best for you. Don't just settle into a comfortable rut. Stretch yourself a little. The exercise will do you good.

Turning an Angry Person into Your Best Customer

I think my favorite example of turning an angry customer around has to be Gloria. I heard that big booming voice say, "No antiques, let's go," as soon as she was in the door. I tried my, "Oh, we have antiques," line on her, and before I knew it she was actually inside looking around. Before she left Gloria had given me a check. Did she buy one of my antiques? No. Then what did Gloria buy? She bought a bright red bandanna dress and she became one of my best customers.

DO YOUR HOMEWORK

1. Take some time to think and write about which of the following ways you would like to try to expand your business.

   • Teaching
   • Designing and publishing
   • Custom work/special orders
   • Writing for magazines and Web sites
   • Selling related commercial items
   • Capitalizing on your location

   Feel free to add your own ideas.

2. Choose one of the above and come up with the first step toward making it a reality.

Custom Work/Special Orders Information Form

Customer's Name _____

Address _____

_____

Phone Number _____

_____

Previous work completed for customer _____

_____

_____

_____

_____

Customer preferences (colors, styles, etc.) _____

_____

_____

_____

_____

Customer sizes (for wearables only) _____

_____

_____

_____

Description of current work contracted (be specific) _____

_____

_____

_____

Projected completion date (are you allowing yourself enough time?)

_____

_____

_____

Estimated cost _____

Amount of payment received at time of order _____

Balance due on completion _____

Signature _____ Date _____

Signature _____ Date _____

Tracking Sheet for Article Submissions

Name of Publication _____

Address _____

_____

_____

Name of Editor _____

_____

Title of Proposed Work _____

Date mailed _____ Date of Response _____

_____

Action taken:

❏ Accepted

❏ Rejected / Reason if given _____

_____

_____

_____

Amount and date of payment _____

Rights sold _____

NEED MORE HELP?

LITERATURE

Applebaum, Judith. *How to Get Happily Published.* 5th ed. New York: Harper Perennial, 1998.

Brabec, Barbara. "Writing Articles for Extra Income." *Crafts Report* (February 1999).

Curtis, Richard, and William Thomas Quick. *How to Get Your E-Book Published: An Insider's Guide to the World of Electronic Publishing.* Cincinnati, Ohio: Writer's Digest Books, 2002.

Gordon, Molly. "Marketing Knitwear: Becoming a Seminar Instructor" (cited: September 2002). Available at: *www.mollygordon.com/resources/ marketingresources/knit/instructor.html.*

Herman, Deborah Levine, and Jeff Herman. *Write the Perfect Book Proposal: 10 That Sold and Why.* 2nd ed. New York: John Wiley and Sons, 2001.

Herman, Jeff. *Writer's Guide to Book Editors, Publishers and Literary Agents 2002–2003.* Rocklin, Calif.: Prima Communications, 2001.

Holm, Kirsten, and Hubbuch, Doug, eds. *2003 Writer's Market Online.* Cincinnati, Ohio: Writer's Digest Books. Published Annually.

Ross, Tom, and Marilyn Ross. *The Complete Guide to Self-Publishing: Everything You Need to Know to Write, Publish, Promote and Sell Your Own Book.* 4th ed. Cincinnati, Ohio: Writer's Digest Books, 2002.

Shinder, Jason, Jeff Herman, and Amy Holman. *Get Your First Book Published and Make It a Success.* Franklin Lakes, N.J.: Career Press Inc., 2001.

Smith, Mack E. *How to Publish and Market Your Own Book: A Simple Guide for Aspiring Writers.* Houston, Tex.: UR Gems Group, 2001.

Strope, Mary. "Earn Extra Income by Teaching." *Crafts Report* (April 2000).

COPYRIGHT INFORMATION

[Contact information is available in Appendix B.]
United States Copyright Office

WEB SITES

[Contact information is available in Appendix B.]
Gotta Write Online

WRITERS MAGAZINES

[Contact information is available in Appendix B.]
Byline
Writer's Digest
Writer's Journal

Lesson 24

DO YOU STILL WANT TO START YOUR OWN BUSINESS?

SOMETIMES, WHEN PEOPLE give business advice to artisans or crafters, they are accused of being negative or nonsupportive. This is rarely the intent. I know that it is not ours as the authors of this book. But if you are starting your own art or craft business you need to hear some of the hard realities along with the feel-good stuff. If you only want everyone to pat you on the back and say you are doing a good job you are headed for trouble.

Starting your own business is hard work. You need to know that. There are rules and regulations to follow. You also need to know that. That's the downside.

But starting your own art or craft business can also be rewarding in so many ways. Of course we all hope it will be rewarding financially. It can also be rewarding emotionally and creatively as you see people paying money for your work.

If you are easily offended you may have to toughen up a little. You may also hear remarks about your work that are not complimentary.

If you are driven to create and spent years in a job where your creativity was stifled, you may find the freedom of working for yourself exhilarating. We all desire the freedom of being our own boss. Just remember, with freedom comes responsibilities.

So, back to the original question. Do you still want to start your own business? After doing your homework and writing a business plan, do you think you need to slow down and start out part-time while keeping your day job? Have you decided that maybe there is more time, effort, or money involved than you have to give right now? There is nothing wrong with that. We hope you will not give up on your creative endeavors. You may want to continue your art or craft work as a hobby, selling a little of your work, or not.

You can also give your work as gifts to friends and family, or donate your work to charity for use or distribution by the organization or for sale to raise funds.

Perhaps reading this book and completing the homework assignments has made your commitment to following your dream even stronger. Do you feel you can't turn back, even if you might want to? Do you believe now, even more strongly than before you started reading this book, that you can do this? You *can* sell your work successfully. Congratulations, you are not only an artist—you are in business!

Appendix A

CAVEAT EMPTOR: RECOGNIZING A LEGITIMATE BUSINESS OPPORTUNITY

WE ALL KNOW ABOUT UNSCRUPULOUS PEOPLE out there waiting to take advantage of unsuspecting folks just trying to find ways of working from home or supplementing their income. Artists and craftspeople are especially vulnerable to this type of activity because we, too often, think it is okay not to understand business. So what are a few of the things you need to watch out for when starting your own business?

✄ WORK-AT-HOME OPPORTUNITIES

You probably know someone who has been taken in by a work-at-home scheme. We have all heard stories of people who have assembled craft items at home to have all but two or three rejected without payment.

There are legitimate ways of working from home, just be careful when choosing a company to work for. To this end I offer the following suggestions.

If something sounds too good to be true, it usually is. Be suspicious if incomes are promised that seem unrealistically high. No one is going to pay you $4 per item if he is selling the item for only $5. Watch the math and be suspicious if the offer is just too good.

Check a company out with the *Better Business Bureau.* If this does not turn up anything it only means that no one has filed a complaint, not necessarily that people have not had bad experiences with the company.

You might also want to check with the *Consumer Protection Agency* in the state where the company is located. But here again, if there is not a complaint on file they may not be much help.

Ask if you have to buy something. If so, what? Are you buying a how-to book or promotional literature? Sometimes advertisements that seem to offer work-at-home opportunities turn out to be actually selling books or other printed or recorded materials.

Know how payment will be handled. When, how, and how much will you be paid? Why might the company refuse to pay? This is often a problem with work-at-home companies.

Be suspicious if you are required to buy your own supplies, either from the company or on your own. Making items on speculation in the hopes that the company will buy them from you is risky business. Reputable work-at-home companies will provide all supplies and materials and then usually pay you a piece rate per item for your labor. Remember, work means you are being paid, not that you are paying the employer.

Learn to recognize network marketing. Now, network marketing is not necessarily a bad thing, just be sure you understand what you are getting into. Does the company emphasize selling product or selling a business plan? How much money and time will you have to invest? What type of training and support is offered? What are the rules, regulations, and restrictions you will be bound to follow? Gather as much information about the company and its sales program as you can. Do not get caught up in the excitement of a large recruitment meeting. Ask those hard questions. It is then up to you to decide if you want to pursue the opportunity.

If you are serious about working from home but do not want to give up the security of a regular paycheck, *consider looking in your own community.* Many mainstream companies are now using home workers. Or, if you have a skill to offer, such as typing, research, mending or altering clothing, or teaching a foreign language, consider placing a small advertisement in your local newspaper. Most papers offer a business and professional services section in their classifieds.

No job is complete without the paperwork. The first piece of paperwork in the work-at-home situation is the contract. Get copies of everything, including statements of materials or supplies you receive from the company you are working for, what you deliver to them, incidental expenses, checks received from them, and other not otherwise mentioned records. Be sure these are signed, or at least initialed, by someone authorized to do so. No contract? Don't accept the assignment. It's just too risky.

✂ LEARN TO RECOGNIZE A SALES PITCH

Work-at-home schemes are not the only pitfalls you must watch for. Once it becomes public knowledge that you are in business, people will start coming out of the woodwork, usually wanting to sell you something. It is important to learn to recognize a sales pitch.

Not all salespeople will tell you that they are selling something. Sometimes salespeople will also call themselves "consultants," "advisors," "inspectors," or "counselors." There are legitimate professionals going by these titles, but the best of these are usually not going to make the initial contact with you, especially by telephone.

Remember, *legitimate city, county, or insurance inspectors will also not try to sell you their services* to fix the problem. They will simply give you a report detailing the problem and tell you to get it fixed.

As annoying as they may be at times, *not all telemarketing calls are part of a scam.* Many fine, ethical, and totally legitimate companies engage in telephone sales. Anytime someone calls another person on the phone and attempts to sell something he is telemarketing. You may have even done this.

There are laws and regulations controlling the way telemarketing is done. These are enforced mainly by the Federal Communication Commission (FCC). For your protection and future reference, keep a special notepad and pen close to your telephone to write down the name of the company and the phone name or ID number of the salesperson. Most companies do not allow telemarketers to use their real names. You may also want to jot down what was promised to you in an offer and how many times you have asked to be removed from the company's phone list. If you are not removed after three requests, you have grounds for a complaint. This is a good rule to follow with all unwanted telemarketing calls, business related or not; however, nonprofit organizations are not required to maintain a do-not-call list.

✂ THE INTERNET

Be very careful when signing up for moneymakers, including affiliate programs, on the Internet. There are legitimate ways of making money online. There are also companies that intend to pay, but when it comes time to write checks the money is just not there. And of course a few businesses are not entirely honest, online or offline. So what do you look for in a legitimate online moneymaker?

How long has the company been in business? *How long have they been online?* Many companies start out with unrealistic expectations when they first go online. Be aware of this when dealing with a company that has been online for less than one year.

How much money do you have to earn before you receive a check? Many affiliate programs online pay monthly or quarterly, but you do not actually receive a check until your account has reached a certain dollar value, often $25. If you are being paid one cent for each customer you send to a Web site, it may take awhile to send the site 2,500 customers to reach that $25 mark. You must decide how long you are willing to wait before you actually see your money.

Are you willing to be paid in merchandise or points to be redeemed for merchandise? This is a popular method of payment for programs where you are paid for visiting certain Web sites. Are you willing to accept this? This can be just as good as cash, as long as the merchandise is something you need or want.

Are you willing to gamble on getting paid? There are many online companies offering to pay you for completing market research surveys. A few pay per survey, but most put your name in a drawing for the cash. How long are you willing to complete questionnaires hoping to be the lucky one to get the money before you actually are? I filled out those questionnaires faithfully for one full year before I realized that I had never won a drawing. After that I decided to only work with the companies that pay per survey.

Are you willing or able to accept a loss if an Internet company goes bankrupt or just shuts down before you get paid? Internet companies come and go at an alarming rate. For this reason don't let the amount of money a company owes you get too large, at least until you have received one or two checks. Even then, you cannot be sure that a company will not suddenly shut down owing you and others money with no plans for paying. This happened to me. Ouch!

I was posting articles on a Web site that promised to pay for traffic brought to their site to read my articles. The articles had been up for one payment period, three months, and I had reached the dollar amount to receive a check. But before the check could arrive, I found a notice in my e-mail saying that the company was declaring bankruptcy. No writers would be paid. I decided not to pursue this since the dollar amount was only $30. Another class in Learning the Hard Way from the School of Hard Knocks.

✂ FILING A COMPLAINT

When you find you have been taken advantage of in any type of business scheme or scam it is a good idea to file a complaint. Unless laws have been broken you will usually want to file your complaint with the local Better Business Bureau. They should be listed in your local phone book or you may contact the Better Business Bureaus for information on your local office. Contact information is in the resource list at the back of the book. Be sure to have the name of the company and their contact information. Keep track of what action you have already taken, names and titles of any people you have spoken with about the problem, and dates of anything pertinent to the situation.

✄ BE AWARE OF YOUR COMMUNITY

If there is a problem in your community with any type of business, it may be on the television or radio news or in the newspapers. If you are approached in a way that seems to fit one of these reports, do not hesitate to call the police or report it in any other way the news report advises.

There is no need to be overly concerned about being cheated as you set up your own business. Just be cautious. Do your research, take time to think before making major decisions, and most importantly, use your common sense.

Appendix B

RESOURCES

Note: Information in this list is the most current available at the time of publication of this book.

Aardvark Art Supply
P.O. Box 434
Belmont, MA 02478
(800) 705-4303
www.aardvarkart.com
[Wholesale painting supplies.]

Abbreviations and Acronyms of the
U.S. Government
*www.ulib.iupui.edu/subjectareas/gov/docs_*
abbrev.html
[Government information.]

Academy of American Doll Artists
73 North Spring Street
Concord, NH 03301
(603) 226-4501
www.aadadoll.org
[Doll-making organization.]

Advancestar Communications
One Park Avenue
New York, NY 10016
(800) 827-7170
(212) 951-6675
www.artexpony.com
[Trade shows.]

Affiliated Wood Carvers Ltd.
P.O. Box 104
Bettendorf, IA 52722
www.awcltd.org
[Woodcarving organization.]

Afloral.com
P.O. Box 526
Celoron, NY 14720
(888) 299-4100
http://afloral.com
[Wholesale floral supplies.]

African American Photographers
Guild
www.aapguild.org
[Photography organization.]

Aftosa
1034 Ohio Avenue
Richmond, CA 94804
(800) 231-0397
(510) 233-0334
www.aftosa.com
[Wholesale ceramic and pottery
supplies.]

Airtex Consumer Products
150 Industrial Park Road
Cokato, MN 55321
(800) 851-8887
(320) 286-2696
www.airtex.com
[Wholesale doll supplies and quilting
supplies.]

All Crafts
http://allcrafts.com
[Links.]

Alliance for Affordable Services
P.O. Box 612547
Dallas, TX 75261
www.affordableservices.org
[Health insurance.]

Alliance of Artists Communities
255 South Main Street
Providence, RI 02903
(401) 351-4320
www.artistcommunities.org
[Professional Organization.]

Ambush
P.O. Box 144
Worcester, MA 01613
(508) 755-2674
www.beads2u.com/
[Wholesale beads and jewelry supplies.]

American Art Clay Company
4717 West 16th Street
Indianapolis, IN 46222
(800) 374-1600
(317) 244-2671
www.amaco.com
[Wholesale ceramic and pottery supplies.]

American Art Pottery Association
P.O. Box 834
Westport, WA 02790-0697
www.amartpot.org
[Ceramic organization.]

American Association of Home Based
Business
P.O. Box 10023
Rockville, MD 20849
www.aahbb.org
[Startup information.]

American Association of Retired
Persons
Membership Center
P.O. Box 199
Long Beach, CA 90801
(800) 424-3410
www.aarp.org
[Membership organization; insurance.]

American Association of Woodturners
3499 Lexington Avenue North, Suite 103
Shoreview, MN 55126
(651) 484-9094
www.woodturner.org
[Woodworking organization.]

American Craft Council
72 Spring Street
New York, NY 10012
(212) 274-0630
www.craftcouncil.org
*[Trade shows; professional, trade, and
industry organization.]*

American Home Business Association
4505 South Wasatch Boulevard #140
Salt Lake City, UT 84124
(800) 664-2422
www.homebusiness.com/FLAX
[Home-based business organization.]

American Institute of Graphic Arts
164 Fifth Avenue
New York, NY 10010
(212) 807-1990
www.aiga.org
[Graphic arts organization.]

American Needlepoint Guild
P.O. Box 1027
Cordova, TX 38088-1027
(901) 755-3728
www.needlepoint.org
[Needleart organization.]

American Quilter's Society
P.O. Box 3290
Paducah, KY 42002-3290
(270) 898-7903
www.aqsquilt.com
[Quilting organization.]

American Sewing Guild
9660 Hillcroft, Suite 516
Houston, TX 77096
(713) 729-3000
http://asg.org
[Sewing organization.]

American Society of Interior Designers
608 Massachusetts Avenue, Northeast
Washington, DC 20002
(202) 546-3480
www.asid.org
[Interior design organization.]

American Society of Picture
Professionals
409 South Washington Street
Alexandria, VA 22314
(703) 299-0219
www.aspp.com
[Photography organization.]

American Watercolor Society
47 Fifth Avenue
New York, NY 10003
www.watercolor-online.com/
AWS/index.shtml
[Watercolor organization.]

Americans for the Arts
1000 Vermont Avenue Northwest,
6th Floor
Washington, DC 20005
(202) 371-2830
www.artsusa.org
[Arts advocacy organization.]

Animation Artist
www.animationartist.com
[Online instruction.]

Appliqué Society
P.O. Box 89
Sequim, WA 98382-0089
(800) 597-9827
www.theappliquesociety.org
[Quilting organization.]

ARA Content
www.aracontent.com
[Web site content: articles.]

Ari Imports
8 South Michigan Avenue
Chicago, IL 60603
(312) 263-3313
www.czechmate.com
[Wholesale beads and jewelry supplies.]

Art and Craft Show Yellow Pages™
CHOICES
P.O. Box 484
Rhinebeck, NY 12572
(845) 876-2995
http://smartfrogs.com
[Craft show listing and directory;
forum and message board; marketing
information.]

Art and Craft Shows.net
www.artandcraftshows.net
[Craft show listings and directories.]

Art and Design Associations on the
World Wide Web
http://web.uflib.ufl.edu/artsorg

The Art Deadlines List
www.artdeadlineslist.com
[Craft show listings and directories.]

Art Fair Source Book
2003 Northeast 11th Avenue
Portland, OR 97212
(800) 358-2045
(503) 331-0455
www.artfairsource.com
[Craft show listing and directory.]

Art Fixtures
P.O. Box 6850
Ketchum, ID 83340-6850
(208) 622-3338
http://artfixtures.com
[Display equipment.]

Arthby's
www.arthbys.com
[Online classifieds.]

Artnet
www.artnet.com
[Craft show listings and directories.]

Art Promote.com
www.artpromote.com
[Free Internet Promotion, Advertising Classifieds, Hosting and Resources.]

Art Resource.com
(866) 465-3294
www.artresource.com
[Wholesale art supplies.]

The Art Store
4004 Hillsboro Pike
Nashville, TN 37215
(615) 298-1112
(800) 999-4601
www.artstoreplus.com
[Wholesale art supplies.]

Art Supplies Wholesale
4 Enon Street
North Beverly, MA 01915
(800) 462-2420
http://allartsupplies.com
[Wholesale art supplies.]

Artgems Inc.
3850 East Baseline Road, Suite 119
Mesa, AZ 85206
(480) 545-6009
www.artgemsinc.com
[Wholesale beads and jewelry supplies.]

The Artist-Blacksmith's Association of
North America
P.O. Box 816
Farmington, GA 30638
(706) 310-1030
www.abana.org
[Metalsmithing and blacksmithing organization.]

Artistic Purr-suits
www.geocities.com/carollhiggs
[Online instruction.]

The Artistan's Commonwealth
Stephen A. Clerico
P.O. Box 192
Free Union, VA 22940
(804) 978-4109
http://members.aol.com/sartisan
[Cooperative information.]

Artists' Health Insurance Resource
Center
Actors' Fund National Headquarters
729 Seventh Avenue, 10th Floor
New York, NY 10019
www.actorsfund.org/ahirc
[Health insurance information.]

Artrider Productions Inc.
P.O. Box 28
Woodstock, NY 12498
(845) 331-7900
www.artrider.com
[Craft show listing and directory.]

Arts and Crafts Association of America
4888 Cannon Woods Court
Belmont, MI 49306
(616) 874-1721
www.artsandcraftsassoc.com
[Professional, trade, and industry organization.]

Arts and Crafts Business @ About.com
www.artsandcrafts.about.com
[Startup information, newsletter, forum, chat.]

The Arts Business Institute
2229 Paseo de los Chamisos
Sante Fe, NM 87505
(800) 224-5106
www.artsbusinessinstitute.org

The Arts and Crafts Society
Events Calendar
1194 Bandura Drive
Ann Arbor, MI 48103
(734) 358-6882
www.arts-crafts.com/index.html
[Craft show listing and directory.]

Arts, Crafts, and Theater Safety
181 Thompson Street #23
New York, NY 10012-2586
(212) 777-0062
www.caseweb.com/acts/index.html
[Safety.]

Artsource
www.ilpi.com/artsource/organizations.html
[List of organizations.]

Artspace
201 East Davie Street
Raleigh, NC 27601
(919) 821-ARTS
http://artspace.citysearch.com
[Arts incubator.]

Association of Crafts and Creative
Industries
1100-H Brandywine Boulevard
P.O. Box 3388
Zanesville, OH 43702-3388
(740) 452-4541
www.creative-industries.com
*[Professional, trade, and industry
organization.]*

Association of Stained Glass
Lamp Artists
5070 Cromwell Drive Northwest
Gig Harbor, WA 98335
www.asgla.com
[Stained glass organization.]

Bally Bead Company
2304 Ridge Road
Rockwall, TX 75087
(800) 543-0280
(972) 771-4515
www.ballybead.com
Wholesale only.
[Wholesale beads and jewelry supplies.]

The Basket Peddler
P.O. Box 44514
Rio Rancho, NM 87174
(505) 896-0050
www.thebasketpeddler.com
[Wholesale baskets.]

Baskets 101.com
P.O. Box 2487
Lexington, SC 29071-2487
www.baskets101.com/index.html
[Wholesale baskets.]

Beada Beada
3500 Hadley Road
Hadley, MI 48440
(866) 38-BEADA
(810) 797-6015
www.beadabeada.com
[Wholesale beads and jewelry supplies.]

Beads Galore
2123 South Priest #201
Tempe, AZ 85282
(800) 424-9577
(480) 921-3949
www.beadsgalore.com
[Wholesale beads and jewelry supplies.]

Beadworks International Inc.
149 Water Street
Norwalk, CT 06854
(203) 852-9108
www.beadworks.com
[Wholesale beads and jewelry supplies.]

The Bemis Center for
Contemporary Art
724 South 12th Street
Omaha, NE 68102
(402) 341-7130
www.bemiscenter.org/index.html
[Arts incubator.]

Bennett's Pottery Supply
431 Enterprise Street
Ocoee, FL 34761
(800) 432-0074
www.bennettpottery.com
[Wholesale ceramic and pottery supplies.]

Best Buy Floral Supply
5715 Sixth Street Southwest
Cedar Rapids, IA 52404
(800) 553-8497
www.bestbuyfloral.com
No minimum order.
[Wholesale baskets.]

Better Business Bureau
4200 Wilson Boulevard, Suite 800
Arlington, VA 22203
(703) 276-0100
www.bbb.org

Beverly's Crafts and Fabrics
100 Cotton Lane
Soquel, CA 95073
(831) 475-2954
http://save-on-crafts.com/bevfabriccrafts
[Wholesale floral supplies.]

Bolek's Craft Supply Inc.
P.O. Box 465
Dover, OH 44622-0465
(800) 743-2723
www.bolekscrafts.com
[Wholesale general craft supplies.]

The Boston Gift Show
George Little Management, LLC
10 Bank Street
White Plains, NY 10606-1954
(914) 421-3200
(800) 272-SHOW
www.bostongiftshow.com
[Trade shows.]

Bplans.com
www.bplans.com
[Business plans.]

Brightman Design
820 Swift Street, Suite D
Santa Cruz, CA 95060
(800) 995-1723
www.displaybright.com
[Display equipment, lighting.]

Buny Works
Kay Cushing
4759 Lakewood Blvd.
Lakewood, CA 90712
(866) 582-5838
http://bunys-e-fabric.twoffice.com
[Wholesale fabric.]

Business Forum Online
www.businessforum.com
[Startup information.]

Business Town
www.businesstown.com
[Startup information.]

Byline Magazine
P.O. Box 5240
Edmond, OK 73083-5240
www.bylinemag.com
[Publication.]

Cabin Craft
3613 Winewood Place
Colleyville, TX 76034
(817) 358-0528
www.ccsw.com
[Wholesale decorative painting supplies.]

Candlemart.com
www.candlemart.com/doorprize.html
[Web site content.]

Caravan Beads
449 Forest Ave.
Portland, ME 04101
(800) 230-8941 (orders)
(207) 761-2503
www.caravanbeads.com/
[Wholesale beads and jewelry supplies.]

Center for Business Planning
www.businessplans.org
[Business plans.]

Charm Woven Labels
2400 West Magnolia Boulevard
Burbank, CA 91506-1738
(800) 463-9543
(818) 841-2459
www.charmwoven.com
[Wholesale fabric labels.]

Chicago Artists' Coalition
11 East Hubbard
Chicago, IL 60611
(312) 670-2060
www.caconline.org/
[Membership organization; insurance.]

Chicago Merchandise Mart
200 World Trade Center Chicago
Chicago, IL 61654
(800) 677-MART
www.merchandisemart.com
[Trade shows.]

Clearsnap Inc.
P.O. Boc 98
Anacortes, WA 98221
(888) 448-4862
www.clearsnap.com
[Wholesale rubber stamping supplies.]

Cloth4Less
(866) 270-0466
www.cloth4less.net
Internet portal for several fabric wholesalers in Los Angeles garment district.
[Wholesale fabric.]

Colored Pencil Society of America
Kay Schmidt, Membership Director
P.O. Box 634
West Linn, OR 97068
www.cpsa.org/index.html
[Colored pencil organization.]

Cover Me Inc.
Pickens, SC 29671
(864) 878-1313
www.tarps.com
[Display equipment: Tarps and canopies.]

"Craft Business" @ About.com
www.artsandcrafts.about.com
[Marketing information.]

Craftown
www.craftown.com
[Online classifieds.]

Craft Canopy
408 Southwest 363rd Place
Federal Way, WA 98023
(800) 457-5644
www.craftcanopy.com
[Display equipment.]

Craft Catalog
P.O. Box 1069
Reynoldsburg, OH 43068
(800) 777-1442
www.craftcatalog.com
[Wholesale general craft supplies.]

Craft Emergency Relief Fund
P.O. Box 838
Montpelier, VT 05601
(802) 229-2306
www.craftemergency.org
[Emergency financial assistance.]

Crafters Catalogs
http://crafterscatalogs.com
[Links.]

Crafter's Community
http://crafterscommunity.net/index.php/169

Crafters Delight
www.craftersdelight.homestead.com
[Links.]

Craftersnet.com
www.craftersnet.com
[Online classifieds.]

Craftfinder
www.craftfinder.com
[E-mail newsletter.]

Craft Link
www.craftlink.net/online_classes.htm
[Online instruction.]

Craft Marketer
www.craftmarketer.com
[Marketing information; Web site construction.]

Craftmaster News
P.O. Box 39429
Downey, CA 90239
(562) 869-5882
www.craftmasternews.com
[Craft show listing and directory.]

Craft Planet
www.craftplanet.com/converstations.index.htm
[Forums.]

Craft Stop
2701 Park Center Drive, Suite B-410
Alexandria, VA 22302
(800) 865-0302
www.craft-stop.com/index.cfm
[Wholesale general craft supplies.]

Craftsite Medic
www.artcraftmarketing.com
[Web site construction.]

Crafts a Million
P.O. Box 7
Compti, LA 71411
www.craftsamillion.com
Small minimum order and case discounts.
[Wholesale floral supplies.]

Crafts Etc.
7717 Southwest 44th Street
Oklahoma City, OK 73179
(405) 745-1200 Extension 1275
(800) 888-0321 Extension 1275
www.craftsetc.com
[Wholesale general craft supplies.]

Crafts Fair Online
www.craftsfaironline.com
[Craft show listings and directories.]

Craftsmarts™
www.craftsmarts.com
[Forums.]

The Crafts Report
P.O. Box 1992
Wilmington, DE 19899
(800) 777-7098
(302) 656-2209
http://craftsreport.com
[Craft business publication, craft show listings, wholesale directory and database.]

Craft Web.com
http://craftweb.com

Craft Yarn Council of America
P.O. Box 9
Gastonia, NC 28053-0009
(704) 824-7838
www.craftyarncouncil.com
[Professional, trade, and industry organization.]

Crafty College
www.craftycollege.com
[Online instruction.]

Crafty Links Mall
http://craftylinks.com/
[Links.]

Create for Less
6932 SW Macadam Avenue, Suite A
Portland, OR 97219
(866) 333-4463
www.createforless.com
[Wholesale quilting supplies, wholesale papercraft supplies.]

Creating Killer Websites
www.killersites.com
[Web site design and construction.]

Creative Containers
P.O. Box 70
Kaufman, TX 75142
(800) 488-6432
(972) 962-8477
www.creativecontainers.com
[Wholesale baskets.]

Cressida's Transformations
www.cressidastransformations.com/
photopaint.html
[Online instruction.]

Crochet Guild of America
P.O. Box 127
Lockport, IL 60441
(877) 852-9190
www.crochet.org
[Crochet organization.]

Dallas Market Center
2100 Stemmons Freeway
Dallas, TX 75207
(800) DAL-MKTS
(214) 655-6100
www.dallasmarketcenter.com
[Trade shows.]

Darcies
P.O. Box 1627
Grants Pass, OR 97528
(800) 453-1527
(541) 471-1254
www.darciesstamps.com
[Wholesale rubber stamping supplies.]

Dealers Supply Inc.
P.O. Box 717
Matawan, NJ 07747
(800) 524-0576
www.dlrsupply.com
[Display equipment: lighting.]

The Denver Merchandise Mart
451 East 58th Avenue, Suite 4270
Denver, CO 80216
(800) 289-6278
(303) 292-6278
www.denvermart.com
[Trade shows.]

DMD Industries
2300 South Old Missouri Road
Springdale, AR 72764
www.dmdind.com
[Wholesale papercraft supplies.]

DMR Distributors Inc.
3500 S.R. 520 West, Building B, Bay 1
Cocoa, FL 32926
(888) 826-4644
www.dmrdist.com
[Wholesale art supplies.]

Dolls by Patricia
www.dollsbypatricia.com
[Links.]

Dried Naturals
37 Center Street
Rainelle, WV 25962
(800) 438-4831
www.driednaturals.com
Low minimum order and volume
discounts.
[Wholesale floral supplies.]

Eclectic Lighting and Electric
Sunrise Center Business Park
6025 Rittiman Plaza
San Antonio, TX 78218
(888) 830-9203
(210) 828-3282
www.eclecticlighting.homestead.com/
home.html
[Display equipment lighting.]

Eco-House Inc.
(506) 366-3529
www.eco-house.com
See Web site for distributor
information.
[Wholesale art supplies.]

Embroiderer's Guild of America
335 West Broadway, Suite 100
Louisville, KY 40202-2105
(502) 589-6956
www.egausa.org/
[Needleart organization.]

Empyrean Beads
P.O. Box 46338
Seattle, WA 98146
(206) 937-4146
www.empyreanbeads.com
[Wholesale beads and jewelry supplies.]

Enterprise Art
P.O. Box 2918
Largo, FL 33779
(800) 366-2218 (orders)
(727) 536-1492
www.enterpriseart.com
[Wholesale beads and jewelry supplies.]

Entrepreneur Magazine
2445 McCabe Way
Irvine, CA 92614
www.entrepreneur.com
*[Forum and message board; startup
information; worksheets.]*

Entrepreneur Startup Costs
Work Sheet
*www.entrepreneur.com/formnet/
frame-fin0016.html*

Evans Ceramics Supply
1518 South Washington
Wichita, KS 67211
(316) 262-2551
www.evansceramics.com
[Wholesale ceramic and pottery supplies.]

Ezine Articles.com
http://ezinearticles.com
[Web site content: articles.]

Fabric Club
(800) 322-2582
www.fabricclub.com
Online business only. No other contact
information available.
[Wholesale fabric.]

Fabric.com
2151 Northwest Parkway, Suite 500
Marietta, GA 30067
(888) 455-2940
http://store.yahoo.com/phoenixtextiles
[Wholesale fabric.]

Factory Direct Craft Supply
315 Conover Drive
Franklin, OH 45005
(800) 252-5223
www.factorydirectcrafts.com
*[Wholesale doll supplies, wholesale general
craft supplies.]*

Fairfield Processing Corporation
P.O. Box 1157
Danbury, CT 06813-1130
(800) 980-8000
www.poly-fil.com
*[Online product use information; wholesale
doll supplies; wholesale quilting supplies.]*

Fashion Fabrics Club
10490 Baur Boulevard
St. Louis, MO 63132
(800) 468-0602
www.fashionfabricsonline.com
[Wholesale fabric.]

Federal Communications Commission
445 12th Street, Southwest
Washington, DC 20554
(888) 225-5322
(888) 835-5322 (TTY)
www.fcc.gov
[Federal Government.]

Federal Citizen Information Center
P.O. Box 100
Pueblo, CO 81002
(800) FED-INFO
www.pueblo.gsa.gov
[Federal Government.]

Festival Network Online
P.O. Box 18839
Asheville, NC 28814
(828) 658-2799
www.festivalnet.com
[Craft show listing and directory.]

Fetpak
70 Austin Boulevard
Commack, NY 11725
(800) 883-3872
www.fetpak.com
[Display equipment.]

fineArt forum resource Directory:
Services
www.msstate.edu/Fineart_Online/
art-resources
[Online directories.]

Findlaw
www.findlaw.com/business.html
[Law Web site.]

Fire Mountain Gems
One Fire Mountain Way
Grants Pass, OR 97526-2373
(800) 423-2319
www.firemountaingems.com
[Wholesale beads and jewelry supplies.]

Flourish Company
3640 Highway 23
St. Paul, AR 72760
(800) 296-0049
www.flourish.com
[Display equipment.]

Folk Art Society of America
P.O. Box 17041
Richmond, VA 23226
(800) 527-3655
(804) 285-4532
www.folkart.org
[Folk art and traditional art organization.]

Frantz Art Glass and Supply
130 West Corporate Road
Shelton, WA 98584
(800) 839-6172
(360) 426-6712
www.frantzartglass.com
[Wholesale beads and jewelry supplies.]

Fred's Studio Tents and Canopies Inc.
7 Tent Lane
Stillwater, NY 12170
(800) 99-TENTS
www.fstcinc.com
[Display equipment.]

Freelance Writer's Report
Writers-Editors Network
CNW Publishing Inc.
P.O. Box A
North Stratford, NH 03590-0167
(603) 922-8338
www.writers-editors.com
[Publication.]

Fun-A-Fair Dolls and Supplies
3150 McMartin Lane
Central Point, OR 97502
(800) 689-9845
(541) 855-7302
http://fun-a-fair.com
[Wholesale doll supplies.]

General Bead
317 National City Boulevard
National City, CA 91950-1110
(800) 572-1302
(619) 336-0100
www.genbead.com
[Wholesale beads and jewelry supplies.]

General Label Manufacturing
P.O. Box 640371
Miami, FL 33164
(800) 944-4696
www.generallabel.com
[Wholesale fabric labels.]

Glass Art Society
1305 Fourth Avenue, Suite 711
Seattle, WA 98101
(206) 382-1305
www.glassart.org
[Glass organization.]

Glass Crafters Stained Glass Inc.
398 Interstate Court
Sarasota, FL 34240
(800) 422-4552 (orders only)
(941) 379-8333 (customer service)
www.glasscrafters.com
[Wholesale stained glass supplies.]

Gotta Write Online
www.gottawritenetwork.com
[Writing and publishing.]

Halstead Bead Inc.
P.O. Box 2491
Prescott, AZ 86302
(800) 528-0535
(928) 778-6776
www.halsteadbead.com
Wholesale only. Minimum order
required.
[Wholesale beads and jewelry supplies.]

The Handcrafted Soap Makers Guild
P.O. Box 71
Sidney, OH 45365
(866) 900-SOAP
www.soapguild.org
[Soap-making organization.]

Hands of the Hills
3016 78th Avenue Southeast
Mercer Island, WA 98040
(206) 232-4588
www.hohbead.com
[Wholesale beads and jewelry supplies.]

Handweavers Guild of America Inc.
1255 Buford Highway, Suite 211
Suwanee, GA 30024
(770) 495-7702
www.weavespindye.org
[Weaving organization.]

Hearts 2 Hands
Writers-Editors Network
CNW Publishing Inc.
P.O. Box A
North Stratford, NH 03590-0167
(603) 922-8338
www.writers-editors.com
[Publication: craft instruction.]
www.hearts2hands.com/online_classes.htm

Hice Sewing
14630 Section Lane Road
Elkmont, AL 35620
(800) 752-4927
Quilt fabric by the pound.
www.hicesewing.com
[Wholesale quilting supplies.]

Hobby Industry Association
P.O. Box 348
Elmwood Park, NJ 07407
(201) 794-1133
www.hobby.org
*[Professional, trade, and industry
organization.]*

Home Based Business News
www.home-based-business-news.com
[Publication: working from home.]

Home-Based Business Owners
Association^SM
(800) 362-6365
(954) 938-8010
www.hboa.com
*[Self-employment and small business
organization; health insurance.]*

Home Business Magazine
PMB 368
9582 Hamilton Avenue
Huntington Beach, CA 92646
(714) 962-7722
www.homebusinessmag.com
[Publication: working from home.]

Home Sewing Association
494 Eighth Avenue, Suite 802
New York, NY 10001-1806
(212) 714-1633
www.sewing.org
[Professional, trade, and industry
organization.]

Home Working Mom.com
www.homeworkingmom.com
[Working from home.]

The Idea Cafe
www.ideacafe.com
[Startup information.]

Idea Marketers
www.ideamarketers.com
[Web site content: articles.]

Indian Arts and Crafts Association
4010 Carlisle Northeast, Suite C
Albuquerque, NM 87107
(505) 265-9149
www.iaca.com
[Folk art and traditional art organization.]

Insta Coach
www.instacoach.com/
[Web site content: articles.]

Insurance Information Institute
110 William Street
New York, NY 10038
(212) 346-5500
www.iii.org
[General insurance information.]

Insurance Resources for Craftspeople
www.craftsreport.com/resources/
insurance.html
[Health Insurance.]

The Internal Revenue Service
Communications Division
1111 Constitution Avenue Northwest
Washington, DC 20224
(800) 829-1040
(202) 622-4010
(800) 829-3676 (Forms, instructions,
and publications)
(800) 819-3377 (TeleTax—recorded
information on tax-related topics)
www.irs.gov
(Check the Small Business Corner on
the Web site or contact your local IRS
office.)
[Federal Government.]

International Cooperative Alliance
www.ica.coop/kids
[Cooperative.]

International E-ZUP Inc.
1601 Iowa Avenue
Riverside, CA 92507
(800) 45-SHADE
www.ezup.com
[Display equipment.]

International Foundation of Doll
Makers
P.O. Box 120187
Clermont, FL 34712
(866) 370-8017
(352) 394-1404
www.ifdm.org
[Doll-making organization.]

International Guild of Candle Artisans
1640 Garfield
Fremont, NE 68025
www.igca.net
[Candle organization.]

International Guild of Miniature Artists
P.O. Box 629
Freedom, CA 95019-0629
(800) 711-IGMA
www.igma.org
[Miniature organization.]

International Sculpture Center
14 Fairground Road, Suite B
Hamilton, NJ 08619-3447
(609) 689-1051
www.sculpture.org/
[Sculpture organization.]

International Society of Glass
Beadmakers
1120 Chester Avenue #470
Cleveland, OH 44114
(888) 742-0242
www.sgb.org
[Glass organization.]

Jenkins Crafted Canopies
3950 Valley Boulevard, Unit A
Walnut, CA 91789
(909) 594-1349
www.jccshade.com
[Display equipment.]

Kansas City Gift Mart Inc.
6800 West 115th Street
Overland Park, KS 66211
(800) 950-MART
(913) 491-6688
www.kcgiftmart.com
[Trade shows.]

Kansas Small Business
Development Center
214 South West 6th Avenue, Suite 301
Topeka, KS 66603-3179
(785) 296-6514
www.fhsu.edu/ksbdc/
[Startup information.]

Knitting Goddess
http://knittinggoddess.com
[Forums and newsletter.]

The Knitting Guild Association
P.O. Box 3388
Zanesville, OH 43702-3388
(740) 452-4541
www.tkga.com
[Knitting organization.]

Laceland
www.laceland.com
[Wholesale fabric.]

Make-Stuff.com
www.make-stuff.com/home_business/
catalogs.html

Make-Stuff.com Home Business
www.makestuff.com/home_business
[Startup information.]

Marasco's Craft King
12750 West Capitol Drive
Brookfield, WI 53005
(262) 781-9660
www.craftking.com
[Wholesale general craft supplies.]

Mary's Craft Classifieds
www.net5000.com/crafts/class8.htm
[Free classified ads.]

Mat Shop Wholesale Frames
3873 Airport Way
Bellingham, WA 98226
(800) 663-7501
www.matshop.com
[Wholesale framing supplies.]

Michaels
www.michaels.com
[Forums.]

Mister Art
913 Willard Street
Houston, TX 77006
(866) 672-7811
www.misterart.com
[Wholesale art supplies.]

Mom's Homework
www.momshomework.com
[Working from home.]

Mommy Tips
www.mommytips.com
[Web site content.]

Mosses Galore
P.O. Box 247
Lake Nebagonmon, WI 54849
(715) 374-2135
www.artcraftmall.com/mossesgalore.htm
[Wholesale floral supplies.]

Motivational Quotes.com
*www.motivationalquotes.com/advertising/
link.shtml*
[Web site content.]

My Free
www.myfree.com
[Forums; classifieds.]

My Internet Craft Show
www.myinternetcraftshow.com
[Links.]

Myron Tobac, Inc.
25 West 47th Street
New York, NY 10036
(800) 223-7550
(212) 398-8300
www.myrontoback.com
[Wholesale beads and jewelry supplies.]

Name Maker Inc.
P.O. Box 43821
Atlanta, GA 30336
(800) 241-2890
www.namemaker.com
[Wholesale fabric labels.]

National Acrylic Painter's Association
Lorraine Strieby, Membership
Chairperson
P.O. Box 4928
Chatsworth, CA 91313-4928
www.napa-usa.org
[Painting organization.]

National Art Craft Company
7996 Darrow Road
Twinsburg, OH 44087
(888) 937-2723
www.nationalartcraft.com
*[Wholesale general craft supplies, wholesale
doll supplies.]*

National Association for the
Self-Employed
P.O. Box 612067
DFW Airport
Dallas, TX 75261-2067
(800) 232-6273
www.nase.org
*[Self-employment and small business
organization; health insurance.]*

National Association of
Independent Artists
NAIA Membership
2785 Stark Road
Harris, WI 55032
http://naia-artists.org
*[Professional, trade, and industry
organization.]*

National Association of Miniature
Enthusiasts
P.O. Box 69
Carmel, IN 46082-0069
www.miniatures.org
[Miniature organization.]

National Candle Association
1156 15th Street, Northwest
Suite 900
Washington, DC 20005
(202) 393-2210
www.candles.org/NCA/index.htm
[Candle organization.]

National Caricaturist Network
c/o Dion Socia
14513 Gateway Point Circle #1307
Orlando, FL 32821
www.caricature.org
[Caricature or cartoon organization.]

National Cartoonists Society
NCS Membership Committee
P.O. Box 713
Suffield, CT 06078
www.reuben.org
[Caricature or cartoon organization.]

National Council for the Traditional Arts
1320 Fenwick, Suite 200
Silver Spring, MD 20910
(301) 565-0654
www.ncta.net
[Folk art and traditional art organization.]

National Council on Education for the
Ceramic Arts
77 Erie Village Square
Eire, CO 80516
(866) CO-NCECA
http://nceca.net
[Ceramic organization.]

National Craft Association
2012 East Ridge Road, Suite 120
Rochester, NY 14622-2434
(800) 715-9594
(716) 266-5472
www.craftassoc.com
*[Professional, trade, and industry
organization; business information or
advice; wholesale directory and database;
trade show listings.]*

The National Endowment for the Arts
1100 Pennsylvania Avenue, Northwest
Washington, DC 20506
(202) 682-5400
http://arts.endow.gov
[Federal government.]

National Foundation for Advancement
in the Arts
800 Brickell Avenue
Suite 500
Miami, FL 33131
(800) 970-ARTS
(305) 377-1140
www.nfaa.org
*[Professional, trade, and industry
organization; scholarships.]*

National Guild of Decoupeurs
820 Idlewilde Lane
Lake Charles, LA 70605
(337) 562-0720
www.decoupage.org
[Decoupage organization.]

National Institute of American
Doll Artists
Kathryn Walmsley, Secretary
8041 Shady Road
Oldenburg, IN 47036
(812) 934-6221
www.niada.org
[Doll-making organization.]

National Polymer Clay Guild
1350 Beverly Road, Suite 115-345
Mc Lean, VA 22101
www.npcg.org
[Professional organization.]

National Quilting Association Inc.
P.O. Box 393
Ellicott City, MD 21041-0393
(410) 461-5733
www.nqaquilts.org
[Quilting organization.]

National Small Business United
1156 15th Street, Northwest, Suite 1100
Washington, DC 20005
(202) 293-8830
www.nsbu.org
*[Membership organization; health
insurance.]*

National Society of Mural Painters
c/o American Fine Arts Society
215 West 57th Street
New York, NY 10019
www.anny.org/2/orgs/0041/mural.htm
[Painting organization.]

National Society of Tole and
Decorative Painters
393 North McLean Boulevard
Wichita, KS 67203
(316) 269-9300
*www.thuntek.net/~rhardy/paint/
nstdp.html*
[Decorative painting organization.]

National Watercolor Society
915 South Pacific Avenue
San Pedro, CA 90731
(800) 486-8670
http://nws-online.org
[Watercolor organization.]

National Wood Carvers Association
P.O. Box 43218
Cincinnati, OH 45243
www.chipchats.org
[Wood-carving organization.]

Natures Best Dried Flowers
P.O. Box 360487
Strongsville, OH 44136
(440) 572-1138
www.nbdriedflowers.com
[Wholesale floral supplies.]

Netcrafts Show Guide
www.netcrafts.com/shows/shows.html
[Craft show listings and directories.]

New Venture Products and
Awning Works Inc.
141158 63rd Way, North
Clearwater, FL 33760
(800) 771-7469
www.newvp.com
[Display equipment.]

New York Artists Equity Association
498 Broome Street
New York, NY 10013
(212) 941-0130
www.anny.org
[Membership organization; insurance.]

The New York Mills Regional
Cultural Center
24 North Main Avenue
P.O. Box 246
New York Mills, MN 56567
(218) 385-3339
www.kulcher.org
[Arts incubator.]

Newton Display Products Inc.
122 Fifth Street
Fort Myers, FL 33907
(800) 678-8677
(941) 936-9199
www.crafthut.com
[Display equipment.]

North American Nature Photography
Association
10200 West 44th Avenue, Suite 304
Wheat Ridge, CO 80033-2840
(303) 422-8527
www.nanpa.org
[Photography organization.]

Offinger Management
Box 3388
Zanesville, OH 43702-3388
(740) 452-4541
www.offinger.com
[Trade shows.]

Onelist
www.onelist.com
[E-mail lists.]

Origami USA
15 West 77 Street
New York, NY 10024-5192
(212) 769-5635
www.origami.com
[Origami organization.]

Ornamental Resources Inc.
1427 Miner Street
P.O. Box 3303
Idaho Springs, CO 80452
(800) 876-6762
(303) 567-2222
www.ornabead.com
[Wholesale beads and jewelry supplies.]

Outdoor Fabrics.com
(800) 640-3539
www.outdoorfabrics.com
[Wholesale fabric.]

Pacific Coast Bach Label Company
1010 East 18th Street
Los Angeles, CA 90021-3008
(888) 225-5222
www.bachlabel.com
[Wholesale fabric labels.]

Paints R Us
P.O. Box 801
Labanon, OR 97355
www.digisys.net/~westfab/paint.html#top
[Wholesale painting supplies.]

Passion4Art
http://passion4art.com
[Free e-mail and online promotion.]

Pastel Society of America
National Arts Club
15 Gramercy Park South
New York, NY 10003
(212) 533-6931
www.pastelsocietyofamerica.org
[Pastel organization.]

Pearl Paint
1033 East Oakland Park Boulevard
Ft. Lauderdale, FL 33334
(800) 221-6845
www.pearlpaint.com
[Wholesale art supplies.]

Penny Products Inc.
P.O. Box 85
Sauk Rapids, MN 56379-0085
(866) 307-3669
(320) 230-0184
www.pennyproductsinc.com
[Wholesale papercraft supplies.]

Penny Soto-Steps to Watercolor
http://worldofwatercolor.com/pennysoto/
pssteps.htm
[Online instruction.]

Photographic Society of America
3000 United Founders Boulevard,
Suite 103
Oklahoma City, OK 73112-3940
(405) 843-1437
www.psa-photo.org
[Photography organization.]

Pinehollow Handcrafts
http://pinehollowhandcrafts.com
[Links.]

Pine Tree Quiltworks Ltd.
585 Broadway
South Portland, ME 04106
(207) 799-7357
www.quiltworks.com
[Wholesale quilting supplies.]

Pioneer Photo Albums, Inc.
P.O. Box 2497
Chatsworth, CA 91313-2497
(818) 882-2161
www.pioneerphotoalbums.com
[Wholesale scrapbooking supplies.]

Pottery Art Studio
4510 Killiam Avenue
Norfolk, VA 23508
(757) 489-7417
www.potteryartstudio.com
[Wholesale ceramic and pottery supplies.]

Presto
1237 Shipp Street
Hendersonville, NC 28791
(800) 334-9060
www.framingsupplies.com
[Wholesale framing supplies.]

The Professional Association of
Custom Clothiers
494 8th Avenue, Suite 802
New York, NY 10001-1806
(877) 755-0303
www.paccprofessionals.org
[Sewing organization.]

Professional Crafters Mailing List
www.professionalcrafters.com
[E-mail lists.]

The Professional Doll Makers Art Guild
530 Tanglewood Loop
North Salt Lake City, UT 84054
(801) 299-9908
www.artdolls.com/artguild.html
[Doll-making organization.]

Quilt University
www.quiltuniversity.com
[Online instruction.]

Quilters Review
www.QuiltersReview.com
[Newsletter.]

Raynor and Associates
P.O. Box 821309
Houston, TX 77282
(800) 424-8372
(281) 497-8372
www.raynorassoc.com
[Wholesale fabric labels.]

Retail Advisors
www.retailadvz.com
[Startup information.]

Rings and Things
P.O. Box 450
Spokane, WA 99210-0450
(800) 366-2156 (orders)
(509) 624-8565
www.rings-things.com
[Wholesale beads and jewelry supplies.]

Rockville Arts Place
100 East Middle Lane
Rockville, MD 20850
(301) 309-6900
www.rockvilleartsplace.org
[Arts incubator.]

The Ronay Guide
A Step Ahead Ltd.
2090 Shadow Lake Drive
Buckland, GA 30625
(706) 342-8225
www.events2000.com
[Craft show listing and directory.]

Rosen Group
3000 Chestnut Avenue, Suite 304
Baltimore, MD 21211
(800) 642-4314
http://americancraft.com
[Trade shows.]

St. Nick Studios
www.stnickstudios.com
[Links.]

Santa's Supply
N9678 North Summit Lane
Summit Lake, WI 54485
(800) 772-6827
(715) 275-4188
www.santasupplies.com/index.html
[Wholesale floral supplies.]

Scrapbook Factory Outlet
3510 Scotts Lane, Building 29
Philadelphia, PA 19129
(800) 739-7277
(215) 842-3600
http://sfodirect.com/enter.htm
[Wholesale papercraft supplies; wholesale scrapbooking supplies.]

Scrapbook Superstore
665 Duluth Highway Suite 804
Lawrenceville, GA 30045
http://store.yahoo.com/scrapbooksuperstore/index.html
[Wholesale scrapbooking supplies.]

Scot Style Web Design
(212) 928-8351
www.scotstyle.com/scotstyle.html
[Web site design.]

Search Engine Guide
www.searchengineguide.com
[Search engine information.]

Search Engines.com
www.searchengines.com
[Search engine information.]

Selling Your Art Online
www.1x.com/advisor
[Marketing information; Web site design; newsletter.]

Service Corps of Retired Executives
(SCORE)
409 3rd Street Southwest 6th Floor
Washington, DC 20024
(800) 634-0245
www.score.org
[Startup information; business advice.]

Sew What's New.com
www.sew-whats-new.com/newsletter.shtml
[Newsletter.]

Sheffield Pottery Inc.
Route 7, Box 399
Sheffield, MA 01257
(888) SPI-CLAY
(413) 229-7700
www.sheffield-pottery.com
[Wholesale ceramic and pottery supplies.]

Shipwreck Beads
2500 Mottman Road Southwest
Olympia, WA 98512
(800) 950-4232
www.shipwreck.com
[Wholesale beads and jewelry supplies.]

Small Business Administration
Answer Desk
6302 Fairview Road, Suite 300
Charlotte, NC 28210
(800) 827-5722 (answer desk)
www.sba.gov
[Federal government; startup information; business plan information.]

Small Business Assistance
Center Network
119 E. Locust Lane
Kennet Square, PA 19348
www.sbacnetwork.org
[Business plans.]

The Small Business Know How
Resource
www.liraz.com
[Startup information.]

Small Business Plan Guides
www.smbtn.com/businessplanguides.
[Business plans.]

Small Business Service Bureau
(800) 343-0939
www.sbsb.com
[Membership organization; insurance.]

The Small Business Know-How
Resource
www.liraz.com
[Startup information.]

Smocking Arts Guild of America
PMB 229
2320 Texoma Parkway
Sherman, TX 75090-2420
(800) 520-3101
www.smocking.org
[Sewing organization.]

Social Security Administration
Office of Public Inquiries
Windsor Park Building
6401 Security Boulevard
Baltimore, MD 21235
(800) 772-1213
www.ssa.gov
Or visit your local office.
[Federal government.]

Society of American Mosaic Artists
P.O. Box 428
Orangeburg, SC 29116
www.americanmosaics.org
[Mosaic organization.]

Society of American Silversmiths
P.O. Box 72839
Providence, RI 02907
(401) 461-6840
www.silversmithing.com
[Metalsmithing and blacksmithing
organization; health insurance.]

Society of Craft Designers
P.O. Box 3388
Zanesville, OH 43702-3388
(740) 452-4541
www.craftdesigners.org
[Professional, trade, and industry
organization.]

Society of Decorative Painters, The
393 North McLean Boulevard
Wichita, KS 67203-5968
(316) 269-9300, Ext.105
www.decorativepainters.com
[Decorative painting organization.]

Society of North American Goldsmiths
(SNAG)
4513 Lincoln Ave #213
Lisle, IL 60532
(630) 852-6385
http://snagmetalsmith.org
[Metalsmithing and blacksmithing
organization.]

SS Traders
2727 Fondren Road #6D
Houston, TX 77063-4114
(713) 789-5553
www.sstraders.com
[Wholesale beads and jewelry supplies.]

Stained Glass Association of America
10009 East 62nd Street
Raytown, MO 64133
(800) 888-7422
www.stainedglass.org
[Stained glass organization.]

Stained Glass Warehouse Inc.
P.O. Box 609
Arden, NC 28704-0609
(828) 650-0992
www.stainedglasswarehouse.com
[Wholesale stained glass supplies.]

STAMPede
3 Terrace Drive
Bethel, CT 06801
(203) 744-6187
http://rubberstampsforless.com
[Wholesale rubberstamping supplies.]

Starving Aritists Law.com
www.starvingartistslaw.com/index.htm
[Startup information.]

The Stencil Artisans League, Inc.
P.O. Box 3109
Los Lunas, NM 87031
(505) 865-9119
www.sali.org
[Decorative painting organization.]

Studio Art Quilt Associates
P.O. Box 2231
Little Rock, AR 72203-2231
(501) 490-4043
www.saqa.com
[Quilting organization.]

Sugarloaf Crafts
Sugarloaf Mountain Works Inc.
200 Orchard Ridge Drive, Suite 215
Gaithersburg, MD 20878
(800) 210-9900
(301) 990-1400
www.sugarloafcrafts.com
[Craftshow listings and directories.]

Sunshine Artist Magazine
Palm House Publishing
3210 Dade Avenue
Orlando, FL 32804
(407) 228-9772
http://sunshineartist.com
[Craft business publication, craft show
listings.]

Sunshine Discount Crafts
12335 62nd Street North
Largo, FL 33773
(800) 729-2878
www.sunshinecrafts.com
[Wholesale general craft supplies.]

The Supply Source Book
The National Directory of Suppliers for
Artists and Artisans
(800) 358-2045
(503) 331-0455
www.artfairsource.com/maher/supply2.htm
[Wholesale directory and database.]

Surfnet Kids
www.surfnetkids.com/daily.html
[Web site content.]

Textile Source
www.textilesource.com
[Wholesale fabric.]

Thomas Register of American
Manufacturers
5 Penn Plaza, 12th Floor
New York, NY 10001
(212) 290-7277
www.thomasregister.com
[Wholesale directory and database.]

Tips and Business Information for
Craftsmen and Artists
www.choices.cc/articles.html

Tipztime
www.tipztime.com/linkto.html
[Web site content.]

Top Craft Suppliers
www.topcraftsuppliers.com
[Wholesale directories and databases.]

Torpedo Factory Art Center
105 North Union Street
Alexandria, VA 22314-3217
(703) 838-4565
www.torpedofactory.org
[Arts incubator.]

Trade Shows Inc.
P.O. Box 2000
Claremont, NC 28610-2000
(828) 459-9894
http://tsishows.com
[Trade shows.]

Uchida of America Corporation
3535 Del Amo Boulevard
Torrance, CA 90503
(800) 541-5877
www.uchida.com
[Wholesale papercraft supplies.]

U.S. Business Advisor
www.business.gov
[Federal information.]

United States Chamber of Commerce
1615 H Street Northwest
Washington, DC 20062-2000
(800) 638-6582
(202) 659-6000
www.uschamber.com/default
Or contact your local Chamber of
Commerce for startup information,
classes, help in planning a grand
opening, etc. Information and services
available may vary by location.
[Startup information.]

United States Copyright Office
Library of Congress
101 Independence Avenue Southeast
Washington, DC 20559-6000
(202) 707-3000
(public information office)
www.copyright.gov
[Federal government.]

United States Patent and
Trademark Office
General Information and
Services Division
P.O. Box 1450
Arlington, VA 22313
(800) 786-9199
(703) 308-4357

(703) 305-7785 TTY
www.uspto.gov
[Federal government.]

United States Postal Service
(800) 275-8777 (Consumer Questions)
www.usps.gov
Or contact your local post office.
[Federal government.]

University of Central Arkansas College
of Business Administration
Small Business Advancement Center
UCA Box 5018
201 Donaghey Avenue
Conway, AR 72035-0001
(501) 450-5300
www.sbaer.uca.edu
*[Startup information; business plan
outline.]*

University of Wisconsin Center for
Cooperatives
230 Taylor Hall
427 Lorch Street
Madison, WI 53706
(608) 262-3981
www.wisc.edu/uwcc
[Cooperative information.]

USA Light
P.O. Box 296
Patton, CA 92369-0296
(800) 854-8794
(505) 891-8696
www.usalight.com
[Display equipment: lighting.]

Utrecht
See Web site for store locations.
(800) 223-9132
www.utrechtart.com
[Wholesale art supplies.]

Val Handmade Crafts
www.valhandmadecrafts.com/
[Links.]

Valley Products Company
York New Salem, PA 17371
(800) 451-8874
www.clothlabels.com
[Wholesale fabric labels.]

The Virtual Quilt
www.planetpatchwork.com/tvqmain
[Online newsletter.]

Warner-Crivellaro
1855 Weaversville Road
Allentown, PA 18109
(800) 523-4242
www.warner-criv.com
[Wholesale stained glass supplies.]

We Are Paper
922 North Noble Street
Chicago, IL 60622
(773) 486-9374
www.wearepaper.com
[Wholesale papercraft supplies.]

Web Builder 101
www.webbuilder101.com
[Web site design.]

Web Resource Center
www.jrzsystem.com/metro
[Search engine information.]

Western Exhibitors LLC
2181 Greenwich Street
San Francisco, CA 94123-3493
(415) 346-6666
www.weshows.com
[Trade shows.]

Whittemore-Durgin Glass Company
P.O. Box 2065
Hanover, MA 02339
(800) 262-1790
(781) 871-1743
www.penrose.com/glass
[Wholesale stained glass supplies.]

Wholesale Frame Service USA
P.O. Box 49067
Greensboro, NC 27419
(800) 522-3726
www.pictureframe-usa.com
[Wholesale framing supplies.]

Wildlife Art Industry Exhibition and
Trade Shows
www.wildlifeartmag.com/industry.htm
[Art show listings and directories.]

Wilson Internet
www.wilsonweb.com
[Web site design.]

Women's Caucus for Art
P.O. Box 1498
Canal Street Station
New York, NY 10013
(212) 634-0007
www.nationalwca.com
[Women in the arts organization.]

The Woodburner
www.woodburner.com/index.htm
[Online forum.]

Woodcrafter.com
P.O. Box 116
Sherrill's Ford, NC 28673-0116
(800) 704-3772
(704) 665-2895
www.woodcrafter.com
[Wholesale woodcraft supplies.]

Woodcrafts and Supplies
206 East Main Street
Oblong, IL 62449
(800) 255-1335
www.woodcraftssupplies.com
[Wholesale woodcraft supplies.]

Wood-N-Crafts Incorporated
P.O. Box 140
Lakeview, MI 48850
(989) 352-8075
www.wood-n-crafts.com
[Wholesale woodcraft supplies.]

Working Today
55 Washington Street, Suite 557
Brooklyn, NY 11201
(866) 420-5807
(718) 222-1099 Extension 103
www.workingtoday.org/
*[Self-employment or small business
organization; health insurance.]*

World Association of China Painters
2641 Northwest 10th
Oklahoma City, OK 73107-5400
(405) 521-1234
www.theshop.net/wocporg/
[China painting organization.]

World Wide Information Outlet
http://certificate.net/wwio
[Web site content.]

Worldwide Quilting Page Quilt
Exhibitions and Museums
http://quilt.com/museums.html
[Craft show lisitings and directories.]

World Wide Recipes
www.wwrecipes.com/link/htm
[Web site content.]

Writer's Digest
4700 East Galbraith Road
Cincinnati, OH 45236
(513) 531-2690, Extension 1483
www.writersdigest.com
[Publication.]

Writers' Journal
P.O. Box 394
Perham, MN 56573
(218) 346-7921
www.writersjournal.com
[Publication.]

Zen and the Art of Website
Promotion
http://zensite.home.att.net
[Web site promotion.]

Index

 **BOOKS FROM ALLWORTH PRESS**

Selling Your Crafts, Revised Edition
by Susan Joy Sager (paperback, 6 x 9, $19.95, 288 pages)

Crafts and Craft Shows: How to Make Money
by Philip Kadubec (paperback, 6 x 9, 208 pages, $16.95)

Business and Legal Forms for Crafts
by Tad Crawford (paperback, 8½ x 11, 176 pages, $19.95)

The Law (in Plain English), for Crafts
by Leonard DuBoff (paperback, 6 x 9, 224 pages, $18.95)

The Fine Artist's Guide to Marketing and Self-Promotion, Revised Edition
by Julius Vitali (paperback, 6 x 9, 256 pages, $19.95)

The Artist-Gallery Partnership: A Practical Guide to Consigning Art, Revised Edition
by Tad Crawford and Susan Mellon (paperback, 6 x 9, 216 pages, $16.95)

The Artist's Guide to New Markets: Opportunities to Sell Art Beyond Galleries
by Peggy Hadden (paperback, 5½ x 8½, 248 pages, $18.95)

How to Grow as an Artist
by Daniel Grant (paperback, 6 x 9, 240 pages, $16.95)

The Quotable Artist
by Peggy Hadden (hardcover, 7½ x 7½, 224 pages, $19.95)

The Fine Artist's Career Guide
by Daniel Grant (paperback, 6 x 9, 304 pages, $18.95)

The Business of Being an Artist, Third Edition
by Daniel Grant (paperback, 6 x 9, 352 pages, $19.95)

The Artist's Complete Health and Safety Guide, Third Edition
By Monona Rossol (paperback, 6 x 9, 416 pages, $19.95)

Licensing Art & Design, Revised Edition
by Caryn R. Leland (paperback, 6 x 9, 128 pages, $16.95)

The Artist's Resource Handbook, Revised Edition
by Daniel Grant (paperback, 6 x 9, 248 pages, $18.95)

Caring For Your Art:
A Guide for Artists, Collectors, Galleries, and Art Institutions, Third Edition
by Jill Snyder (paperback, 6 x 9, 256 pages, $19.95)

Legal Guide for the Visual Artist, Fourth Edition
by Tad Crawford (paperback, 8½ x 11, 272 pages, $19.95)

Please write to request our free catalog. To order by credit card, call 1-800-491-2808 or send a check or money order to Allworth Press, 10 East 23rd Street, Suite 210, New York, NY 10010. Include $5 for shipping and handling for the first book ordered and $1 for each additional book. Ten dollars plus $1 for each additional book if ordering from Canada. New York State residents must add sales tax.

If you would like to see our complete catalog on the World Wide Web, you can find us at *www.allworth.com*.